LAW *and* LEGITIMACY
in the SUPREME COURT

Law *and* Legitimacy
in the Supreme Court

Richard H. Fallon, Jr.

The Belknap Press of Harvard University Press

Cambridge, Massachusetts

London, England   2018

First printing

Library of Congress Cataloging-in-Publication Data

Names: Fallon, Richard H., Jr., 1952- author.
Title: Law and legitimacy in the Supreme Court / Richard H. Fallon, Jr.
Description: Cambridge, Massachusetts : The Belknap Press of Harvard
    University Press, 2018. | Includes bibliographical references and index.
Identifiers: LCCN 2017032270 | ISBN 9780674975811 (hardcover : alk.
    paper)
Subjects: LCSH: United States. Supreme Court. | Political questions and
    judicial power—United States. | Judicial process—United States. |
    Constitutional law—United States.
Classification: LCC KF8748 .F284 2018 | DDC 342.73—dc23
LC record available at https://lccn.loc.gov/2017032270

To the memories of my mother, Jean Murray Fallon, and my friend and colleague Daniel J. Meltzer

Contents

Preface ix

Introduction 1

1   Legitimacy and Judicial Authority 20

2   Constitutional Meaning
Original Public Meaning 47

3   Constitutional Meaning
Varieties of History That Matter 71

4   Law in the Supreme Court
Jurisprudential Foundations 83

5   Constitutional Constraints 105

6   Constitutional Theory and Its Relation to
Constitutional Practice 125

7   Sociological, Legal, and Moral Legitimacy
Today and Tomorrow 155

Notes 177

Acknowledgments 215

Index 217

Preface

As MY TITLE OF *Law and Legitimacy in the Supreme Court* suggests, this is an ambitious book. By design, it blends three perspectives on constitutional law. The first is that of the longtime constitutional law professor that I am. As a law professor, I take constitutional law and doctrine seriously. I believe that what the Supreme Court says in one case matters for future cases, both in lower courts and in the Court itself. I also credit the idea that debates in the Supreme Court are about law, not just politics.

The book's second perspective is that of philosophy. Although I am not a philosopher, it is impossible to talk about law in the Supreme Court without embracing positions on multiple jurisprudential questions. These include issues involving the relationships between law and language and, perhaps especially, between law and political morality. In an era when we refer unhesitatingly to judicial liberals and judicial conservatives, anyone who cares about constitutional law also needs to think about political theory.

The book's third perspective is that of political science. As political scientists remind us, we should not let normative preoccupations cause us to skip over questions about how the Supreme Court got the power that it has, about why people put up with judicial power as we know it, and about what the Justices need to do to maintain their power.

The perspectives of law, philosophy, and political science intersect, diverge, and overlap in many interesting ways, including in their concerns with judicial "legitimacy." Legitimacy is a concept with multiple senses. It sometimes means different things to lawyers, philosophers, and political scientists. Among my ambitions is to sort out confusions and to set the stage for a multidisciplinary inquiry into matters of pressing common concern.

The late Justice William J. Brennan used to counsel law clerks that "the most important number in the Supreme Court is five." When the clerks asked why, he would reply, "With five votes, you can do anything." For reasons that I shall explore, Brennan was wrong: there are some things—indeed, many things—that the Justices cannot do, even with five votes. But suppose Brennan was right. By what moral and legal right could five Justices impose their views on the rest of us? Or, perhaps more aptly, how would the Justices need to decide the controversial cases that come before them in order to justify, legally and morally, their claims to obedience? Yes, the Justices have the power to decide many important issues as a matter of political fact. In addition, the Constitution's language and history do not dictate clear answers to many of the questions that the Justices confront. Thus comes the inevitability that the Justices' moral and political views will sometimes influence their decisions. Yet the Justices are not merely politicians in robes, or at least they ought not to be. Questions of justification— both of judicial power generally and of the exercise of judicial power in particular ways—are this book's dominant concern.

Political conservatives have often railed against "judicial activism." Political liberals have more recently shuddered at Supreme Court threats to scuttle progressive legislation and to pare back protections of abortion. Everyone has a stake. Nearly every thoughtful person experiences disquiet, if not outrage, at some Court decisions, especially when the Justices are narrowly divided into conservative and liberal coalitions that pit those appointed by Republican presidents against those named to the Court by Democrats.

At a time when many people have lost confidence in the Supreme Court and have come to regard it as a "political" institution in a pejorative sense, the book's questions about the relationships among law, language, and legitimacy deserve urgent attention. But they are intellectually risky questions to pursue, not so much because they are politically controversial as because of the need to cross disciplinary lines in the quest for answers. Academic specialization, which is often a virtue, can leave no one properly credentialed to confront large intellectual challenges. As I have said, I am not a philosopher, nor am I a political scientist. Yet the most important questions about law, language, and legitimacy in the Supreme Court do not lie within the exclusive province of any single discipline. Those questions involve law but are not narrowly legal. Issues concerning the meaning of language are highly pertinent, as are issues of moral justification. But our worries about law in the Supreme Court have empirical and practical dimensions that require much more than purely philosophical knowledge. And while we cannot grasp the full complexity of our current predicament without focusing on the political scientific question of how political and judicial power work within our constitutional regime, political scientists have no distinctively moral or legal expertise.

Perhaps no one knows enough to speak with state-of-the-art sophistication about all of the matters that bear on my topic of law and legitimacy in the Supreme Court. Nevertheless, I venture the risk of speaking beyond my expertise because I am convinced that vital current issues cannot be understood except through an approach that links legal, philosophical, and political scientific inquiries. Within our politically and morally divided nation, all of our institutions may be destined for, or indeed may be in the midst of, legitimacy crises. But the Supreme Court is at least as vulnerable as Congress and the president, and in the long run it may be more so. The Court's members have no renewable democratic mandate stemming from periodic elections. Questions involving the entitlement of narrow majorities of the Justices to impose their will are likely to arise with even greater urgency in the future than they have in the recent past.

In my experience, the people with the deepest, most corrosive cynicism about law and legitimacy in the Supreme Court are often those who began with unrealistic expectations that the Justices' decision making could be wholly apolitical or untouched by ideological influence. Upon coming to see that the Justices' political views matter, they then apprehend that the Justices' political views are all that matter, and they resent what they perceive as the Justices' hypocrisy in purporting to be bound either by law or by a consistent methodology. As an antidote, we need to recognize that political views will have an inescapable role and, having done so, develop conceptions of law in the Supreme Court and legitimacy in judicial decision making that accommodate this realization. Judicial legitimacy should be a practical ideal for us, not a piece of utopian pie in the sky. But our conceptions of law and legitimacy in the Supreme Court cannot be so flaccid that they would permit the Justices, with five votes, to do anything that they might be able to get away with. Embracing the challenge, this book offers conceptions of law and legitimacy in the Supreme Court to which concerned citizens should hold the Justices, beginning today. Never in my lifetime has it been more important to bring all relevant resources to bear in addressing how the Justices of the Supreme Court would need to decide cases such that even those of us who disagree with their conclusions ought to respect the Court and its rulings.

LAW *and* LEGITIMACY
in the SUPREME COURT

Introduction

IN THIS COUNTRY we accept judicial review by the Supreme Court as an article of constitutional faith. Academic writers occasionally question whether judicial review is a good idea.[1] But most Americans know that nothing practical hinges on the discussion. We may not like what the Supreme Court has done in some cases. We may vow to support only presidential candidates who will appoint different kinds of Justices from those who dominate the Court now or have done so in the past. Nevertheless, few Americans want to abolish the Court or eliminate its central powers.

Anxieties and Puzzles

At the same time, many of us feel anxiety about the Supreme Court's authority. The doubts arise from questions about the nature and force of law as it applies, if at all, to the Court's decision making. To a greater or lesser extent, sophisticated Americans have absorbed the basic teachings of Legal Realism. Informed citizens know that the Court divides, roughly, into judicial conservatives and judicial liberals. All but the most uninformed or naïve among us accept that the Justices' moral or political views influence their votes in some cases and that huge political consequences hinge on their decisions.[2]

A vivid illustration of Realism regarding the Supreme Court came in the aftermath of the death of Justice Antonin Scalia in February 2016. Scalia was a conservative, one of five Justices who were usually so identified at the time he died. If President Barack Obama could have appointed his successor, the Court's balance might have tipped from conservative to liberal for the first time since the 1970s. Republican senators recognized the stakes and refused even to consider confirming an Obama nominee, even though their stance left the Court short-handed for more than a year. Senate Republican leaders argued that the winner of the 2016 election, with a more recent mandate from the American public, should get to make the politically charged nomination of a Justice whose moral and political views would help to shape the direction of the Supreme Court.

If we are Realists, however, most of us are not Cynical Realists, who believe that the Justices simply vote their political preferences in constitutional cases, without regard to law, or that they are merely politicians in robes. The Supreme Court regularly decides upwards of 40 percent of its cases by unanimous vote.[3] In those cases, the Justices' political views play no obvious role. Moreover, although the trend lines may be troubling, leading political scientists report that, despite the advent of Legal Realism, public support for the Supreme Court typically survives even its most unpopular decisions.[4]

Somewhat ironically, another demonstration that most Americans are not Cynical Realists came from a widespread reaction to *Bush v. Gore*.[5] Some people of course thought that the Supreme Court ruled correctly when it halted a Florida recount that threatened to move the state from George W. Bush's column to that of Al Gore and thus make Gore, not Bush, the victor in the 2000 presidential election. A more interesting reaction emanated from the Gore side. Many Gore supporters denounced the decision not just as mistaken—for nearly everyone thinks many Court decisions mistaken—but as *illegitimate*.[6] Others have responded in similar ways to decisions invalidating campaign finance regulations, striking down gun control laws, and upholding a right to gay marriage. Legal and moral legitimacy, and the ways in which they relate to but differ from legal correctness and incorrectness, are among my central concerns in this book.

In a book on the Supreme Court written in 2008, the journalist Jeffrey Toobin reports that although *Bush v. Gore* initially caused ruptures among the Justices, most returned relatively swiftly to a business-as-usual approach.[7] According to Toobin, the notable exception was Justice David Souter. Toobin writes that Souter sometimes sat at his desk and wept about the decision. He did so not because he had suffered a political disappointment, and not because he thought the Court had erred (he dissented in myriad other cases without reacting similarly), but because he believed that the Justices in the majority had engaged in a betrayal. But a betrayal of what?

Over the course of this book, I hope to answer the question, What is the nature of the judicial responsibility that the Justices must not betray? The answer is not simple, but neither is the question. We might start here: if Toobin's tale about *Bush v. Gore* is accurate, it captures the sense—shared by many Americans—that an important but blurry line divides cases of reasonable, predictable, and understandable disagreement in the Supreme Court, including disagreement along ideological lines, from those in which the law, or norms of permissible and appropriate judicial decision making, clearly apply. With respect to the former, we are Realists. Dissent and disagreement are routine. But for a Justice to cross the line in a clear case should occasion outrage.

Also reflected in Toobin's account is an implicit picture of the nature and limits of constitutional law in the Supreme Court. When we think of examples of law, we may think of stop signs or the tax code. When we come to stop signs, we know we have to stop. The tax code is different, because it is more complicated. Many of us hire accountants or use computer programs to calculate our obligations. Still, we think there is an answer to nearly all questions on which those who know the tax code in all its intricacies would agree. After the calculations are done correctly, we owe the government one exact sum.

Law in the Supreme Court does not conform to the model of the stop sign or the tax code, even though betrayals of basic constitutional obligations remain possible. Law in the Supreme Court sometimes, maybe often, calls for the exercise of judgment, including judgment with an ideological component. Even in those cases, however, there are some constraints that the Justices cannot ignore without breaching obligations of fidelity to the Constitution and laws of the United States.

Although the foregoing distillation includes an important core of truth, it remains too simplistic. Among other things, we still need an account of the nature and sources of the supposedly clear lines that the Justices must not transgress. But here matters grow complicated. We might start with the cases in which the Justices seem genuinely outraged with one another and hurl accusations that their colleagues have behaved not just mistakenly but constitutionally indefensibly or illegitimately.

Judicial conservatives and judicial liberals both castigate their colleagues for perceived misbehavior. But their perceptions vary in interesting, ideologically correlated ways. Conservatives tend to deride judicial liberals as having lapsed into illegitimacy or abuse of power when liberals deviate from the "original public meaning" of constitutional language or, roughly speaking, what that language meant to the generation that wrote and adopted it. Examples come from cases involving abortion and gay rights. In *Roe v. Wade*, for instance, then-Justice William Rehnquist excoriated the majority for holding that the Fourteenth Amendment's Due Process Clause protects a woman's right to have an abortion when that conclusion deviated from apparent historical understandings.[8] "To reach its result, the Court necessarily has had to find within the scope of the Fourteenth Amendment a right that was apparently completely unknown to the drafters of the Amendment," he wrote.[9] In *Obergefell v. Hodges*, the Court's decision holding that there is a constitutional right to same-sex marriage, Justice Scalia accused the majority of engaging in "constitutional revision" that "robs the People of the most important liberty they asserted in the Declaration of Independence and won in the Revolution of 1776: the freedom to govern themselves."[10]

By contrast, liberals' howls of outrage have come most recently in cases in which a conservative majority overturned long-standing judicial precedents. *Citizens United v. FEC* furnishes a case in point.[11] In a decision holding that the First Amendment prohibits statutory restrictions on corporate expenditures for electioneering communications, the Court overturned two prior precedents and effectively eviscerated a congressionally enacted framework of campaign finance laws.[12] In "emphatically dissent[ing]" from the Court's ruling, Justice John Paul Stevens criticized the majority for "reject[ing] a century of history" and "blaz[ing] through our precedents."[13]

Again, however, complexity lurks just beneath the surface. If conservative Supreme Court Justices sometimes pillory liberals for deviating from the original meaning of constitutional language, it would be a mistake to think that conservatives always adhere to original public meanings themselves. Affirmative action cases furnish a good example. Few originalists—or those who believe that the original public meaning of constitutional language should normally control modern cases—argue that any provision of the Constitution was originally understood to bar preferences for historically disadvantaged minorities.[14] Abundant evidence suggests that the Framers and ratifiers of the Fourteenth Amendment's Equal Protection Clause did not view it as barring all race-based classifications.[15] Reconstruction Congresses, including the one that proposed the Fourteenth Amendment, specifically voted a number of appropriations for diverse categories of "colored" people, including widows as well as soldiers and sailors.[16] Even more striking, no one suggests that the Due Process Clause of the Fifth Amendment, which conservative Justices have relied on in attacking affirmative action programs enacted by the federal government, was originally viewed as barring race-based preferences for historically disadvantaged groups. (The Equal Protection Clause provides that "no State shall . . . deny to any person within its jurisdiction the equal protection of the laws," but makes no reference to Congress or the federal government.) When the Fifth Amendment's Due Process Clause was ratified in 1791, race-based discrimination was commonplace. Accordingly, in voting to invalidate affirmative action programs, the conservative Justices have relied almost entirely on judicial precedents, sometimes of their own creation. So far, none has cited the Constitution's original meaning as a ground for decision in these cases.

It would be equally mistaken to infer from liberals' assaults on conservatives' abandonment of long-standing precedents—in cases such as *Citizens United*—that liberals think that the Constitution or norms of judicial legitimacy require adherence to precedent in every case. To take just two examples, liberal majorities have recently overturned or narrowly distinguished Supreme Court precedents in gay rights cases, as well as in cases in which they have held the death penalty unconstitutional as applied to some categories of defendants. In *Lawrence v. Texas*, which held that the Constitution forbids states from criminalizing same-sex sodomy, the Court's five-Justice majority overruled *Bowers v. Hardwick*, a seventeen-year-old precedent that had upheld a state anti-sodomy law.[17] Writing for the majority, Justice Anthony Kennedy reasoned that "*Bowers* was not correct when it was decided, and it is not correct today. It ought not to remain binding precedent."[18] In *Lawrence*, it fell to one of the conservative Justices to chastise the liberal majority for infidelity to precedent.[19] Similarly, in *Atkins v. Virginia* and *Roper v. Simmons*, liberal majorities overruled precedents while holding it unconstitutional for states to execute people with mental retardation and juveniles, respectively.[20]

As these examples illustrate, in the sometimes angry back-and-forth about how the Court should resolve particular, disputed cases, contending coalitions of Justices—and their supporters in the public and the legal academy—recurrently appeal to what they suggest are the clear rules that divide legitimate from illegitimate judicial action. But their protestations may generate little faith that such rules actually exist. To the contrary, the heated arguments may foster two deeper worries.

One is that the Justices are rank hypocrites. Although they pledge fidelity to the Constitution and to rigorous methodologies for its interpretation, they stand ready to betray their commitments whenever they can promote their political ideologies by doing so. The other, related worry is that even if the Justices are not self-conscious hypocrites, constitutional adjudication in the Supreme Court may be like tennis without a net. There are no real rules or standards—and thus no real law and no objective legal standards of either correctness or legitimacy in constitutional interpretation. When all is said and done, the ideal of law in the Supreme Court is like the Great and Powerful Oz: a false front with a charlatan, or set of nine charlatans, behind the curtain.

Does either of these situations obtain? I do not think so, but neither do I believe that the worries are wholly unfounded. Explaining why is the first project of this book. Prescribing correctives is the second.

The Challenges of Legitimacy

The central organizing concept for the book—which links the perspectives of law, philosophy, and political science—is that of legitimacy. "Legitimacy" is a word with many meanings. When we speak about legitimacy, it is easy to talk ourselves into confusion. In this book, I draw a number of clarifying distinctions—for example, between the kind of sociological legitimacy that centrally interests political scientists and the legal and moral legitimacy that predominantly concern lawyers and philosophers. Among the book's principal ambitions is to draw together the perspectives of law, political science, and political theory in unraveling and ultimately solving some of the puzzles that surround law and legitimacy in the Supreme Court.

In the legal and especially the moral sense of "legitimacy" that defines the core of the book's inquiry, invocations of the concept seek to answer questions along the lines of, By what moral right does the government of the United States, and especially the Supreme Court, establish controversial rules of law, some of which many people think mistaken or even morally repugnant, and then enforce its dictates coercively? Or, perhaps better, How would the Supreme Court of the United States need to decide the cases that come before it—both procedurally and substantively—in order to justify imposing its will on those who reasonably disagree with its conclusions about the bearing of the Constitution on politically charged issues?

The book offers original answers to these questions. Some emerge from a vision of the nature of the law that binds the Supreme Court. As Chapter 4 argues at length, law, in the relevant sense, resides in norms of judicial practice that structure and constrain but do not always uniquely determine legal judgment. Such norms allow room for reasonable disagreement but mark some positions as legally untenable or unreasonable. What complicates matters is that even the norms that exclude some conclusions as legally unreasonable can themselves have vague, disputable fringes. In other words, we have, and need to understand the possibility of, debates about whether some judicial rulings are beyond the pale of the legally tenable. The frequent indeterminacy of constitutional language—which the book will explain, especially in Chapter 2—contributes to the need for, and helps to explain disagreements concerning the nature of, sound judicial judgment.

With law and language often failing to determine uniquely correct answers to hard constitutional questions, legitimacy emerges as a crucial concept—legally, morally, and sometimes sociologically. In the legal and moral senses with which I am most concerned, legitimacy differs importantly from correctness. We cannot reasonably expect every judicial judgment to be correct. Human judges are incorrigibly fallible. Nor can we expect the Supreme Court always to decide cases in ways that we applaud. Reasonable legal disagreement, like reasonable moral disagreement, has always existed and will not go away. We need to come to terms with it. We also need to come to grips with the idea that presidents with political ideologies different from ours will appoint Justices whose judicial philosophies we disapprove of—up to a point.

In conditions of relatively widespread reasonable disagreement, legal and moral legitimacy connote respect-worthiness. Even when we disagree with Supreme Court judgments, we can respect them, provided that they satisfy certain conditions. At this point in the book I can offer only a first approximation of the considerations that bear on the legitimacy or respect-worthiness of the Court's decisions. But it is vital to understand the nature of the decisions that the Court renders and the nature of the domain in which it claims an entitlement to respect.

The Court holds itself out as a legitimate authority. This is a complex term that I shall unpack later. In political theorists' terminology, however, a legitimate authority is a decision maker with the capacity to change the normative obligations of others.[21] Throughout U.S. history, the Supreme Court has famously claimed the authority to alter others' duties—and not just those of the immediate parties to cases before it. In *Cooper v. Aaron*, the Court upbraided Arkansas's governor and legislature for refusing to accede to the Court's school desegregation ruling in *Brown v. Board of Education*, even though the Arkansas governor and legislature were not parties to the earlier case.[22] In the course of its opinion, the Court appealed to "the basic principle that the federal judiciary is supreme in the exposition of the law of the Constitution."[23] Similarly, in *Planned Parenthood of Southeastern Pennsylvania v. Casey*, a case involving abortion rights, the Court claimed the authority to direct citizens to "end their national division by accepting a common mandate rooted in the Constitution."[24] When the Court refers to others' obligations of obedience to its decisions, I take it to speak in a moral, and not just in a legal, sense.

A few brief examples will illustrate the consequences. Following the Court's decisions in *Roe v. Wade* and *Planned Parenthood v. Casey*, officials cannot punish abortion, even if they think it immoral. State officials must furnish licenses to gay couples who seek to marry, even if those officials believe that same-sex marriage contravenes God's law. When Kim Davis, a county clerk in Rowan County, Kentucky, defied the Supreme Court's decision in *Obergefell v. Hodges* by refusing to issue marriage licenses to same-sex couples, a judge held her in contempt of court and ordered her jailed. *Obergefell* also bars legislators from enacting laws that some believe necessary to maintain a decent society.

If we ask how or by what right the Supreme Court gets to change not only legal but also moral obligations, we may be tempted to answer by stating that the Constitution gives the Court this power. But this response begs a central question. Does the Constitution in fact give the Supreme Court the power to alter people's legal and moral obligations if it deviates from the original meaning of constitutional language (as it may have done in upholding abortion rights in *Roe v. Wade* and rights to gay marriage in *Obergefell v. Hodges*) or if it overturns its own precedents for nonoriginalist reasons (as the majority may have done in *Citizens United*)? In considering this question, we can see again the sting of accusations that the Justices are in essence merely politicians, or politically motivated lawmakers, in robes.

Analysis of the Court's legitimate power needs to delve deeper. Although the Supreme Court claims to be a legitimate authority, its legitimate authority is derivative. We accept the Court's authority because we accept, and most of us feel obliged to support, the Constitution and the American legal system as a whole. And within that framework, the Justices' legitimate authority depends, in the first instance, on their carrying out the mandate of prior legitimate authorities. In other words, the Court's principal function is to determine what prior authorities—and, in particular, the Constitution—have decided or established, and to apply the dictates of prior authorities to the cases that come before it.

A difficulty, of course, is that prior authorities—centrally including the Constitution—do not always speak clearly or determinately. As a result, the Supreme Court must sometimes establish law for the future. At the barest minimum, it must make clear what the Constitution's language left unclear. (For example, the Constitution provides that no one can be deprived of life, liberty, or property without "due process of law"—but no one thinks that this phrase determinately establishes exactly what "process" a state must provide before it can temporarily remove a child from the custody of a parent whom state officials believe to be unfit in the twenty-first century.)[25] In instances in which the Court functions for all practical purposes as a lawmaker, it must so behave as to constitute itself and its decisions as legitimate authorities in their own right and as capable of changing the normative obligations of others going forward.

The Court's claims to legitimate authority are, accordingly, Janus-faced. They look simultaneously backward, to what prior legitimate authorities have established, and forward, to the future, as the Court strives to make decisions that qualify as legal and moral authorities to whose dictates others ought—in the moral sense of that term—to adhere. The notion of moral authority is crucial. It depends not on brute force but on the Court's claimed capacity to make good decisions in both the backward-looking and the forward-looking senses. When the Court speaks in the name of the law in resolving contentious issues, it almost necessarily claims to make the morally and practically best decisions that the law allows. The Constitution vests the Court with its powers based on the premise that its decisions will produce better and fairer results—within the limits that the law allows—than would occur otherwise.[26] Most of us accept the Court's legitimate authority on the same basis.

So far, so good, you may say, but haven't I myself begged one of the main questions that I set out to answer: What should we say about the legitimacy of the Supreme Court's decisions in cases in which we believe that the Justices have erred, maybe even badly? In such cases, legitimacy in the relevant sense depends on a compendium of considerations that bear on respect-worthiness. It will take most of this book to discuss those considerations in adequate detail, but three play especially central roles. First, the Justices must stay within the bounds of law, or at least exhibit reasonable judgment about what they can do within the bounds of law. Second, the Justices must exhibit good or at least reasonable practical and moral judgment—another matter about which we must expect some disagreement. But in both cases, I emphasize, we should not take too exacting or unforgiving a stance. We need to expect reasonable legal and moral disagreement. We should not come too readily to angry or cynical conclusions about the Justices or their constitutional conclusions.

In this context, a third consideration becomes crucial. In the name of legitimacy, we can and should demand that the Justices support their judgments with arguments that they advance in good faith. Like legitimacy itself, the concept of good faith will loom large in this book. Here I can introduce it but not explicate it fully.

When the Justices take positions in such cases as *Bush v. Gore*, *Roe v. Wade*, *Citizens United v. FCC*, and *Obergefell v. Hodges*, they need to offer supporting legal arguments. Sometimes those arguments assume substantive premises—for example, about the values that the First Amendment, the Equal Protection Clause, or the Due Process Clause protects. Sometimes, moreover, the Justices' arguments involve methodological commitments—for example, about the significance of the original public meaning of constitutional language or about the judicial obligation to follow precedent. These substantive and methodological commitments need not be simple, much less simplistic. For example, a Justice can reasonably believe that the original meaning of constitutional language should control in some, but not all, cases, or that precedent binds in some cases but not in others. Arguing in good faith does not entail the denial of complexity in constitutional reasoning.

Good faith does, however, require that the Justices—like the rest of us—sincerely believe what they say when engaging in constitutional argument. Leaving the Justices temporarily aside, imagine that you and I engage in an extended constitutional discussion that includes a sequence of cases. We can respectfully disagree about many substantive and methodological points as we proceed. But suppose I reject your argument in one case, involving a claim that there is a constitutional right to gay marriage, by asserting that "there can be no such right because the originally understood meaning of constitutional language is always controlling; otherwise the Constitution would not be law." Suppose then that in discussing a subsequent case, I take a position contrary to the original meaning of constitutional language—for example, by insisting that the Due Process Clause of the Fifth Amendment bars affirmative action—and you challenge me by pointing out that when that provision was ratified, in 1791, no one understood it as doing so. If I insist that affirmative action by the federal government is unconstitutional even so, I may have a plausible explanation. For example, I might say that in the first case, I mistakenly or carelessly spoke too categorically: what I actually believe is that the original public meaning should always determine constitutional outcomes unless clear and contrary judicial precedents that have become woven into the fabric of our law dictate otherwise. If so, I could reasonably ask you to respect my reasoning in both cases.

But suppose my response in the second case is, "Although I said that the original understanding controlled the first case, I did so only for rhetorical purposes, without really believing it, and I certainly don't feel bound by history now." At this point you would reasonably conclude that arguing with me about constitutional law is pointless due to my lack of good faith in argumentation. My side of the argument would be a charade. You would have no reason to respect me or the conclusions that I reach unless you agreed with them anyway. And I would justifiably respond to you in the same way if you said that recent judicial precedents should always be followed when it suited your purposes but as readily renounced precedent-based reasoning whenever you did not like the conclusions to which it pointed.

As we would respond to each other, so we should respond to the Justices of the Supreme Court. Within the bounds of reasonable legal disagreement, we can respect Justices with whom we disagree, provided that the disagreement is principled. We can even respect Justices who change their minds, so long as they provide reasons for doing so that they genuinely believe and intend to adhere to in the future. But our respect for the Justices—and our appraisal of the Court's decisions and its institutional legitimacy—would rightly suffer grievously if we came to view the Justices as cynical manipulators whose arguments possess no integrity.

Argumentative good faith is not, of course, the only criterion that bears on the legitimacy of judicial decision making in the Supreme Court. Even if all the majority Justices in *Roe v. Wade* sincerely believed the Court's arguments to be good ones, some critics would think the Court's conclusion too legally and morally unreasonable to deserve their respect. In response to those critics, we might have more to say on the merits, but we should get the point with regard to legitimacy. Sometimes we will disagree about legal and moral legitimacy. Disagreement about legitimacy should not happen as frequently as about the correctness of judicial decisions, but it will not vanish entirely.

If disagreements about legitimacy persist, we should also be ready to pursue a conversation—to which Chapter 7 seeks to contribute—concerning how sociological legitimacy relates to moral legitimacy. To oversimplify greatly for the moment, we should prepare to consider when, if ever, the Justices should allow other people's perceptions of the moral legitimacy of their decisions to affect their actual decision making.

As this preliminary discussion will have signaled, my approach to issues of law, language, and legitimacy in the Supreme Court will sometimes involve close attention to the meaning and application of legal concepts, centrally including that of legitimacy. Subsequent chapters will also probe the concept of law as it applies to adjudication in the Supreme Court and the meaning of constitutional "meaning." In light of the deeply practical nature of my interests, some may regard this angle of approach as naïvely misguided. I believe otherwise. In adopting a conceptual framework for addressing matters of profound practical import, I borrow an insight from the great economist John Maynard Keynes. In their economic thinking, he maintained, the world's most ostensibly practical people are "usually the slaves of some defunct economist."[27] In constitutional law, too, I believe that practical people are often in the grip of

long familiar theories and sometimes resulting confusions that
drive and explain their actions, even if they are not conscious of it.

For those who resist this claim, my conceptual approach offers
something weaker but still significant. I shall seek to explain how
it *could* be the case, even if currently it is not, that the Justices' debates
about the requirements of law and legitimacy in the Supreme Court
might be meaningful, genuine ones, despite the obvious fact of ideologically inflected disagreement. In other words, I shall offer an account of what law and legitimacy might be such that we could have
them right now, manifest in the Supreme Court, despite what might
look on the surface to be cacophonous inconsistency. And if we do
not have genuine law and meaningful legitimacy in the Court, then
we should insist on getting them. If persuaded that some high-
sounding ideals are unattainable, we should not succumb directly
to Cynical Realism but should seek instead to identify more modest
yet significant standards of legitimate judicial decision making,
under law, even in and by the Supreme Court. Especially in the
current climate of political discord, we should view judicial legitimacy as a practically meaningful ideal, not a species of pie-in-the-sky
utopianism.

A Preview of the Argument Ahead

My analysis begins in Chapter 1 with further examination and
explication of the concepts of judicial legitimacy and legitimate judicial authority. Chapter 1 carefully distinguishes sociological,
legal, and moral conceptions of legitimacy and explains how they
relate to one another. The chapter also explains why these different
senses of legitimacy matter. (The book recurrently emphasizes that
in discussions of concepts such as law and legitimacy, it is vitally
important to maintain a focus on what, practically, is at stake or
why anyone ought to care.)

Chapter 1 also develops the important thesis that moral legitimacy
needs to be conceptualized in partly dualist terms. It defines both a
minimum, beneath which a political regime (or a judicial decision)
should command no respect at all, and an ideal. We should demand
minimal legitimacy from the Supreme Court and hope for it to ap-

proximate the ideal as closely as possible. Nevertheless, it is important not to think of moral legitimacy, including the moral legitimacy of Supreme Court decision making, in all-or-nothing terms.

With the notion of judicial legitimacy as applied to the Supreme Court having been preliminarily explicated in Chapter 1, Chapter 2 begins an exploration of the Supreme Court's backward-looking obligations by probing the notion of constitutional "meaning." We agree that the Supreme Court must enforce the Constitution and that, in order to do so, it must determine what the Constitution means. But when we talk about the meaning of the Constitution, to what do we refer?

In many if not most of the important cases that come before the Supreme Court, Chapter 2 argues, constitutional language frames the challenge for judicial resolution but does not determine a uniquely correct outcome. In light of reflection on history and language, this conclusion should provoke no surprise. We know that the Founding generation disagreed about many issues. And beyond purely historical disagreements lie deep conceptual issues about what "meaning" means.[28] With respect to these issues, Chapter 2 argues that meaning is a concept with many senses, not just one, and that there will often be multiple candidates to supply the Constitution's original meaning—even if we assume that the original meaning should always control. In short, the chapter establishes that although language is surely relevant to constitutional adjudication in the Supreme Court, hard cases are seldom ones in which outcomes can hinge exclusively on matters of historical or linguistic fact.

With Chapter 2 having argued that the Supreme Court must often choose among competing candidates to supply the Constitution's meaning, Chapter 3 pursues the question of how and why historical practice and precedent subsequent to the Founding era matter to constitutional adjudication. In the *Federalist Papers*, James Madison and Alexander Hamilton both acknowledged the indeterminacy of constitutional language, but both appeared to think that practice and precedent would help to alleviate the problem.[29] Constitutional meaning would become fixed over time, they maintained.

Chapter 3 explores that hypothesis but comes to nearly the opposite conclusion from the one that Madison and Hamilton reached.

The modern worry about a legally unconstrained Supreme Court may be as much exacerbated as alleviated by judicial precedents. Nearly everyone agrees that past judicial rulings can alter what otherwise would be the Justices' backward-looking obligations in some cases. Yet no one thinks that the Supreme Court must always adhere to precedents that it regards as mistaken. To take perhaps the most noncontroversial example, nearly everyone agrees that the Supreme Court acted rightly when, in the middle of the twentieth century, it swept aside a number of precedents that had permitted state-mandated segregation on the basis of race.

With cases such as these in view, we need to think about what the Supreme Court should or must do, as a matter of law, when it must consider not only the Constitution's original meaning but also the meaning ascribed to relevant constitutional language by other authoritative decision makers at subsequent times. Given a conflict of authorities, do the Justices simply get to choose as they will?

Chapter 4 takes up the challenge of conceptualizing "law" in the Supreme Court. It begins with a familiar but fundamental premise: the Constitution is law not because it claims that status, or because the Framers commanded that subsequent generations should obey the Constitution, but because Americans today accept it as the governing charter of the United States. In the leading practice-based theory of law, Professor H. L. A. Hart identified judges and other officials as the decisive cohort whose "rules of recognition" fix the meaning of legal and constitutional norms.[30] Chapter 4 accepts Hart's basic portrait of the foundations of our constitutional order but with one possible modification and with another change of emphasis. First, Chapter 4 insists that the practices of Justices and other officials in recognizing the Constitution as valid are nested in and conditioned by the attitudes and practices of other officials and ultimately the American public. Second, Chapter 4 emphasizes that the rules or standards of recognition that apply to contested cases in the Supreme Court are often vague and indeterminate. In such cases, the Justices must exercise moral and practical judgment, albeit within bounds that the law defines.

The result is a roughly (but only roughly) two-tiered picture of law in the Supreme Court. One tier consists of the myriad easy cases to which applicable rules or practices of recognition yield a clear resolution. The other encompasses hard cases in which prevailing rules or standards of proper Supreme Court adjudication call for the exercise of moral or practical judgment. There is of course no sharp dividing line between these two categories. Among other things, cases can become hard because of their moral stakes, which different Justices will appraise differently. Nevertheless, recognition that the Justices confront many easy cases, and understand them as such, should help to reassure us that there is law in the Supreme Court. Even apart from "easy" cases, Chapter 4 argues that important, tacitly recognized rules guide and sometimes determine the Justices' decision making. To back up that claim, it offers a number of meaningful examples.

Chapter 5 continues the discussion of law in and binding on the Supreme Court by examining the topic of constitutional constraints. Who can enforce the law that ostensibly binds the Justices? And if the answer were "no one," should we conclude that constitutional adjudication in the Supreme Court is like tennis without a net after all? Having posed these questions, Chapter 5 confronts and rejects the argument that because no other institution can enforce the Constitution against the Supreme Court, the Court cannot be bound by law in any meaningful sense. In particular, this chapter identifies a number of mechanisms through which other institutions can and do constrain the Justices. To borrow a phrase from political scientists, the Justices operate—and know that they operate—within politically constructed bounds.

The existence of political and other constraints on the Justices of course generates the possibility of collisions between the Justices' felt constitutional obligations and the checks that the Constitution creates against judicial power. The problem here is probably an insoluble one, well expressed in the ancient query "Who will guard the guardians?"[31] Chapter 5's important empirical point, however, is that the law that applies in the Supreme Court can sometimes be enforced against the Justices, however imperfectly, by other institutions of government and their officials.

Chapter 6 examines the role of constitutional theories and methodological argumentation in the Supreme Court. Theories such as originalism and various versions of living constitutionalism aim to serve two functions. They seek to identify optimal or correct answers to disputed questions and, equally importantly, to provide assurances that judicial rulings are both substantively and procedurally legitimate.

Without disparaging the importance of methodological premises in constitutional argument, Chapter 6 aims to transform and transcend the increasingly tired and stylized debate about the comparative merits of well-known constitutional theories. As a brief review makes plain, all of the familiar theories are too incomplete or underspecified to resolve all possible cases. As a result, constitutional theories and the Justices' articulated methodological principles frequently misfire in their aspiration to provide assurances of legitimacy in judicial decision making. Absent further specification, commentators recurrently excoriate the Justices, and the Justices embarrass each other, with charges of unprincipled manipulation. But the proper response, Chapter 6 argues, does not lie in the ex ante development of algorithmically determinate substitutes. The possibility of such rigidly mechanical theories should frighten rather than inspire us. The flow of experience inevitably churns up unforeseen issues. We should not risk the disastrous constitutional outcomes that rigid theories developed in advance of experience might impose.

As a better approach, Chapter 6 proposes a Reflective Equilibrium Theory, modeled on John Rawls's celebrated methodology of moral and political deliberation.[32] When the Justices' case-by-case intuitions about constitutional justice are at odds with their prior interpretive methodological assumptions or commitments, Reflective Equilibrium Theory prescribes that they—like the rest of us who care about constitutional law and engage in constitutional argument—should consider and reconsider our case-specific convictions and our views about sound interpretive methodology at the same time, in search of an equilibrium solution. Most often, case-specific judgments should yield to demands for the consistent application of sound interpretive principles. This is the hallmark of principled decision making. Occasionally, however, unshakeable convictions about the constitutional correctness of particular outcomes should instigate a reformulation or revision of prior methodological commitments (as may have occurred for some of the Justices in the iconic school desegregation case of *Brown v. Board of Education*). In cases of revision or reformulation, we should hope that the complexities of a new case enrich a Justice's perspective and provoke her to adjust her theory of constitutional interpretation in order better to realize the simultaneously backward- and forward-looking aspects of legitimacy in judicial decision making. Even and especially in such cases, however, the Justices should acknowledge an unyielding obligation of argument in good faith, which requires them to make only arguments in which they believe and to rely only on interpretive premises that they genuinely endorse, looking forward to future cases.

Chapter 7 concludes the book by offering legitimacy-based appraisals of the Supreme Court today and of the prospect for better tomorrows. It discusses evidence of the Court's diminishing sociological legitimacy, explains why this evidence should occasion concern, and offers prescriptions.

1

Legitimacy and Judicial Authority

THE SUPREME COURT claims to be a legitimate authority, capable of altering people's obligations.[1] At the very least, the Court's decisions create legal rights, responsibilities, powers, and disabilities that did not exist previously. Following *Roe v. Wade*, for example, women had new rights.[2] Correspondingly, state officials faced new legal disabilities. Supreme Court decisions can impose new affirmative duties as well. In the wake of *Brown v. Board of Education*, local officials learned that they had an obligation not just to stop discriminating but also to eradicate the vestiges of prior school segregation "root and branch."[3] What is more, the Court's claims of legitimate authority appear to extend from law into the domain of moral obligation. Although the Court did not purport to change the moral status of abortion in *Roe* or of white supremacist attitudes in *Brown*, it claimed to establish that morally conscientious citizens should not interfere with the legal rights that it had recognized.

But a puzzle lurks behind these claims. The legitimacy of Supreme Court authority is not, to say the least, a simple, obvious, or uncontestable fact. Many people argue that the Court's decision in *Roe* was illegitimate. Other people hurl charges of illegitimacy in other contexts. For example, many who applauded *Roe* maintained that the Court's decision in *Bush v. Gore*—which halted a presidential recount in the state of Florida and effectively blocked any possibility that Al Gore might prevail in the 2000 presidential election—was illegitimate.[4] Perhaps relatedly, many observers predicted that both *Roe* and *Bush v. Gore* would cause the Court to lose its legitimacy in some more general, further-reaching sense. Similar controversies swarm around more recent decisions involving the constitutionality of same-sex marriage, campaign finance regulation, and gun control.

This chapter examines the meaning of claims involving legitimate judicial authority and the legitimacy and illegitimacy of Supreme Court decisions. When people talk about legitimacy, what are they talking about? By what standards should we judge claims of legitimacy and illegitimacy in Supreme Court decision making? What is at stake? And, most important, why should we care?

Although this chapter will answer these questions, we need to begin by drawing distinctions. First, we need to distinguish among sociological, moral, and legal concepts of legitimacy.

Sociological legitimacy involves prevailing public attitudes toward governments, institutions, or decisions. It depends on what factually is the case about how people think or respond—not on what their thinking ought to be. A regime or decision can be widely approved (and thus sociologically legitimate) but morally misguided and illegitimate. For example, the Nazi regime in Hitler's Germany may have enjoyed widespread sociological legitimacy. Conversely, a decision could be legally and morally sound but deeply unpopular and widely defied. As these contrasts suggest, sociological legitimacy is not the only kind of legitimacy with which we have reason to be concerned. We also have reason, and sometimes greater reason, to care about moral legitimacy. Moral legitimacy is at bottom a moral concept, concerned with the attitudes that we *ought* to hold (regardless of what others say or think) toward claims of authority. Finally, legal legitimacy is a legal rather than a sociological or moral concept. It will require complex unpacking to sort out the relations among sociological, moral, and legal legitimacy.

Second, we need to distinguish claims about different possible *objects* of legitimacy judgments. These include particular court decisions (such as *Roe v. Wade* or *Bush v. Gore*), the Supreme Court as an institution, and the American legal system as a whole.

Through most of this book, my main concerns will be the legal and especially the moral legitimacy of Supreme Court decision making in particular cases. But legitimacy judgments involving cases almost inevitably presuppose the sociological and moral legitimacy of the surrounding legal system. Accordingly, large chunks of this chapter will focus on issues involving the overall constitutional order in which the Supreme Court is situated. Judgments involving the Court's legitimacy as an institution will receive attention mostly only as they bear on judgments about its decisions in individual cases.

Distinguishing Sociological and Moral Legitimacy

For a myriad of purposes, it is vital to distinguish between *sociological legitimacy*, on the one hand, and *moral or political legitimacy*, on the other. Proceeding initially in sociological terms, we sometimes ask whether there is a functioning legal system within a particular territory (such as Libya, for example). Where functioning legal systems exist, we might say that they have de facto authority. This assertion implies only that enough people, and especially officials, accept the dictates of identifiable laws or recognized officials for law, rather than anarchy, to prevail.

Slightly distinct from the question whether there are functioning governments with de facto authority is the question of sociological legitimacy. This is the question whether people (and, if so, how many of them) believe that the law or the constitution deserves to be respected or obeyed for reasons that go beyond fear of adverse consequences.[5] Libya might again function as an example. During the Gaddafi regime, we might say, Libya's government had de facto authority but lacked widespread sociological legitimacy. In the history of political theory, Max Weber most famously emphasized the importance of sociological legitimacy to the effective functioning of governments.[6] For Weber, legitimacy numbered among several foundations of de facto political authority. In modern states, he thought, many people obey the law not just because they fear the consequences of noncompliance but because they think they ought to obey.

Loosely following Weber, I shall associate sociological legitimacy with beliefs that the law and formal legal authorities within a particular regime deserve respect or obedience and with a further disposition to obey the law for reasons besides self-interest. As so defined, sociological legitimacy depends wholly on facts about what people think, not an independent moral appraisal of how people ought to think. In addition, sociological legitimacy is relative in a double sense. First, it is relative to individuals and to groups. Within the United States, for example, many people almost surely obey the law for reasons that go beyond self-interest, but others undoubtedly deny that the Constitution and laws inherently deserve obedience or even respect. Such attitudes, moreover, can vary over time. Second, some have much stronger attitudes of respect and dispositions to obey or demand obedience than do others. Accordingly, sociological legitimacy can exist in degrees.

With due recognition of these qualifications, I shall assume, going forward, that most Americans believe that they and their fellow citizens, and especially public officials and Justices of the Supreme Court, ought to obey the law, centrally including the Constitution.[7] In so assuming, I rush past a number of important issues. Among the questions to which I shall return is what it means for judges and officials to obey the Constitution.

For now, suffice it to say that we should care about sociological legitimacy insofar as we care about whether, and, if so, to what extent, people living within the United States—including Supreme Court Justices, other public officials, and ultimately the public—will be disposed to respect and obey the Constitution and laws of the United States and the decisions of the Supreme Court.[8] As I shall emphasize in later chapters, we should not take compliance for granted in all circumstances.

When legitimacy functions as a *moral* (rather than a sociological) concept, the answers to questions about its nature and significance differ markedly. The question of moral legitimacy is not whether the Justices or anyone else in fact respects or endeavors to obey the Constitution and laws of the United States. It is, rather, whether, morally speaking, people ought to do so or whether governmental officials are morally justified in coercing compliance.[9] We might frame the circumstances or problem of legitimacy in the following terms: Nearly everyone lives within the jurisdiction of a government that enacts laws that it enforces coercively. Nearly all of us, however, believe that some of the laws to which we are subject are unduly burdensome, unwise, or unjust. Why should we think that we or others ought to obey (if we do)? Or how might officials justify their actions, morally, in coercing those who press the question, "What moral right do you or does the state have to coerce me in this way?"

The nature and significance of the concept of moral legitimacy emerge from these questions. As a first approximation, we invoke the concept of moral legitimacy, or illegitimacy, to answer the questions whether citizens have an obligation to respect or obey their governments and whether governments have a right to rule those within their territory. A morally legitimate regime is one with the power to alter normative obligations (though I postpone, for the moment, the question of which normative obligations). In order to have that moral power, a legal regime must satisfy certain moral conditions. Conversely, if the overall body of law within a legal regime falls beneath some standard, or if morality would forbid conformity to enough of its dictates, it will lack legitimate authority in the moral sense, even if it enjoys broad support among its population. This situation may have existed with Hitler's Third Reich.

Ideal, Minimal, and Two-Level Theories of Moral Legitimacy

The leading theories of moral and political legitimacy divide into two main categories. One consists of *ideal* theories, which attempt to specify the necessary conditions for legal orders or assertions of state authority to be perfectly morally justified or to deserve unanimous obedience. The other consists of *minimal* or relative theories, which address a different question, involving when governments that may be far short of ideal, and even unjust in significant respects, are nevertheless good enough to deserve respect or obedience (in preference to anarchy) or to justify officials in coercively enforcing the law. A third category embraces theories that aspire to combine an account of the irreducible minima needed for legitimacy to exist with the ultimate ideals of legitimacy to which a regime ought to aspire. In my view, only a theory of this third type could satisfy all of the demands that we reasonably make of the concept of moral legitimacy.

Ideal theories of legitimate authority figure prominently in the literature of political theory, from Plato through Jean-Jacques Rousseau to Robert Nozick.[10] But such theories have an implication that might make us doubt their practical usefulness in answering questions about law and legitimacy in the Supreme Court. That implication is that in the history of the world, there has never been, and likely never will be, a legitimate government.[11] Certainly the leading ideal theories would mark the Constitution of the United States and its surrounding legal system as failing to possess legitimate authority.

Ideal theories come in two classic varieties and, possibly, a more modern hybrid version. The first classic type looks to the consent of the governed to provide the foundations of legitimate authority: people who have consented to be governed by specified principles cannot reasonably object when the government enforces those principles.[12] For consent to justify coercion, theorists in the social contractarian tradition have usually maintained that it must be unanimous.[13]

The Constitution of the United States never received unanimous consent. At the time of its ratification, many white males opposed it. Women could not vote. Many African Americans were enslaved. Nor would the Constitution win unanimous consent in a yes-or-no vote today.

A second asserted foundation for moral legitimacy lies in ultimate standards of justice: a perfectly just constitutional regime would be legitimate even in the absence of consent.[14] If we ask today whether the Constitution and legal system of the United States are perfectly just, few would answer in the affirmative. To cite just one example, conservatives would complain that the government engages in too much redistribution of resources from the better off to the less well off, liberals that it does too little.

Perched between consent-based and substantive theories are those that root governmental legitimacy in hypothetical consent.[15] Such theories ask whether everyone would consent to a scheme of governing principles, or would have good reason to consent, under fair conditions. John Rawls's "liberal" theory of legitimacy epitomizes this approach.[16] Rawls takes it for granted that all or nearly all of us will regard some laws as improvident and possibly even as seriously unjust. On this assumption, the problem of legitimacy is to identify terms on which we should respect or obey the government despite disagreements with some of its policies that trace, ultimately, to disagreements with our fellow citizens about what the law ought to be. So defining the problem, Rawls looks to the constitution to solve it. Given the facts of disagreement about particular laws and the urgent need for a government to keep the peace, Rawls says that we should give our respect, cooperation, and obedience to the prevailing governmental regime if it operates under "a *constitution* . . . [that] all citizens may reasonably be expected to endorse in the light of principles and ideals" that should be acceptable to them "as reasonable and rational."[17] People are "reasonable," Rawls stipulates, insofar as they "are willing to govern their conduct by a principle from which they and others can reason in common; and reasonable people take into account the consequences of their actions on others' well-being."[18] In short, a governmental regime is legitimate if it operates under a constitution that all reasonable people would or ought to accept under circumstances of reasonable disagreement.

Rawls's theory of legitimacy places great weight on the notion of reasonableness. But his explication of that crucial concept is ambiguous. On one possible interpretation, the ideal of reasonableness that matters for moral legitimacy implies that constitution writers have given due and equal consideration to the interests of everyone in framing a constitution that all ought to be able to endorse in light of shared "principles and ideals." On this interpretation, if the constitution deviates from principles and ideals (in its "essentials") that I, as a reasonable person, could be expected to "endorse" as reasonable—suppose, for example, that it denies equal rights to some groups or gives some people more voting power than others—then I need not view it as morally or politically legitimate. This, of course, would be a very stringent standard of legitimacy. If a constitution is unjust or unfair in any substantial respect or embodies the self-interested and unreasonable demands of those who simply happened to possess controlling power at the time of its adoption, it would fail the relevant test.

If we adopted this conception of moral or political legitimacy, it would be easy to identify ways in which reasonable people might withhold consent from the U.S. Constitution. At the time of the Constitution's ratification, the most palpably objectionable aspect involved its toleration of and support for chattel slavery in states where slavery existed. Although the abolition of slavery addressed this problem, other grounds for objection continue to exist. In considering whether all reasonable people would assent to the current version of the U.S. Constitution, we might focus on the guarantee that each state must have equal representation in the Senate, regardless of population.[19] This constitutionally entrenched repudiation of the one-person, one-vote principle reflects a historical compromise, forged as a result of hard and self-interested bargaining by representatives of small states at the Constitutional Convention, not a "principle" that all reasonable people could be expected to "endorse."[20] I would expect that other reasonable people could offer further examples of what they regard as constitutional deficiencies. Accordingly, if Rawls's concept of the reasonable were stringently interpreted, in a way that made his "liberal theory of legitimacy" an ideal theory, then I think the U.S. Constitution would fail to satisfy it, just as it would fail to meet the demands of universal consent and perfect justice.[21]

If the U.S. Constitution and legal system come up short under ideal theories of legitimacy, we should wish to do better. We should all want a legal system that is more just and democratic and to which all reasonable people—taking others' views and interests into account, but also insisting that others must afford them the same consideration—would give their assent. This, roughly, is why we should care about ideal theories of legitimacy. Such theories give us targets at which we ought to aim, even if we can never expect to score a bull's-eye.

But even, and indeed especially, if the U.S. Constitution is not ideally legitimate, we can consider the alternative question whether the Constitution is legitimate enough to generate obligations of respect or obedience or to justify coercive enforcement of the law. We can see a recognition of the practical urgency of this question in Rawls, who—at a crucial point—begins to push his inquiry toward identifying minimal, rather than ideal, governmental legitimacy. The test for legitimacy, he thus writes, is not whether a constitution is "perfectly just" but whether it is "sufficiently just" or "just enough in view of the circumstances and social conditions."[22]

In turning the inquiry from moral ideals to what reasonable people would take to be sufficiently just under less than ideal conditions, Rawls appears to rely on an interpretation that would require reasonable people sometimes to accede to unreasonable demands by others in endorsing a constitution in order to achieve a reasonably just, law-governed social order. If we adopt this interpretation, we might conclude that the question for reasonable citizens with regard to the U.S. Constitution is whether to take it or leave it. I may think it unreasonable for the citizens of small states to insist on the same representation in the Senate as California, but the question for me may not be whether the Constitution now on offer is just or even reasonable in all respects but whether it would be reasonable to reject the Constitution with no option besides anarchy currently on the table.

This approach to thinking about what reasonable people should accept and acknowledge as a morally legitimate legal regime both resonates with a familiar usage of the term "legitimacy" and captures important considerations in thinking about the appropriate moral stance toward less than perfect governments. Even in a world in which no governments are ideally legitimate, we frequently use the term "legitimacy" in a different sense and say, for example, that the governments of France and Canada are legitimate but those of North Korea and Turkmenistan are not. In this usage, our practical, moral concern in inquiring into legitimacy is likely to be whether a particular regime is minimally good enough to deserve support or respect, or whether public officials are morally justified in coercively enforcing its laws.[23]

Proponents of minimal theories typically begin with the premise that decent human lives would be impossible without government and law. Against this background, such theories maintain that the need for effective government generates a moral duty to support any reasonably just legal regime, absent a fair prospect of its swift and relatively nonviolent replacement by better institutions.[24]

If we wish to appraise legal regimes for minimal or relative rather than ideal legitimacy, a question of course arises concerning the metric that we ought to use. In response, we most appropriately rely on the same normative ideals that feature in discussions of ideal legitimacy, even though we may have to be minimally satisfied with less than the ideal in light of concerns about whether there are realistic options between support for an imperfect regime and civil war or anarchy. The first ideal involves relative substantive justice. Is the regime's set of institutions and rights guarantees at least reasonably just? The second involves political democracy and fair allocations of decision-making power. In a less than ideal world characterized by reasonable moral and political disagreement, we cannot sensibly insist on unanimous agreement as a test of legitimacy. Nevertheless, we can respect the principle that everyone's interests and opinions count by insisting that all citizens should have rights of democratic participation. Accordingly, democratic decision making is an important source of moral and political legitimacy, even if it is not the exclusive source under less than ideal conditions.[25] A third criterion concerns fairness in the application of reasonably just and reasonably democratic laws. Fair procedures for judicial and quasi-judicial decision making can also contribute to a regime's moral legitimacy in the minimal or relative sense.

As measured by the spare and uninspiring premises that support minimal theories of moral or political legitimacy, the Constitution and laws of the United States seem to me to pass muster rather easily. I believe—as I think most other Americans do—that the American legal system is reasonably just and that it is sufficiently democratic to be worthy of respect. I also think that our judicial system is reasonably fair, despite deficiencies that disadvantage the less well off relative to the better off.

In reaching this judgment, only one issue gives me substantial pause. In the domain of moral argument, eloquent voices have asserted that our nation's historic and continuing mistreatment of racial minorities has rendered the American legal system morally illegitimate, at least from the perspective of minority groups.[26] This argument raises important issues about the role of perspective in appraising moral legitimacy.

When we make claims about moral legitimacy, as much as when we aver that murder is wrong, we assert judgments about what is morally the case, without regard to perspective. When I say that murder is wrong, I mean that murder is wrong, full stop. Slaughtering Jews may have been morally acceptable from the perspective of the Nazis, but insofar as we are making moral rather than sociological judgments, we need to judge—on the basis of reflection and argument—how we and everyone else *ought* to think about the matter. Morality cannot depend on perspective in a sense that could make the slaughtering of Jews right for the Nazis, given their perspective, but wrong for you or me, given ours. At first blush, the claim that our moral judgments are judgments about what is right or wrong for everyone may sound arrogant and imperial. As reflection should attest, however, it merely describes the inescapable presuppositions of moral judgment and argumentation.[27] When we confront moral questions, we must each—as morally responsible beings—decide for ourselves what morality requires. If we are morally responsible, we cannot cede responsibility to the Supreme Court or any purported body of experts, any more than the citizens of Nazi Germany could responsibly let Hitler judge for them. Once again, moreover, our claims of moral correctness or incorrectness imply the falsity of contrary views.

When we judge the moral legitimacy of political regimes, however, we need to consider whether perspective, or something analogous to perspective, might matter in a different sense. More concretely, we must consider whether the severe disadvantaging of some groups relative to others might make a legal order morally illegitimate—even in what I have called the minimal sense—with respect to members of those disadvantaged groups but not to other members of the community. An example may come from the pre–Civil War legal regime in the United States. I would hesitate to say that it lacked minimal moral legitimacy insofar as it purported to impose obligations on white Americans. But I would confidently deny that it imposed any of the obligations on enslaved African Americans that we ordinarily regard the notion of moral legitimacy as importing. From this example, I conclude that even the minimal moral legitimacy of a political regime can be relative to groups or group status, as judged from the perspective of a reasonable member of the relevant, disadvantaged groups.

If this conclusion is correct, it has potentially uncomfortable implications for well-off Americans, and especially for well-off whites, such as me: we need to take seriously the question whether the American legal system is minimally morally legitimate today in its relationship to all minority groups in our society. This is far too large a question for me to take on here. Among its daunting aspects, it has complex empirical as well as normative dimensions. In going forward, I shall assume, as I have said, that the American legal regime is morally legitimate in its relationship to most if not all citizens, but not without anxiety that the question, "morally legitimate with respect to whom?" deserves more searching examination than I can give it here.

The possibility that moral legitimacy might be relative to groups helps to highlight the importance of a question that deserves close attention. So far, I have not said exactly what practical consequences follow from a conclusion that a government either possesses or fails to possess moral legitimacy. On the traditional view, when a state has legitimate authority, then those subject to its jurisdiction have a general obligation to obey its laws.[28] (Nearly all agree that if a general obligation of obedience exists, it is defeasible in the case of seriously unjust laws, such as those that once imposed and supported chattel slavery.) On a slightly weaker view, the overall moral legitimacy of a legal regime affords a moral justification for officials in coercively enforcing the law but entails no duties on the part of those against whom the laws are enforced.[29]

Among philosophers and political theorists, the question whether there is a "general" moral obligation to obey the laws of a legitimate regime is deeply controversial. Controversy is possible because many laws—such as those forbidding murder—largely track what morality would require anyway. Emphasizing rather than denying that people have moral duties to one another, so-called philosophical anarchists do not suggest that people should be able to rob, pillage, or murder as they please. Rather, they insist that it does not take a moral obligation to obey the law to generate a moral obligation not to murder, steal, commit fraud, or the like.[30] Because the philosophical anarchists are correct about this point, the question whether there is a general moral obligation to obey the law becomes salient only when the law purports to change people's moral obligations.

Apart from enforcing moral obligations that people would have anyway, minimally legitimate legal systems routinely make general obligations specific. For example, I may have a freestanding moral obligation to contribute my fair share to pay for police and fire protection and to support the destitute, but the law specifies what my fair share is. Once again, ingenious efforts have been made to show that what matters even in this case is not the legal mandate of the tax code but an extralegal obligation to coordinate my efforts to do what is right with those of others.[31] Others have tried to explain constitutionalism and adherence to legal norms as equilibria in complex coordination "games" in which the participants, acting entirely for self-interested reasons, adjust their conduct in response to the actual and anticipated reactions of others.[32] Having little to add to the debates on these subjects, I shall not attempt to join them. Here I can say no more than that there are cases in which law's contribution to our moral situation and our resulting moral duties seems to me to be distinctive. Accordingly, with acknowledgment that I am leaving deep issues unplumbed, I believe that those within the jurisdiction of a minimally legitimate government have a general obligation at least to *respect* its law—with the obligation of respect capable of being satisfied if, for example, someone treats the laws and the reasons that lie behind them as entitled to significance in practical deliberation about how to behave.[33] In this formulation, someone who is stopped by a traffic light at an intersection and can clearly see that no other vehicles are remotely proximate has a duty at least to weigh respectfully whether the duly enacted traffic laws, and the reasons that support them, morally oblige her to remain stopped under the circumstances, but they do not necessarily generate even a weak duty to obey.

Partly independent of duties of obedience or respect is the question whether a governmental regime's legitimacy justifies the regime's officials in coercively enforcing its law, at least in cases not involving extreme injustice. In my view, the answer to this question must be yes. This is the minimal entailment of a conclusion that a government is morally legitimate.

With these thoughts about the moral implications of legitimacy judgments in mind, we should reconsider the kind of theory of moral legitimacy that we ought to embrace. We have practical needs to make determinations of minimal legitimacy. In the absence of perfect justice, one of our central concerns in gauging the moral legitimacy of our Constitution and the legal regime that surrounds it is to determine how we—you and I—ought to behave in a less than perfect world. But another question involves how officials with power to make, enforce, and interpret laws ought to conduct themselves. With that question in mind, we might have reason to care whether possible actions by government officials in establishing law for the future would enhance or detract from the relative moral legitimacy of the legal regimes that they serve. For example, we might want to assess whether a particular change in governing norms, if brought about by a court (such as our Supreme Court), would make our legal regime more or less morally legitimate overall.

In making that assessment, we should once again attend carefully to the standards by which we ought to gauge minimal or relative legitimacy—standards that include not only substantive justice but also fair allocations of decision-making power. If we focus on decision making by the Supreme Court with both of these criteria in mind, the question will not be a simple one of whether a judicially mandated change would make the regime more substantively just. Even if so, the change might make the legal regime less relatively legitimate if, for example, effecting the change required a usurpation of power by a relatively non–democratically accountable Supreme Court. For instance, we might think a legal regime would be more just if it afforded universal rights to free college education and medical care but believe that a judicial mandate to provide those benefits—absent a historically identifiable constitutional command, and in the face of opposition by political majorities—would make the regime less, not more, legitimate or respectworthy overall. As I shall emphasize repeatedly hereafter, minimal or relative moral legitimacy is a multifaceted concept with partly incommensurate elements.

In cases in which concerns of substantive justice are in partial tension with democratic or procedural values, we could undoubtedly assess what decision makers with de facto authority ultimately ought to do without invoking the concept of moral legitimacy. Nevertheless, the concept of moral legitimacy marks the complexity of the calculation—due to its multidimensionality—that ought to be made.

Recognizing that we care about moral legitimacy as an action-guiding concept in a world in which both unanimous consent and perfect justice seem realistically unattainable should lead us to conclude that the best overall theory of legitimacy would transcend the distinction between "ideal" and "minimal" theories around which I have organized the discussion thus far. More specifically, we should seek to develop a theory that specifies both a minimum and what we might think of as a relative ideal—that is, an ideal fitting for or relative to a world in which we cannot expect unanimous agreement on all important matters and in which, in the face of reasonable disagreement, we should all exhibit humility in our judgments of what perfect justice would require. Recasting our theoretical ambitions in these terms, we should aspire not only to identify what is minimally good enough for legitimacy but also to develop a theory—partly inductively, on a case-by-case basis—that includes prescriptions for citizens and officials who want to move progressively closer to the ideal. In doing so, moreover, we should recognize that moral legitimacy is a complex compound, partly distinct from such relevant contributing ideals as those of pure substantive justice, unanimous consent, and perfect democratic or procedural fairness. Indeed, when moral legitimacy is conceptualized in the appropriately compound sense, we should recognize it as a trumping ideal in the realm of political morality. Its trumping status emerges if we agree, for example, that a regime that is more legitimate should be preferred to one that is more substantively just if the substantive justice would have to come at the cost of too large a reduction in fair allocations of democratic power (such as through a judicial usurpation of democratic prerogatives).[34]

In the remainder of this book, I shall therefore assume that the concept of moral legitimacy marks both a minimum and an ideal in a world in which unanimous agreement on the requirements of perfect justice cannot reasonably be expected. Governments must satisfy the minimum in order to deserve support and respect and to justify their officials in exercising coercive force (except in situations in which the same coercive force would be justified if it were exerted by any other institution or person—for example, to stop a murder or a rape). But governments and their officials should also aspire to move their regimes closer to the ideal that legitimacy defines, involving mixed elements of substantive justice, democratic decision making, and procedural fairness that could possibly exist in partial tension with one another.

Legal Legitimacy

As we make the transition from appraising legal regimes as a whole to assessing institutions and decisions within a particular legal regime, another complication enters the picture. This is the concept of *legal legitimacy*. Judgments of legal legitimacy involve legal authorization. When we talk about Supreme Court decisions as being legitimate or illegitimate, we are concerned with whether the Justices' decisions accord with or are permissible under constitutional and legal norms.

To grasp the distinctive nature of legal legitimacy, and its complex relationship to moral legitimacy, we can begin by noticing that when talking about the legal system as a whole, we can offer appraisals of moral, but not of legal, legitimacy. It is pointless to ask whether a legal system is legally legitimate. There is no outside legal standard by which an entire legal system can be judged—even though there are moral standards. Legal legitimacy, in the sense in which I shall use the term, depends on intrasystemic criteria.

In maintaining that we cannot cogently ask whether entire legal systems are legally legitimate, I make a terminological choice. A traditional "natural law" view maintains that an unjust law is "no law at all."[35] Without engaging the long-standing debate between positivists and natural lawyers, I would readily acknowledge that we can use the terms "law," "legal," and "legal legitimacy" in senses permitting the conclusion that a seriously unjust political regime is, at the very least, so defective as a species of law as to have a compromised claim to be called a legal system at all. We understand perfectly well what someone means if she says, for example, "There is no law in North Korea." So recognizing, I shall nonetheless reserve the term "legal legitimacy" to mark judgments based solely on a legal system's internally recognized norms. Limiting the use of the term in this way makes it possible to draw distinctions that I believe clarifying in some cases. For example, it lets us talk about whether officials were morally justified in enforcing the fugitive slave laws that once existed in the United States in light of both their intrasystemic validity and their moral depravity—an important question that is not wholly captured by the alternative inquiry whether there were any true laws and constitutional provisions, or only purported ones, protecting slavery in the United States.

If we use the term "legal legitimacy" in the sense that I have stipulated, we can ask whether a statute enacted by a state legislature is legally valid under the Constitution, or whether the Supreme Court has reached a legally correct decision about its validity. At some point, however, the chain of legal validation will run out: there will be no more law against which a claim of legal legitimacy or validity can be tested. We come very close to the end of the chain, if we have not already arrived there, when someone asks whether the Constitution is legally valid or legitimate. Postponing foundational inquiries into the Constitution's lawful status until Chapter 4, let us assume here that the Constitution and surrounding norms of interpretation possess unchallengeable legal validity. If so, the Constitution and surrounding norms of interpretation furnish the measure of whether Supreme Court decisions are legally correct or legitimate.

This assumption frames an important question about the significance of law and legal legitimacy in gauging the *moral* legitimacy of Supreme Court decision making. If the Constitution is law that legally binds the Supreme Court, and if it is also minimally morally legitimate, then whether the Justices have behaved morally legitimately will almost necessarily depend on whether the Justices have acted legally correctly or legitimately. The Justices have sworn an oath to enforce the Constitution. If the Constitution is minimally legitimate, then that promise has moral significance.[36] When ruling on disputed cases, the Justices purport to speak in the name of the law. Having promised to support and obey the Constitution, the Justices have an obligation not to speak falsely.

In saying that the moral legitimacy of decisions by the Supreme Court will normally depend on their legal legitimacy, I do not mean to claim that the Justices could never be morally justified in deviating from constitutional norms. A brief discussion of *Bolling v. Sharpe* will help make this possibility concrete.[37] *Bolling*, a companion case to *Brown v. Board of Education*, held that the Due Process Clause of the Fifth Amendment barred the federal government, to which the Equal Protection Clause does not apply, from mandating racial segregation in the District of Columbia public schools.[38] The Fifth Amendment's Due Process Clause says nothing about racial segregation, which was commonplace at the time of its ratification in 1791. No intervening precedent strongly supported the Court's ruling in *Bolling*.[39] Accordingly, the legal case for *Bolling* was weak. Nevertheless, I would say that the Supreme Court acted morally legitimately in deciding *Bolling* as it did, even if—as some have suggested—its ruling was erroneous or possibly even illegitimate as a strictly legal matter.[40]

A variety of practical imperatives impelled the Court to decide as it did. Among the relevant considerations, the lack of a constitutional norm forbidding the federal government from discriminating against racial minorities was a serious moral defect in the preexisting constitutional regime. In addition, a failure of the Justices to bar discriminatory schooling in the District of Columbia would likely have looked hypocritical to many nonlawyers and, thus, might have undercut the moral authority of the Court's simultaneous ruling in *Brown* that state and local governments must not maintain racially segregated schools.[41] In my view, the moral importance of the situation would have justified the Court in appealing less to the letter of positive law than to principles of moral right in calling on the parties and the nation to accept its decision as deserving of lawful status.

This is of course a controversial and even dangerous form of argument. It might be objected that by forging a new constitutional requirement, the Court offended principles governing the fair allocation of political power: the Court should leave the implementation of constitutional change to political majorities acting through the amendment process that Article V of the Constitution provides, not arrogate a power of innovation to itself.[42] It bears emphasis, however, that the status quo ante had been established by political processes from which racial minorities were almost wholly excluded. Under those circumstances, the argument that the Court should have stayed its hand based on concerns about the fair allocation of political power rings slightly hollow. Even if my analysis of *Bolling* is correct, however, *Bolling* is an anomalous case. Having taken an oath to support our morally legitimate Constitution, the Justices almost invariably ought to do so in the moral as well as the legal sense of the word "ought."

Once we allow the concept of legal legitimacy to enter into our thinking about moral legitimacy, we should ask more precisely what "legitimacy" in the legal sense means and inquire more broadly into why we should care about it. For example, is saying that a judicial decision is legally legitimate just another way of saying that it is correct, or is calling a decision legally illegitimate—which is a familiar charge in debates about Supreme Court decision making—just another way of criticizing it as erroneous?

The answer is no. The supporting argument comes from practical reasons that bear close attention. Our centuries-long experience with constitutional law teaches that we must expect reasonable disagreement about many of the constitutional issues that reach the Supreme Court. For purposes of argument, let us stipulate that those questions all may have one best, correct, or optimal answer—the one that Professor Ronald M. Dworkin's ideal judge Hercules, or instead perhaps the one that we ourselves, would give.[43] Despite the stipulation, we know well that the Justices will sometimes disagree among themselves, and with us, about what the best or correct answer is. Reasonable disagreement is an ineradicable fact of both political and constitutional life.[44]

One of our most central interests in making judgments about the legal legitimacy of Supreme Court decisions emerges in response to reasonable legal disagreement—just as our interest in making judgments of moral legitimacy arises from the phenomenon of reasonable moral disagreement. If the concepts of legal legitimacy and illegitimacy are to do any useful work, they must signify something other than the correctness or incorrectness (in the speaker's judgment) of a judicial opinion. One of our practical interests is in determining when we owe respect or obedience to judgments that we think erroneous.

When parsed against this background, claims that a Justice or a majority of the Justices have acted illegitimately communicate a much more serious indictment than assertions that the Justices reached an erroneous conclusion.[45] In a world in which all of us have to expect that a majority of the Justices will disagree with us some of the time, charges of illegitimacy attempt to mark normative breaches or judicial misconduct that we should not have to expect and that, if the pattern were extended, we as a nation perhaps ought not tolerate. (Chapter 5 will discuss some possible responses.) Correspondingly, an acknowledgment of the legal legitimacy of a judicial decision often functions as less than a full-throated endorsement: it may import no more than that a court committed no egregious breach of applicable norms.[46]

In thinking about whether and, if so, when the Supreme Court strays outside the domain of reasonably contestable judgment and into the terrain of legal illegitimacy, the notions of abuse of discretion and of jurisdiction to decide—both of which are well known to lawyers in other contexts—commend themselves as analogies. Although officials often possess discretion about how to make decisions, legal discretion characteristically exists within a limited domain. Indeed, a charge that an official has exceeded her discretionary authority has serious reverberations, triggering the term "abuse of discretion."[47] In some cases officials may exceed their discretion by acting for the wrong kind of reason: they may base their decisions on considerations that they have no lawful power to weigh.[48] But an abuse of discretion can also occur when an official shows particularly bad judgment in assessing relevant considerations.[49]

The other helpful concept in thinking about legal legitimacy and illegitimacy is that of jurisdiction.[50] Although the concept of jurisdiction is itself chameleonlike, changing from context to context, in one use it connotes a power that can be exercised either rightly or wrongly, at least within bounds.[51] In this usage, not every legal error provides a ground for jurisdictional objection. In other words, the lawfully conferred power includes the authority to commit mistakes.[52]

The concept of legal legitimacy appears to function somewhat analogously to the concepts of discretion and jurisdiction when applied to judicial decision making. More particularly, a claim of judicial legitimacy characteristically suggests that a court (1) had lawful power to decide the case or issue before it; (2) in doing so, rested its decision only on considerations that it had lawful power to take into account or that it could reasonably believe that it had lawful power to weigh; and (3) reached an outcome that fell within the bounds of reasonable legal judgment. Conversely, claims of judicial illegitimacy suggest that a court (1) decided a case or issue that it had no lawful power to decide; (2) rested its decision on considerations that it had no lawful authority to take into account or could not reasonably believe that it had lawful authority to consider; or (3) displayed such egregiously bad judgment that its ruling amounted to an abuse of authority, not a mere error in its exercise.

To see the utility of notions of abuse of discretion and lack of jurisdiction in explicating claims of illegitimacy in Supreme Court decision making, we need look no further than well-known debates about *Bush v. Gore* and *Roe v. Wade*. Critics who claimed that the Supreme Court acted illegitimately in *Bush v. Gore* mostly implied that the majority abused its discretion by ruling based on partisan motivations and exceeded its jurisdiction by acting on reasons that it had no lawful authority to consider. More particularly, some thought that the majority breached the requirement that judges must apply legal principles consistently, without regard to the parties or to a case's partisan impact.[53] Similarly, suggestions that the Court behaved illegitimately in *Roe v. Wade* have often reflected views that the Court lacked lawful authority to recognize substantive due process rights not firmly rooted in the nation's history or abused its discretion by extending precedents recognizing personal rights of bodily integrity to encompass a morally insupportable entitlement to destroy innocent human life.[54]

In view of my concern with the practical significance of legitimacy judgments, two final points deserve attention. First, insofar as legal legitimacy depends on reasonableness in the exercise of legal judgment, and insofar as the bounds of acceptable legal judgment have partly sociological foundations—as I shall argue in Chapter 4 that they do—legal as well as sociological legitimacy can be compromised and made vulnerable by moral fissures within a society. As a result, questions can arise about how, morally, Justices should respond to or seek to repair such fissures. I shall be concerned with this question throughout, but especially in Chapter 7.

Second, as protests against *Roe, Bush v. Gore*, and other controversial decisions indicate, a charge of legal illegitimacy need not, though in some cases it might, imply that a Supreme Court decision has no legal claim to obedience. It will therefore prove helpful to distinguish between the *substantive* legal legitimacy of judicial rulings, which reflects their reasonableness as a matter of law, and their *authoritative* legitimacy or legally binding character, which may depend on standards that allow an even larger margin for judicial error or misconduct. We may think a Supreme Court decision contemptible or unworthy of respect but still think that it is legally binding until overruled and that we ought to obey it based on an obligation to support what remains, overall, a reasonably just and at least minimally legitimate legal regime. Our obligations to obey specific judicial rulings may be more stringent than our obligations with regard to laws that we believe unwise or unjust, due to the potentially anarchic consequences if people refused to yield to judicial judgments specifically addressed to them.

Legally and Morally Legitimate Decision Making by the Supreme Court

In thinking about issues of legal and moral legitimacy in the Supreme Court, it is tempting to focus almost exclusively on standards of illegitimacy, as if our sole concern were to mark bounds outside which the Court must not stray. But to do so would be a mistake. If our constitutional regime is less than ideally morally legitimate, and if the constitutionally defined role of the Court includes a responsibility for making decisions that require the exercise of judgment, we have reason to care whether the Justices' decisions enhance or diminish the overall moral legitimacy of the American constitutional order.

The constitutional role of the Supreme Court is, of course, a matter of contentious debate. For present purposes, I shall offer only a shallow description that I hope all or nearly all could accept, even though a deeper or fuller account would admittedly occasion controversy. My description unfolds in three steps.

First, within the legal regime of the United States, the written Constitution is a legally and morally legitimate authority, binding on the Supreme Court as on other institutions and officials.

Second, in order to obey, enforce, and maintain the Constitution, the Justices must ascertain what it means. Sometimes, perhaps typically, we understand perfectly well what the Constitution means or how it applies to a particular case based on simple linguistic and well-known historical facts. In other cases, however, a first-blush examination of relevant linguistic and historical facts may leave us puzzled or uncertain.

Third, resolution of uncertainties through judicial interpretation sometimes requires normatively inflected judgment. In asserting this claim, I mean to stake out as few controversial positions as possible at this stage. Reasonable people will differ on how and why adjudication sometimes requires normative judgment. Two views stand out.

On one, interpretation is a one-step, ultimately determinate process.[55] Suppose, for example, that we want to ascertain the scope of the president's unilateral authority to remove other officials of the federal government from their positions. The Constitution expressly authorizes the president to "nominate, and by and with the Advice and Consent of the Senate, . . . appoint," high or principal officers of the United States.[56] Article II further specifies that "the Congress may by Law vest the Appointment of such inferior officers, as they think proper, in the President alone, in the Courts of Law, or in the Heads of Departments."[57] But the Constitution says nothing about authority to remove either "principal" or "inferior" officials except by impeachment, a process requiring action by both houses of Congress based on misconduct constituting "Treason, Bribery, or other high Crimes and Misdemeanors."[58] When questions about the president's removal power arose early in American history, members of the Founding generation—to whom the original meaning of the Appointments Clause was presumably an everyday fact of life—differed in their judgments.[59] In the face of linguistic indeterminacy, they viewed the matter as one that required "interpretation" to resolve.

Acknowledging the possibility of reasonable disagreement on this and similar points, some would say that the Justices of the Supreme

Court should take all pertinent considerations into account in arriving at the best or even the correct interpretation of the Constitution under the circumstances. Most who take this view would acknowledge the need for normatively inflected judgment as one moves from core cases—perhaps some will view it as obvious that the president must be able to remove the secretary of state for any reason that the president deems good or adequate—to more peripheral ones, involving, for example, whether Congress could restrict the president's authority to dismiss federal prosecutors or the chair of the Federal Reserve Board.[60] (Understandably, the Court has divided over matters of interpretation closely analogous to these.)[61]

Others take the view that "interpretation" in a more appropriately restricted sense of that term will sometimes reveal no more than that constitutional language is relevantly vague, ambiguous, or otherwise indeterminate.[62] "Interpretation," on this view, is the search for "meaning," and meaning, in many contexts, is simply vague or ambiguous. Consider once more the question whether the Appointments Clause of Article II establishes a unilateral presidential power to remove some or all executive branch officials from office. Addressing this question, those who regard the Constitution as irreducibly vague or indeterminate on this point would say that the Justices must exercise partly independent normative judgment about how best to render determinate what the language left uncertain. Some originalists use the term "construction" to refer to the judicial function of resolving ambiguities and giving content to vague constitutional commands.[63]

For present purposes, there is no need to choose between these rival accounts of the nature of the judicial role in cases of vague or reasonably disputable constitutional meaning. The important points are that such cases inevitably arise and that it is a task of the Supreme Court to resolve them authoritatively. The Court, moreover, cannot reach determinate decisions by relying on any simple historical or linguistic fact of the matter. When the historical and linguistic facts fail to determine a precise resolution of a legal issue, the Court must exercise some kind of normative judgment, either to determine what the law means or to make the law more precise than it was previously.[64]

With cases in which the Constitution's meaning (or preinterpretive meaning) is vague or indeterminate on the table, we should recognize—as noted in the Introduction—that the role of the Supreme Court under the Constitution is Janus-faced in a way that the concepts of interpretation and moral legitimacy bring out. The Court has a backward-looking obligation to obey and enforce the Constitution in resolving current-day disputes. This obligation follows from the uncontroversial premise that the Constitution is itself a legitimate authority, binding on the Court on terms determined in part by the legal system's surrounding interpretive norms (which are also legitimate authorities).

At the same time, the Court's role in resolving disputes about the meaning or appropriate construction of indeterminate language has a forward-looking aspect, as introduced and mediated by the concept of interpretation.[65] The forward-looking aspect involves partly independent exercises of normative judgment as the Court resolves constitutional indeterminacies in a way that will produce more or less normatively desirable outcomes for the future. (Chapter 6 will consider restrictions on the kinds of normative reasons on which the Justices can legally and morally legitimately rely when speaking in the name of the law.)

The Court's Janus-faced role in constitutional interpretation has deep historical roots. In cases of ambiguity or uncertainty, Justices at least since John Marshall have gravitated toward the candidate to furnish the correct legal meaning that would produce the wisest, best, or most sensible outcomes. As Marshall put it in *McCulloch v. Maryland*, "general reasoning" refutes the proposition that, given a choice, a court should adopt an interpretation of the Constitution that would render the achievement of its largest purposes "difficult, hazardous, and expensive."[66]

We arrive at the same conclusion concerning the need for the Supreme Court to issue morally based judgments in some cases by reflecting on the Court's role as an institution that claims legitimate authority in the moral as well as the legal sense. Insofar as the Court claims legitimate authority to resolve a question on which the prior law was indeterminate, it necessarily claims a capacity to reach a more morally or practically apt decision, under the legal circumstances, than other potential decision makers could make if left to decide for themselves. The Court's claims of legitimate legal and moral authority can be rooted in the first instance in institutional roles: the Constitution vests the Justices with decision-making authority, and if we accept the Constitution as a legitimate authority, then we will acknowledge the Court's entitlement to decide authoritatively. Nonetheless, if we probe the foundations of the Justices' claim of legitimate moral authority to bind us in a particular way, not determined by the Constitution's language or meaning, that precise claim of legitimate authority must rest on moral foundations of some kind.[67]

Those foundations need not involve a claim or assumption that the Justices have better legal and moral judgment than everyone else. The most persuasive justification for judicial review depends on the premise that the overenforcement of rights should normally be preferred to their underenforcement.[68] Given that premise, we appropriately charge both legislatures and courts with determining independently whether a statute comports with constitutional norms. Nevertheless, claims of legitimate Supreme Court authority must reflect the premise that the legal system will arrive at better legal and moral outcomes than it would otherwise—for example, by achieving national uniformity on a point of law or by erring on the side of overprotecting constitutional rights—if the Justices exercise their best legal and moral judgment in resolving a particular case in a particular way.

If my claim concerning the need for moral justification of particular exercises of judicial authority to resolve open questions sounds extravagant, we should reflect on the implications of denying it. Surely the Supreme Court could not decide legally or morally legitimately on the basis of whim, caprice, or personal like or dislike for the parties. A ruling rendered on such a basis would not be either legally or morally legitimate—even if it possessed the formal authority of law and, as a result, altered moral as well as legal obligations. In resolving questions concerning which the Constitution previously was indeterminate, the Court cannot claim that its particular decisions embody the will of the people or otherwise reflect the fair operation of political democracy. Rather, the Court's authority to decide in particular ways and bind others for the future must rest on its claimed and presumed capacity to bring our legal system to better ultimate decisions—within such limits as applicable law allows—than other officials have already made (if, for example, the Court invalidates legislation) or would make otherwise.[69]

2

Constitutional Meaning

Original Public Meaning

Chapter 1 argued that for the Supreme Court to maintain its legal and moral legitimacy, it must treat the Constitution as a legitimate authority, capable of imposing binding obligations. In order to determine what obligations the Constitution imposes, however, the Justices must determine what the Constitution means. Sometimes this may be an easy task, sometimes a difficult one. To understand it, we need to consider the relationship between constitutional meaning and linguistic meaning.

In discussing constitutional interpretation in the Supreme Court, I assume that the Constitution's various provisions have meanings. I further assume that legally legitimate interpretation requires adherence to the Constitution's meaning. But in order to ascertain what the Constitution's meaning is, we need to probe what "meaning" means.

On the surface, the claim that we need to pause over the meaning of "meaning" may seem sophistical, possibly a prelude to what Justice Antonin Scalia once called "interpretive jiggery-pokery."[1] Today, most originalists maintain that the Constitution's meaning is its "original public meaning"—defined, roughly, as the meaning that a reasonable and informed member of the public would have ascribed to it at the time of its promulgation.[2] Some advance the further claim that there is a linguistic or legal fact of the matter concerning what the Constitution's language meant at the time of its ratification and that this fact of the matter determines how the Supreme Court should resolve cases today. An example may clarify the kind of claim that some originalists frequently (though, as I shall emphasize, do not always) make. The Eighth Amendment prohibits "cruel and unusual punishments."[3] Today, many people believe that the death penalty is not only morally reprehensible but also "cruel and unusual." To appraise such arguments, originalists say that we must look backward to the original meanings of constitutional terms. When drafting and ratifying this language, some originalists further assert, the Founding generation clearly did not contemplate that it would ban the death penalty.[4] Therefore, originalists of this stripe conclude, the death penalty cannot be categorically unconstitutional within the meaning of the Eighth Amendment.[5]

As this example may help to illustrate and as Chapter 3 discusses, some of the puzzles about the meaning of constitutional language may stem from the possibility—and I would say the fact—that meanings can change over time. But we may not even need to consider the possibility of changed meaning in order to make sense of disputes about the meaning of the Eighth Amendment and its application to the death penalty. Without prejudging that question, in this chapter I begin with the originalists' notion of the Constitution's "original public meaning." I do so for two reasons. First, some originalists think that original meaning is all that matters.[6] Second, everyone agrees that original meaning matters sometimes.[7]

Recognizing the importance of the original public meaning to constitutional interpretation—even to nonoriginalists—we can ask, When we look back in history to determine the Constitution's original meaning, what exactly should we look for? As the example of the Eighth Amendment brings out, some originalists assume that the relevant inquiry should focus on how people in the Founding generation would have expected relevant language to be applied. But this is not the only possibility. As we shall see, the notion of meaning—as a linguistic as well as a legal matter—can be fluid. To put the point only slightly differently, there are multiple senses of meaning, different ones of which may seem more apt or salient in some contexts than in others, depending on the reasons for which the question of an utterance's meaning arises. In so claiming, I do not mean to take a nihilist, radical subjectivist, or Alice-in-Wonderland view of the way in which language works in constitutional law or in life more generally. But we should recognize the limits of linguistic determinacy in many of the cases that come before the Supreme Court.

Originalism and Disagreement

We get a window into the difficulty of imagining that history could endow constitutional language with unique, determinate meanings in cases that come to the Supreme Court by recognizing that originalists disagree among themselves about which historical facts we should look at in order to determine what constitutional provisions mean.[8] Some originalists have equated the Constitution's original meaning with the intentions or purposes of the Framers of constitutional language.[9] But there are obvious difficulties in identifying the intentions of multimember bodies.[10] To begin, different members may have had different intentions.

Equally fundamentally, we might question whether and, if so, why the Framers' intentions should control if their intentions differed from what they said. If we discovered that the Framers had written the Constitution in a secret code, in order to achieve results that they knew the public would not have supported, it would be unconvincing to insist that we should treat their deliberately concealed intentions as determining the meaning of the Constitution that others ratified and embraced as the supreme law of the land.

In acknowledgment of constitutional law's inherently public character, other originalists have taken the position that what matters—when we look back to history—is not what the Framers intended but what participants in the various state ratifying conventions and other members of the public originally understood the Constitution's language to mean.[11] In my view, original public understandings should count for a great deal in cases in which we can be confident that nearly all members of the Founding generation shared a relatively determinate understanding of what a constitutional provision meant or how it applied.[12] With respect to many issues, however, we know as a matter of historical fact that no determinate consensus existed.

For example, members of the Framing generation notoriously disagreed about whether one or more provisions of Article I of the Constitution authorized Congress to charter a Bank of the United States—an institution with many of the attributes of a private corporation but also a number of quasi-public functions in managing the availability of credit on a national scale.[13] When an uncertain President George Washington asked the advice of Secretary of State Thomas Jefferson and Secretary of the Treasury Alexander Hamilton, Jefferson said no, but Hamilton answered affirmatively.[14]

There appear to have been similar disagreements about the meaning of the First Amendment's guarantee of the freedom of speech. Historians have reached a variety of conclusions about the originally understood meaning of the Free Speech Clause. Among the data points with which they have had to struggle is the decision of an early Congress, in 1798, to enact the Alien and Sedition Acts, which made it a crime to criticize the president. As viewed from a modern perspective, those enactments look like flagrant violations of the freedom of speech. Some took that position in the 1790s. But others, at the time, defended the Alien and Sedition Acts as consistent with the First Amendment's meaning.[15]

Partly in recognition of problems such as these, most contemporary originalists now say that the object of historical inquiry by the Supreme Court should be the "original public meaning" of constitutional language. By this phrase, originalists signify that we should look for the meaning that a reasonable, well-informed person would have understood constitutional language to have at the time of its ratification.[16] There are obvious questions about what it means for a person to be reasonable and about exactly what a well-informed person should be assumed to know. I shall come back to the first of these questions later. For now, I would emphasize that the movement from a search for what everyone (or even most people) agreed on—which references to "the original understanding" appear to contemplate—to what a reasonable person would have thought is a telling one. Whether directly or indirectly, originalists rely on the concept of reasonableness or that of a reasonable and well-informed person to help resolve doubts and indeterminacies, including some that we know existed even at the time of the Constitution's ratification.

For the time being, I have no reason to register disagreement with this general strategy. Language is often vague. It is not unfamiliar to encounter uncertainties—that then need to be resolved—about what legal provisions mean. And nearly all agree that it is the function of the Supreme Court to resolve such indeterminacies, one way or another. But recognition of possibilities for doubt and disagreement leads directly to the question that the introduction to this chapter framed: What does "meaning" mean when we or others talk about the "original public meaning" in disputed cases?

Diverse Senses of Constitutional "Meaning"

As I hope reflection will suggest, "meaning" can have many senses. As I shall explain later, I believe this to be as true of ordinary language use as it is of constitutional law. But I begin with examples drawn from constitutional law in identifying no fewer than five senses in which the word "meaning" has been or can be used in disputes about constitutional meaning in the Supreme Court: (1) contextual meaning, as framed by the shared presuppositions of speakers and listeners, (2) literal or semantic meaning, (3) moral conceptual meaning, (4) reasonable meaning, and (5) intended meaning.

Among these, perhaps the paradigmatic sense of "meaning" is *contextual meaning, as framed by the shared presuppositions of speakers and listeners*, including shared presuppositions about application and nonapplication. To be sure, sophisticated analysts sometimes find fault with this account of meaning on the ground that meaning is one thing, expected applications something else.[17] Although they may well be right, reliance on a sense of meaning that emphasizes widespread original presuppositions about application and nonapplication is common in constitutional law. An example of this sense comes from debates about the Eighth Amendment's prohibition against cruel and unusual punishments, to which I referred in the introduction to this chapter. Although many people today believe that the death penalty is cruel and unusual, almost no one seems to have thought that the Eighth Amendment prohibited capital punishment at the time of the amendment's ratification in 1791. To the contrary, the Fifth Amendment, which was ratified at the same time, clearly appears to contemplate that the government could deprive people of "life" under some circumstances, just as it could deprive them of liberty or property, as long it first provided "due process of law."[18] Citing this and other evidence, Justice Scalia and others have protested vehemently that modern, judicially enforced prohibitions against the death penalty contravene the original public meaning of the Eighth Amendment.[19]

Justice Scalia seems right that we often, perhaps most often, treat an utterance's contextual meaning, as framed by contemporaneously shared expectations concerning applications and nonapplications, as determining its actual meaning. As applied to constitutional law, however, this equation could easily occasion embarrassments. For example, a good deal of historical evidence suggests that most of those who lived at the time of the ratification of the Fourteenth Amendment did not understand the Equal Protection Clause as barring racially discriminatory public schools, at least as long as states provided separate facilities for whites and nonwhites that were more or less materially equal.[20] Most of those who have examined that evidence have concluded that the original contextual meaning permitted segregated schooling to survive.[21] Although the relevant evidence includes many complex strands, an important datum is that of the states that mandated segregated public education in 1868, when the Fourteenth Amendment was ratified, none appears to have changed its policies, or to have thought that it had to do so.[22] Through the remainder of the nineteenth century and well into the twentieth, a number of other states established segregated schools without evident constitutional embarrassment.

When the Supreme Court addressed the question whether public school segregation violated the Constitution in 1954, in *Brown v. Board of Education*, some of the Justices apparently hoped that evidence of the contextual meaning of the Fourteenth Amendment, as framed at least in part by the shared presuppositions of speakers and listeners, might help to justify their conclusion that segregation was unconstitutional.[23] But after asking the lawyers in the case to submit briefs addressing the historical meaning of the equal protection guarantee, Chief Justice Earl Warren, in an opinion for a unanimous Court, pronounced the evidence "at best . . . inconclusive."[24] Eschewing any aspiration to "turn the clock back," the Court opinion then swiftly redirected its gaze to the present and future and decided the case on grounds—involving the psychologically adverse and sociologically unequal effects of segregated education on black children—that admittedly were not solely historical.[25]

Neither, however, did historical meaning vanish entirely from the picture. On one plausible interpretation, the Supreme Court's argument in *Brown* reflects a shift from the shared presuppositions and expectations of the generation that framed and ratified the Equal Protection Clause to the *literal or semantic meaning* of the Fourteenth Amendment in 1868.[26] The Equal Protection Clause provides that "no State shall . . . deny to any person within its jurisdiction the equal protection of the laws."[27] Focusing on this language, the Court needed to inquire into the meaning of "equal protection." For decades, under the regime of *Plessy v. Ferguson*, the Court had contemplated that separate facilities for whites and blacks could be "equal" and that, if so, the demands of the Fourteenth Amendment were satisfied.[28] But *Brown* refuted that position, based on the effect of separate schools in demeaning and stigmatizing black children. Given the social realities, Chief Justice Warren wrote, "separate educational facilities are inherently unequal."[29] In so reasoning, the Court concluded that the plaintiff schoolchildren were denied the equal protection of the laws in a literal sense.

If we appeal to the literal meaning of the Equal Protection Clause in this way, do we necessarily abandon fidelity to the Fourteenth Amendment's original meaning? I would say not. "Literal meaning" is as familiar a sense of meaning as is that of contextual meaning, as defined by shared assumptions about application and nonapplication. An example illustrating the point involves a statute that forbids school attendance by anyone with a "contagious disease."[30] Imagine that when the statute was enacted, both the legislature and the public believed psoriasis to be a contagious disease. When later research reveals that psoriasis is not a contagious disease, would we say that "the original public meaning" of the hypothetical statute continues to bar anyone with psoriasis from attending public school? In answering that question, we could say, not only intelligibly but correctly, that there can be a gap between a statute's meaning—at least in the literal or semantic sense—and its originally understood or anticipated applications. And in a case of this kind, we could say that literal or semantic meaning ought to control the legal outcome.

In my view, we can sensibly understand modern constitutional doctrines under the Equal Protection Clause that bar discrimination based on race and also on gender—which elicited little concern in 1868—as enforcing the literal or semantic meaning of the Fourteenth Amendment, even if few in the generation that wrote and ratified the Fourteenth Amendment would have anticipated its application in these ways. These, of course, may be contestable examples. Some might say that the original historical evidence reveals widely shared assumptions that would have made prohibitions against race discrimination in the public schools expected rather than unexpected applications—even though actual state legislatures did not experience a constitutional compulsion to change their discriminatory practices, and even though courts permitted segregated schools to persist for nearly a hundred years.[31] Moving from race to gender, others might protest that interpreting the Equal Protection Clause to bar discrimination against women deviates from the original public meaning of the Fourteenth Amendment, largely because that interpretation varies from originally expected applications.[32]

But my point here is not to resolve specific constitutional debates. It is, rather, to maintain that there is a possible sense of "original public meaning"—which constitutional law has sometimes adopted—that equates original meaning with original literal meaning and that recognizes the possibility of a gap between original meaning and originally expected applications.[33] Apart from the Equal Protection Clause, an important example may come from the First Amendment, which provides that "Congress shall make no law . . . abridging the freedom of speech."[34] According to a number of historians, many if not most members of the Founding generation understood this language as having quite an astonishingly narrow reach (by modern standards).[35] These historians believe that few if any of the Founders would have expected the First Amendment to be applied to protect sexually explicit books or pictures, blasphemy, false statements of purported fact about those who were not public officials or candidates for public office, or commercial advertising, to take just a few examples. Even if these historians were correct, we might say, as the Supreme Court has effectively held, that the literal meaning of the First Amendment sweeps much more broadly and appropriately controls constitutional outcomes.[36]

We might reach similar conclusions about the proper application of the First and Fourteenth Amendments by appealing to another possible sense of "original meaning," *moral conceptual meaning*. Some prominent lawyer philosophers argue that when legal provisions employ moral terms—as "equal protection" and "freedom of speech" arguably are—then the original meaning of constitutional provisions that contain those terms might depend on what is morally true or correct.[37] To use a nonlegal example, if I tell my children, "Always do the right thing," I do not mean—and they should not understand me as meaning—"Always do what I think is right." "Right" means right. If this analysis carries over to constitutional law, then moral conceptual meanings would open another path to the conclusion that the original public meaning of the Equal Protection Clause, when properly understood, actually forbids racially segregated public schools and many forms of gender-based discrimination. If these practices are inconsistent with the moral ideal of equality or equal protection, then the Equal Protection Clause forbids them and in principle has always forbidden them, even if the generation that ratified the Fourteenth Amendment did not so recognize.[38] Some have applied a similar analysis to the case of "cruel and unusual" punishments.[39]

Yet another important sense of "meaning" in constitutional law is *reasonable meaning*. Constitutional law exhibits many examples of reliance on reasonable meanings, even if they are not always recognized as such. A paradigm case comes from the interpretation of otherwise absolute constitutional language, such as that of the First Amendment's guarantees of freedom of speech and religion ("Congress shall make no law . . . abridging the freedom of speech"), as contemplating at least some exceptions. In perhaps the most historically and rhetorically celebrated example, Justice Oliver Wendell

Holmes Jr. pointed out that "the most stringent protection of free speech would not protect a man in falsely shouting fire in a theatre and causing a panic."[40] Today, the Supreme Court regularly recognizes that restrictions on the rights of speech and the free exercise of religion are permissible if necessary to protect a "compelling" government interest.[41] Why do we assume that otherwise applicable rights involving speech, religion, and the equal protection of the laws must sometimes yield to compelling governmental interests? The answer lies in widely shared, and thus in widely imputed, notions of reasonableness. The assumption frequently goes without saying, and certainly without a felt need for supporting historical research, that the Constitution is not a suicide pact and that its rights guarantees must incorporate the reasonable limitations that reasonable people surely would have wanted and presumably would have understood them to incorporate.

A final possible sense of "original public meaning" is *intended meaning*, especially as informed by the publicly known purposes of those who drafted particular language. Although it is now well known that problems attend the ascription of unitary intentions to multi-member bodies,[42] the concepts of intention and purpose are difficult entirely to dispense with in ascribing meaning to legal language that was adopted by rational beings with an evident aim of communicating. Accordingly, even those who debunk "subjective" notions of legislative intent acknowledge the need for interpreters sometimes to impute an "objective intent" or purpose to constitutional provisions and to those who enacted, drafted, or ratified them.[43] Those imputed intentions or purposes will sometimes support a sense of "meaning" as "intended meaning."

An example may come from *Plaut v. Spendthrift Farm, Inc.*, which posed the question whether Congress could validly nullify a judicial judgment after it has taken effect due to the unavailability of further appeals.[44] The relevant constitutional language was that of Article III, which endows the federal courts with the "judicial power" of the United States. Although Article III says nothing about the nullification of judgments, the Court interpreted it by ascribing intentions and purposes to those who had drafted and ratified it and then relying on a sense of meaning derived from those intentions or purposes. According to Justice Scalia's majority opinion, the Framers, who had "lived among the ruins of a system of intermingled legislative and judicial powers," wished to insulate final judicial judgments from legislative revision.[45]

Others insist that the intent of those who ratified the First Amendment was to protect political democracy. Beginning with this premise, they would extend the protective scope of the Free Speech Clause to some kinds of speech that many in the Founding generation would not specifically have anticipated.[46]

In claiming that participants in constitutional debates, including the Justices of the Supreme Court, sometimes rely on at least five different senses of meaning, I do not deny that there is overlap and interpenetration among them. Sometimes the same evidence that would underlie a claim about intended meaning might also support a claim about contextual meaning, and vice versa. Examples involving other conceptions of meaning abound. But my main point is that the idea of "constitutional meaning" is often not a sharply determinate one and that constitutional law relies on different senses of "original meaning" in different cases.

This conclusion draws an important corollary with it: the variety of possible senses of meaning, including possible conceptions of a provision's original public meaning, creates occasions for the exercise of judicial judgment in determining which is most salient in a particular context. Imagine that a disparity exists between the Equal Protection Clause's contextual meaning, as framed by shared understandings and expectations at the time of its ratification, and its literal or its moral conceptual meaning—as applied, for example, to cases of gender discrimination. Which sense of meaning ought to control outcomes in the Supreme Court? The decision requires a normative judgment—a point to which I shall return, and for which I shall offer argument, later.

Constitutional Meaning and Linguistic Meaning

Although I have used legal examples to make a point about how Supreme Court Justices' backward-looking search for constitutional meaning can reveal diverse candidates, similar ambiguities or indeterminacies exist in the way that ordinary people speak of meaning in conversation more generally. This is a potentially important point about the relationship between constitutional law and ordinary language use. Parts of the Constitution employ technical legal terms with associated technical meanings. On one plausible view, legal language is pervasively technical, with even quite ordinary terms—such as "and" and "equal"—assuming specialized meanings in legal contexts.[47] But there are reasons to doubt that constitutional meaning could float wholly free from ordinary linguistic meaning. The Constitution is written in English and was addressed to the general public, not just to lawyers. As Chief Justice John Marshall wrote in *Gibbons v. Ogden*, "The enlightened patriots who framed our constitution, and the people who adopted it, must be understood to have employed words in their natural sense, and to have intended what they have said."[48]

If there were only one sense of meaning in ordinary language use, and if the Supreme Court frequently deviated from it, then we would need to confront questions of judicial legitimacy in the backward-looking sense that do not arise if the Court's practices have analogues in other linguistic contexts. In the end, I think that the Court's practice of relying on diverse senses of meaning could be justified legally and morally in some cases, for reasons that will emerge in Chapter 4, even if it defied conventions of nonlegal usage. In my view, however, the permissibility of the Court's reliance on multiple senses of meaning finds support not only in arguments about the nature of law but also in partial parallels between meaning in law and meaning as a concept in everyday, nonlegal discourse.

Sketching the parallels involves admitted complications. In ordinary conversation, we sometimes distinguish kinds of claims of meaning with a more precise categorical scheme than I employed in describing constitutional debates. Outside law, we can distinguish among *sentence* meaning, *utterance* meaning, and *speakers'* meaning. So distinguishing, we can regard sentences as having meanings that do not vary across contexts, but also emphasize that the *utterance* or use of a sentence in one context can mean something entirely different from the utterance of the same sentence in another context. Think of sarcasm. The same sentence, the "sentence meaning" of which does not change, can be used in utterances with opposite meanings. In ordinary conversation, we can also distinguish a speaker's intended meaning from the meaning of the sentence that she spoke or the meaning of her utterance. Sometimes people fail to say what they intended to say. Nonetheless, we may sometimes (but not always) grasp their intended meanings.

For a variety of reasons, these distinctions are seldom made in constitutional argument. More importantly, they may often prove less helpful in constitutional law than in conversation. The idea of speakers' meaning becomes difficult because of uncertainties or confusions about who the relevant speaker is—the drafters of a constitutional provision or those who ratified it and thereby endowed it with legal authority? Indeed, it is not obvious that there even is a unitary speaker in the same sense as in ordinary conversations. It is a further, equally deep and perplexing question whether we should regard the Constitution as a series of utterances in the sense in which philosophers of language use the term "utterance" in discussing remarks made by a single speaker to an anticipated set of readers or listeners in a particular time and place. By all accounts, the meaning of utterances depends crucially on background information (for example, of the kind on which we draw in concluding that a speaker meant a remark sarcastically). But when we speak of a Constitution authored by one set of people, ratified by another, and framed as law that could be applied to unforeseeable circumstances in remote centuries, there is no agreement and no simple fact of the matter concerning what information ought to count as forming the relevant background.

Despite all of these differences, I think it illuminating to recognize that people in ordinary conversation recurrently invoke the term "meaning" in ways that reflect all of the interests and concerns that are exhibited in the five senses of legal meaning that I distinguished previously. In ordinary conversation, we are perhaps most typically concerned with *contextual meaning, as framed by the shared presuppositions of speakers and listeners.*[49] Consider sarcasm, to which I referred passingly earlier. If I say, "Sam was a big help," my remark may mean that Sam was a big help, but it can also mean, in context, precisely the opposite of its literal meaning. Typically, my conversational partners will care which and will describe the meaning of my remark accordingly. In addition, we often understand much more than literal words convey. If I ask my wife if she would like to go to the movies tonight, and she tells me she has a meeting, she has told me that she does not want to go to the movies, even though she has not literally said anything of the kind.

Nevertheless, we sometimes equate meaning with, or assign priority to, the *literal or semantic meaning* of sentences. Suppose a college president publicly instructs the director of admissions to "admit the most-qualified students." Now suppose that the child of a wealthy donor applies, and the admissions director decides not to admit him. Further suppose that the admissions director has no difficulty in anticipating that her decision will disappoint, and possibly anger, the college president. The president, she knows, will think she should have understood, in context, that the directive to "admit the most-qualified students" included an implied reservation for cases involving the children of wealthy donors. But, the admissions director insists, "an instruction to 'admit the most-qualified students' does not mean 'admit the most-qualified students except in cases involving the children of wealthy donors.'" Whether or not we approve of the admissions director's response, she has not committed a crude linguistic mistake. There is a literal sense of meaning in which "admit the most-qualified students" indeed means "admit the most-qualified students."

The notion of *moral conceptual meaning* is also at least as at home in ordinary conversation as in constitutional law. As I noted previously, when I tell my children, "Always do what is right," "right" means what is really right, not what I think is right (even if, when I disagree with some of their actions, I may want to say, "But that is not what I meant"). Admittedly, moral conceptual meaning could be viewed as a subspecies of literal meaning insofar as moral terms have meanings fixed by objective morality. (We can thus say that slavery was always wrong, even if the ancient Greeks did not think so and would not have applied the word "wrong" to some cases of slavery.) Even if so, the familiar and important distinction between facts and values endows moral conceptual meaning with a status that warrants singling out.

Reasonable meaning similarly has a place in ordinary language use, especially in cases involving unforeseen circumstances. If my dean instructs me, "Come to my office at 2 p.m.," I do not understand her as having commanded me to arrive at that time even if, for example, I encounter someone on the way who urgently needs me to drive her to the hospital. I can say, accordingly, that the dean's directive did not mean that I must come, regardless of any emergencies that might arise.

We also speak commonly of *intended meaning* as the most salient sense of meaning. If I puzzle over the meaning of my doctor's instructions, my concern is with what the doctor intended to communicate, not what she literally said or even, necessarily, what her words—apart from her intentions—would most naturally be understood to have meant in the context of their utterance. The doctor may not have said what she meant to say, but the meaning of her instructions, in the sense most relevant to me, is their intended meaning. In so saying, I want to emphasize, I do not mean to suggest that this is the only possible sense of "meaning," even in this context. If someone asserts, "The meaning of the doctor's instructions was at variance with what she intended to say," there is a sense in which this is true, under the circumstances that I have imagined. My point, once again, is that there can be different senses of "meaning," even when we speak about the meaning of a particular utterance on a particular occasion.

The Perspectives of Lawyers, Philosophers of Language, and Ordinary People

In offering claims about senses of "meaning" in ordinary conversation, I venture onto treacherous grounds. Some of the most distinguished philosophers of language who have interested themselves in legal interpretation reject my analysis of "meaning" as a concept with multiple senses, in its application both to ordinary conversational utterances and to legal texts, or they reject the kind of parsing exercise in which I have engaged as beside any relevant point. In probably the prevailing view among philosophical experts, when we speak of the meaning of a legal text or a conversational utterance, what we should always be concerned with is its "asserted or stipulated content."[50] The highly respected philosopher of language Scott Soames thus writes, "In general, what a speaker uses a sentence S to assert or stipulate in a given context is, to a fair approximation, what a reasonable hearer or reader who knows the linguistic meaning of S, and is aware of all relevant intersubjectively available features of the context of the utterance, would rationally take the speaker's use of S to be intended to convey and commit the speaker to."[51]

In appraising the views of Soames and the lawyer-philosophers who agree with him, I am strongly disposed to accede to most but not to all of their strictly linguistic claims—so long as those claims are construed narrowly—but to disagree with some asserted implications for constitutional law. I also have at least one quibble that is not peculiar to law or constitutional law, though it may have implications for law. As is often the case with conceptual debates, however, it is important to stay focused on the practical stakes, if any.

To begin, Soames and those who follow him focus their law-related analyses on the meaning of *utterances* on particular occasions.[52] Though emphasizing that references to meaning sometimes pick out the meanings of sentences and speakers' intended meanings, they regard these senses of meaning as irrelevant to legal analysis (and to claims about linguistic meaning in ordinary conversation) except as they relate to utterance meanings.[53] In partial contrast, I have suggested that when we refer to meaning in ordinary conversation, we sometimes pull various senses of meaning apart—distinguishing, for example, among the literal or semantic meaning of sentences; the contextual meanings of those sentences, as measured partly by expected applications; and speakers' intended meanings—and seek to determine which is most salient in a particular case. The view of Professor Soames and other leading philosophers who have interested themselves in legal interpretation would seem to be that the various senses of meaning that I have identified are not alternatives among which we sometimes have to choose in determining what an utterance or legal provision means. Rather, they are more nearly like component elements that contribute to an utterance's or a legal provision's overall meaning as a reasonable person would identify it in its conversational or legal context.[54] As one philosopher of language puts the point, "The relation here is more like parts to the whole, not like a choice between 'it can mean X or it can mean Y.'"[55] If so, we might still conclude that the meaning of an utterance or legal provision in any particular context is best specified in terms that would correspond to what I have called the contextual, literal, moral conceptual, reasonable, or intended senses of meaning. But, Professor Soames and some others would insist, there is one sense of meaning that is always most fundamental—and that sense is utterance meaning or, more specifically, an utterance's "communicative content."[56]

With this point we get a glimmer of the stakes of the debate about the meaning of "meaning" as engaged by philosophers who interest themselves in constitutional adjudication. Those stakes involve whether, when we talk about the meaning of the Constitution, we should approach it as if it consisted of a string of utterances of the kind familiar in conversation. Whether constitutional provisions should be understood in the same way as conversational utterances is obviously a legal question, or even partly one of political theory, not a linguistic question that philosophers of language could resolve decisively. (In fairness, some parties to the debate scrupulously so recognize.[57]) This question about the relationship of constitutional meaning to the meaning of utterances in ordinary conversation is also understandably difficult and controversial, as I signaled in my earlier reference to the possibility that legal meaning might differ from linguistic meaning in important ways. When we see the controversial character of that question, however, we also get a reminder of why it may matter whether the claim that meaning has many senses among which we sometimes need to choose needs to be defended as distinctive to law, without close parallel in ordinary conversation. As I have said, claims that the Supreme Court must sometimes choose among multiple possible senses of legal meaning may look less vulnerable to objection if there also are multiple possible senses of meaning in ordinary conversation (even on the assumption, which can be challenged separately, that we should approach the Constitution as if it consisted of a string of utterances conceptually indistinguishable from conversational utterances).

Of special importance to me in insisting that "meaning" can have multiple senses, in ordinary conversation as well as in law, is a sense of meaning that I have not so far introduced because it is not strictly relevant to the idea of "original public meaning" with which this chapter is centrally concerned. That sense is one of "interpreted" or "precedential" meaning. In life, as in law, it is often natural to say that a directive has acquired an "interpreted meaning." Imagine that a golf or tennis club has a long-standing written rule that says only members may eat in the dining room. Further imagine that a practice develops under which members are routinely permitted to bring guests into the dining room as long as they personally accompany those guests. At some point we might begin to say that, whatever the rule originally meant, it has acquired an interpreted or precedential meaning under which guests are in fact permitted into the dining room as long as they are personally accompanied by members. If so, we might similarly say—more nearly in parallel with than in defiance of extralegal linguistic practice—that whatever the original meaning of the Equal Protection Clause, for example, it has acquired a precedential meaning that bears on how courts should apply it. It seems impossible to reconcile the notion of "interpreted meaning" with Professor Soames's equation of meaning with the asserted content of an utterance in its linguistic and historical context.

Nor, with the case of *interpreted meaning* in mind, do I feel constrained to yield to the distinctive expertise of philosophers of language regarding what "meaning" is or means. "Meaning" is a concept routinely used by ordinary people for ordinary purposes.[58] Philosophers of language can propose better, more perspicuous understandings of concepts than most ordinary speakers have achieved already. But philosophers have no distinctive authority to determine how concepts in ordinary use can be employed correctly in the contexts in which ordinary people ordinarily use and understand them. When philosophers offer claims about the concept of meaning as it functions in ordinary language, we—you and I—are entitled to test their theoretical claims against our own linguistic intuitions and related explanatory judgments, each for himself or herself.[59] Even outside law, I am comfortable in saying that utterances, prescriptions, stipulations, and written rules all can have multiple meanings, of the kinds that I have identified, among which we may sometimes need to choose based on which is most salient for particular purposes in a particular context. Philosophers of language have no authority to legislate how you and I properly use nontechnical concepts.

The Consequences of Vagueness and Indeterminacy

As I have said, however, we should not become so preoccupied with linguistic questions that we lose focus on the practical stakes of debates about constitutional meaning. For practical purposes, little may hinge on my claim that meaning can have many senses and that we sometimes have to determine (whether in law or in ordinary conversation) which is most apt or salient for relevant purposes. For the moment, for the sake of argument, let us assume that we should gauge the linguistic meaning of constitutional provisions in the same way we ascertain the meaning of conversational utterances. In addition, let us further assume that utterances ultimately have just one linguistic meaning, defined as Professor Soames maintains, with no room for multiple senses. Even if we make this assumption, there would be many cases in which I would remain deeply uncertain about what a particular constitutional provision means or, looking backward, what its original meaning was. The Eighth Amendment prohibition of cruel and unusual punishments and the Fourteenth Amendment guarantee of the equal protection of the laws can again serve as examples. In resolving questions about their meaning, we must—according to those who hold that constitutional provisions can have just one linguistically correct meaning—rely on the notion of a "reasonable" listener or reader who knows not only the linguistic meaning of words but also any other "intersubjectively available" and relevant facts.[60] In this formulation, the notion of reasonableness obviously bears great weight. In trying to make legal and practical sense of the thought processes of an imagined "reasonable" listener or reader, for purposes of identifying a constitutional provision's original public meaning, we should bear in mind the admonition of historian Jack N. Rakove: "An imaginary . . . reader who never existed historically can never be a figure from the past; the reader remains only a fabrication of a modern mind."[61]

An example may help to sharpen Rakove's point about the limitations of purely historical analysis in resolving questions of constitutional meaning. Consider once again the historically debated question whether Article I of the Constitution, when properly interpreted, empowered Congress to create a Bank of the United States. With Hamilton having said yes and Jefferson having said no, and with numerous followers having concurred with each of them, what would we need to do in order to decide what a "reasonable" person would have concluded? On what basis could we say that Hamilton was right and Jefferson wrong, or vice versa?

One possibility would be to endow the concept of reasonableness with considerable normative content: given vagueness or indeterminacy in constitutional language, a reasonable person would adopt the eligible interpretation that was most reasonable in the sense of best or wisest from a practical perspective. Chief Justice Marshall modeled this approach to constitutional analysis when upholding the Bank of the United States against constitutional challenge in *McCulloch v. Maryland*.[62] Believing that a narrow interpretation of Congress's power would have an untoward effect, Marshall upheld the constitutionality of the Bank on the basis of frankly normative, forward-looking reasoning that he thought called for a broad interpretation of congressional power.[63]

Although endowing an imagined "reasonable" person with moral, political, and practical judgment would facilitate resolution of many historically disputed and disputable questions, it would also make the idea of reasonableness deeply contestable, even ideologically charged. In the case of the Bank, for example, those who maintained that Congress had no power to create a Bank, from Jefferson through Andrew Jackson, believed it normatively better, or more reasonable, to adopt a narrow understanding of congressional power, not the broad one that Marshall endorsed.[64]

The dispute about the Bank is by no means atypical. As James Madison acknowledged in *The Federalist No. 37*, the Constitution as it emerged from the Constitutional Convention and ratification process was understandably vague, ambiguous, or indeterminate in many respects.[65] And, as one might anticipate, divisions among the Founding generation about how to resolve the indeterminacies often provoked ideologically rooted division. An example comes from the Alien and Sedition Acts, enacted in 1798, which made it a crime to criticize the president. Almost without exception, members of the opposition Democratic-Republican Party argued that the prohibition violated the First Amendment, while the incumbent Federalists overwhelmingly maintained that it did not. If one asks what a reasonable person would have concluded, any honest answer would need to begin by acknowledging the absence of any simple, dispositive, historical fact of the matter.

I should emphasize here that Professor Soames and others who resist my claim about the potential multiplicity of senses of meaning would not disagree that constitutional meanings can be vague or indeterminate as a matter of linguistic fact. If so, Soames and some originalists would say, the Supreme Court has no choice but to play a creative role to "precisify" vague language or to "construct" its meaning.[66] In constitutional law, precisification or construction takes the form of judicially crafted rules and doctrines to decide constitutional questions that the Constitution's linguistic meaning left unresolved.

In my view, acknowledgment of the need for the Supreme Court to exercise practical judgment and sometimes creativity to make the Constitution determinate and workable is an important step toward a clear understanding of the Court's function in our constitutional order. In taking that step, originalists and others who accept the need for the Supreme Court to engage in constitutional precisification or construction come into approximate (even if not total) alignment, for practical if not for theoretical purposes, with those who think that there can be different senses of constitutional meaning among which the Justices of the Supreme Court sometimes have to choose. They recognize that the Justices must sometimes, perhaps frequently, make normative judgments in order to reach appropriate, determinate conclusions in constitutional cases.

One example of the convergence—which I choose largely because I take it to be uncontroversial—emerges from constitutional provisions, including the First and Fourteenth Amendments, that speak in exceptionless terms. The First Amendment says that "Congress shall make no law . . . abridging the freedom of speech," the Fourteenth Amendment's Equal Protection Clause that "no State shall . . . deny to any person within its jurisdiction the equal protection of the laws." Nevertheless, the Supreme Court, during the 1970s, devised a formula under which it will uphold legislation that would otherwise violate the First and Fourteenth Amendments (among others) if it is "necessary" to protect a "compelling" governmental interest.[67]

The precise terms of this "strict scrutiny" test have no roots in either the language or the history of the First or Fourteenth Amendment. In my view, it is a sensible formula, well within the legitimate authority of the Supreme Court to craft to implement vague or indeterminate constitutional language. Given the availability of "reasonable meaning" as a plausible sense of constitutional meaning, I would regard the First and Fourteenth Amendments as relevantly open-ended, vague, or in need of judicial precisification, construction, or implementation through judicially created doctrine. However one judges that claim, the strict judicial scrutiny formula—to which few originalists have offered any categorical objection on the ground that it deviates from the Constitution's original public meaning—required independent normative judgment by the Supreme Court in a double sense. First, the Court had to determine that it was proper to read literally exceptionless language as in fact contemplating or authorizing exceptions for cases involving urgent governmental interests. Second, the Court had to devise a formula to express the bounds of the exception to otherwise applicable norms.

Myriad other examples would amplify, but not fundamentally alter, the point that purely linguistic and historical facts could not, even in principle, establish a sufficiently determinate original meaning to resolve most of the kinds of constitutional cases that come to the Supreme Court. For the Justices, there is no escaping the burdens of moral and practical judgment.

Language and Its Limits

In bringing this chapter to a close, I should highlight perhaps the most important conclusions of a long argument about the meaning of constitutional meaning, and in particular about the original public meaning of constitutional language, especially in reasonably disputable cases in the Supreme Court. The Constitution is written in

English for English speakers. For the most part, in seeking to ascertain what the Constitution means, we begin with the ordinary meanings of English words, phrases, and sentences. We do not always or necessarily need to end there—a point that will emerge more fully in Chapter 4. But beginnings are important.

In the Supreme Court, I have argued, ordinary language, including the language of the Constitution, often does more to frame issues or choices than it does to resolve them. Among other things, "meaning" can have various senses, more than one of which may stand as candidates to control the outcome of a particular constitutional dispute. Originalists sometimes talk as if there were a linguistic fact of the matter concerning the Constitution's meaning, or its original public meaning, that those whom they deride as living constitutionalists seek to evade. In fact, it much more frequently happens that there are many relevant facts, linguistic and otherwise, that bear on disputes in the Supreme Court about what the Constitution means, establishes, or requires. Language may shape and constrain without ultimately controlling the proper conclusion of the Court's analysis.

Does the effect of linguistic indeterminacy or multiple plausible senses of meaning make constitutional adjudication in the Supreme Court like tennis without a net? No more so, I would say, than our efforts to discern the meaning of utterances in a variety of conversational contexts. Nonetheless, we need to acknowledge openly that a lot of room can exist for the exercise of judicial judgment. There is also, accordingly, a lot of room for worry about how the Justices do and ought to decide disputed cases.

Without purporting to dispel that worry, I should draw attention, in conclusion, to a point that I made passingly earlier and that Chapter 4 will develop at length. In appraising the Justices' backward-looking obligations in identifying constitutional meaning, we need to be concerned not just with linguistic meaning, or even just with linguistic meaning and moral or practical desirability, but also with law. In assigning meaning to constitutional provisions, law—through legal rules of interpretation—could impose obligations of forward- and especially backward-looking legitimacy that language and linguistic meaning do not. Again, however, consideration of that possibility will come later. For now, suffice it to say that although language and linguistic meaning, like morality, are woven into the law in complex ways, they leave many questions unresolved. Among other things, "meaning" can have multiple senses, even when the meaning in question is the original public meaning of constitutional language.

3

Constitutional Meaning

Varieties of History That Matter

IN CHAPTER 2 I wrote as if the only legal authority to which the Supreme Court needs to look back when deciding constitutional cases were the Constitution itself. But I took that approach only for purposes of orderly exposition, not to endorse it. Although appeals to history occur nearly ubiquitously in constitutional law, many involve postoriginalist history. More specifically, the Supreme Court often acknowledges the interpretive significance of actions taken and judgments made by public officials, judges, and the American people in the time since the Constitution's adoption.

Somewhat simplistically, we can conceptualize constitutional history as unfolding in a three-stage sequence. At Time One (T1), the Constitution was written and ratified and acquired its original meaning. At Time Two (T2), also in the past, judges and other officials interpreted or applied the Constitution. In some cases, we may assume, these T2 actions or decisions concerned matters with regard to which the Constitution's original meaning was vague or disputable—for example, about whether the Constitution authorized the creation of a Bank of the United States or whether the Equal Protection Clause forbade racially segregated schools or discrimination against women. But we must also assume that T2 interpreters, being fallible, sometimes may have erred in their ascription of T1 meaning to the Constitution. Now, in the present, or Time Three (T3), we need to determine what bearing T2 judgments have on constitutional adjudication in the Supreme Court.

We can usefully distinguish four questions. First, can T2 decisions authoritatively resolve any vagueness or indeterminacy that otherwise might have existed in T1 meaning and thereby bind the Supreme Court at T3? Second, can decisions made at T2 ever alter the meaning of the Constitution or give rise to new senses of constitutional meaning, such that, for example, language the meaning of which did not forbid race or gender discrimination by the federal government at T1 can forbid such discrimination today, at T3? Third, insofar as there can be disparities between or among T1 and T2 authorities, does one or the other possess lexical priority over the other, or can there be genuine conflicts among legally legitimate authorities? And fourth, if so, how does and should the Supreme Court resolve those conflicts in light of its legal obligations and backward- and forward-looking considerations of moral legitimacy? I shall address the fourth question in later chapters. This chapter advances answers to the first three.

Sources of T2 Meanings

In order to make questions about the bearing of postoriginalist history on constitutional adjudication meaningful, we need some examples of T2 history to which the Supreme Court sometimes appeals and of T2 judgments that the Court sometimes treats as authoritative.

Liquidation through practice. Recognizing that the Constitution was vague or ambiguous on many important points, James Madison maintained that "difficulties and differences of opinion" in interpreting it "might require a regular course of practice to liquidate [and] settle the meaning of some of" its provisions.[1] Today, in thinking about the resolution of constitutional uncertainties, our minds run most familiarly to judicial precedents. But Madison had a broader understanding, encompassing the settlement of constitutional questions by the practice of Congress and the executive branch, as well as the judiciary. Consistent with Madison's expectation, the Supreme Court sometimes treats long-ago or long-standing actions by Congress and the executive branch as having determined the Constitution's meaning. Three examples, two from early U.S. history and the third from more recent times, illustrate the phenomenon.

One early example involves the function of Supreme Court Justices. The very first Congress enacted a law, the Judiciary Act of 1789, that effectively required the Justices to serve in dual capacities: part of the time they performed functions that we associate with the role of a Justice, but for many months of the year the Judiciary Act required them to travel around the country and to act, in effect, as lower court judges.[2] Some members of the Founding generation thought that the law requiring the Justices to perform "circuit-riding" duties breached Article III of the Constitution by failing to respect the distinction that it arguably draws between Justices of the Supreme Court and lower court judges.[3] But when the Court finally had occasion to pronounce on that question in 1803, it ruled that "practice and acquiescence under it" had settled the constitutional issue.[4] (Congress alleviated some of the burdens of circuit riding in 1869 but did not abolish the practice altogether until 1911.)[5]

The Court took a similar approach when the contested issue of the constitutionality of the Bank of the United States finally came before it in 1819, in *McCulloch v. Maryland*.[6] By that time, the first Congress had chartered a Bank, with the approval of George Washington. After the original Bank's twenty-year charter had lapsed, Madison, who had opposed the original Bank as unconstitutional, changed his mind largely on the basis that prior practice had settled the issue.[7] As president, he signed a bill chartering a second Bank in 1816. When the Supreme Court upheld the Bank in *McCulloch*, Chief Justice John Marshall cited among his reasons that "it would require no ordinary share of intrepidity to assert that a measure adopted under these circumstances was a bold and plain usurpation, to which the Constitution gave no countenance."[8]

A more recent example of liquidation of constitutional meaning through the decisions of Congress and the executive branch comes from *Printz v. United States*, in which the Supreme Court carefully examined the practices of early Congresses before ruling that the federal government cannot compel state executive agencies and their officials to enforce federal law. In parsing the historical record, the

Court noted that "early congressional enactments provid[e] contemporaneous and weighty evidence of the Constitution's meaning" and further observed that "contemporaneous legislative exposition of the Constitution . . . , acquiesced in for a long term of years, fixes the construction to be given its provisions."[9]

Historical "gloss." Closely related to the idea of settlement of constitutional meaning through liquidation, but possibly more capacious, is that of long-standing and seldom questioned practice as a "gloss" on constitutional meaning.[10] The classic formulation of the notion of a historical gloss on constitutional language comes from Justice Felix Frankfurter's concurring opinion in *Youngstown Sheet & Tube Co. v. Sawyer*, in which he maintained that "a systematic, unbroken, executive practice, long pursued to the knowledge of the Congress and never before questioned, engaged in by Presidents who have also sworn to uphold the Constitution, . . . may be treated as a gloss on [the meaning of the term] 'executive Power' [that is] vested in the President by . . . Art[icle] II."[11]

Depending on how the concept of "liquidation" is construed, the idea of a "gloss" on constitutional language may sweep more broadly. For example, nothing inherent in the notion of "gloss," as Justice Frankfurter described it, restricts the glossing power to the Framing generation or limits settlement through practice to a range of meanings that was originally contemplated as permissible.[12] In the 2014 case of *NLRB v. Noel Canning*, for example, Justice Stephen Breyer's majority opinion asserted that "[the] Court has treated practice as an important interpretive factor even when the nature or longevity of that practice is subject to dispute, and even when that practice began after the founding era."[13]

As an empirical matter, the Supreme Court has most frequently credited the argument that long-standing historical practice can put a gloss on constitutional meaning in matters involving the separation of powers.[14] But it has pursued similar analyses in other contexts. For example, the Court relied on historical practice in rejecting arguments that federal and state tax exemptions for religious institutions constitute respect or support for an "establishment of religion," in violation of the First Amendment.[15] Similarly, all of the sitting Justices recently agreed that early congressional action in hiring a chaplain defeats the argument that prayers at the beginning of legislative sessions violate the Establishment Clause.[16] (Notwithstanding agreement on this point, the Justices divided sharply about whether and, if so, how much early congressional practice with regard to chaplains affects the constitutionality of governmentally sponsored prayers at other public events.[17])

Overall, the Justices seem prepared to assume that even if original or early congressional practice might have deviated from the best understanding of the Constitution's T_1 meaning, any possible deviation would no longer require correction, at least in some cases. Rather, the long-settled practice would constitute a gloss on the Constitution's original meaning. The point is complicated because the Supreme Court seldom if ever says that it has determined to follow T_2 practice in preference to a T_1 meaning that it describes as pointing toward a different conclusion.[18] More commonly, it describes T_2 meanings as authoritative after having characterized T_1 meanings as vague or ambiguous. As a practical matter, however, that distinction marks little if any difference. On any plausible account, the Court grows more prone to characterize original meanings as vague or ambiguous when T_2 meanings might otherwise seem in tension with the most linguistically plausible understanding of T_1 meaning.[19]

Historical traditions. Historical traditions, sometimes involving the practices of state officials or the American people as much as those of Congress and the president, often shape Supreme Court interpretations of the Constitution. The roles played by traditions in doing so are quite various. In some cases, inquiry into the content of traditions may overlap with other forms of historical inquiry, such as those involving original public meanings, liquidation, and historical gloss. But sometimes the Justices' reliance on traditions as having resolved matters of constitutional import appears less obviously connected, if connected at all, with determinations of original public meaning, liquidation, or even historical gloss.

For instance, Justices who otherwise disagree about the grounds and permissibility of "substantive due process" adjudication appear to converge in accepting that the Due Process Clause "protects those fundamental rights and liberties which are, objectively, 'deeply rooted in this Nation's history and tradition.' "[20] Some Justices believe that the substantive protection of the Due Process Clause should extend further, to embrace now-important liberties that prior generations would not have recognized.[21] Others, with greater allegiance to originalism, have expressed doubts that the Due Process Clause originally conferred any substantive protections at all.[22] Nonetheless, nearly all seem to agree that historical tradition in recognizing an asserted right—such as a right of parents to control their children's upbringing or of competent adults to refuse unwanted medical care—provides support for claims that the right in question enjoys protection under the Due Process Clause.[23]

In another form of reliance on historical tradition, some Justices have also maintained that evidence of open, long-standing practice can defeat claims of constitutional right that otherwise might succeed. For example, Justice Antonin Scalia argued strenuously that judicially developed tests for gauging constitutionality "cannot supersede—and indeed ought to be crafted so as to reflect—those constant and unbroken national traditions that embody the people's understanding of ambiguous constitutional texts."[24] Others of course disagree. In *United States v. Virginia*, a majority of the Supreme Court, over Justice Scalia's protest, barred the traditionally sanctioned exclusion of women from the Virginia Military Institute.[25] In *Loving v. Virginia*, the Court similarly held that prohibitions against interracial marriage violate the Equal Protection Clause, despite plausible arguments that such prohibitions accorded with long-settled tradition.[26] For current purposes, the important conclusion is that even if evidence of traditional practice does not always determine the outcome of constitutional cases, some Justices depict it as decisive or authoritative under some circumstances.

Judicial precedent. Today, the best-known and most widely discussed form of T2 authority is judicial precedent, which can play at least two roles in the Supreme Court. First, it can function as a form of liquidation, implementation, or construction of vague or ambiguous meanings that renders determinate what otherwise would be indeterminate. Second, T2 judicial decisions might authorize or mandate T3 decisions that deviate from the T1 meaning of constitutional language. I begin with the first of these roles before turning, separately, to the second—which is much more controversial—in the next section of this chapter.

Supreme Court opinions recurrently and mostly uncontroversially cite the Court's own precedents as determining current meanings and controlling present controversies. As others have pointed out, the vast majority of constitutional adjudication in the Supreme Court involves the meaning and proper application of the Court's own precedents, with little renewed attention to the Constitution's language or original meaning.[27] Consistent with Madison's enduring insight that the Constitution's original meaning was vague in many respects and thus needful of "liquidation," even most originalists recognize a legitimate role for precedent in shaping the Court's decisions.[28]

Although mostly uncontroversial, reliance on precedent to resolve original constitutional indeterminacies occasionally gives rise to debate. For those who believe that T1 meanings ordinarily ought to control and that precedent constitutes a legitimate authority only insofar as it accords with original meanings, questions obviously can arise about how much T1 indeterminacy is enough to license subsequently controlling T2 judicial lawmaking via liquidation or construction.

Another question involves the circumstances under which the Supreme Court, at T3, should revisit the wisdom of a T2 precedent, rather than simply treating it as authoritative. In its discussion of the authority of T2 precedents, the Court often says, in effect, that precedents bind unless subsequent developments have shown them unwise or unworkable—on the assumption, which I am continuing to make, that the T2 precedent was not flatly inconsistent with the Constitution's T1 meaning.[29] Even when the Court articulates this understanding, however, it characteristically insists that the question whether to adhere to precedent is one of policy, not constitutional mandate.[30]

The Possibility of New Constitutional Meanings

We come now to the question whether T2 decisions can change the meaning of constitutional language, create new meanings, or otherwise alter the obligation of the Supreme Court to adhere to the

Constitution's T1 meaning (or to one of its senses of T1 meanings). There are two senses in which I believe the answer to this nested set of questions to be yes, depending on the construction that one gives them.

First, consistent with ordinary language usage, the Constitution, like other texts, can sometimes acquire new meanings, which we then might contrast with its original meanings.[31] This is one linguistically natural way to account for the role of at least some leading precedents in constitutional law. For example, some Justices, as noted previously, have maintained that the Supreme Court's extensive body of substantive due process doctrine deviates from the Constitution's T1 meaning, yet they continue to apply some aspects of that doctrine—for example, to hold that the Due Process Clause of the Fourteenth Amendment makes nearly but not absolutely all of the Bill of Rights, which initially applied only to the federal government, applicable against the states.[32] To explain their practice, we might say that the Due Process Clause has acquired an "interpreted" or "precedential" meaning, which contrasts in some respects with what some Justices believe the clause's original meaning to have been, that they accept and apply for some purposes.

A less charged example may come from the First Amendment. The First Amendment says that "Congress shall make no law . . . abridging the freedom of speech."[33] Yet the modern Supreme Court largely ignores the language—and what one might accordingly expect to have been its original meaning—in holding that the First Amendment creates important protections against executive branch and judicial actions that restrict speech, as well as against prohibitions adopted by Congress.[34] Given long-standing precedents applying the First Amendment to presidential and judicial action, we might say that the First Amendment has acquired a precedential meaning that sweeps more broadly than its original meaning, which restricted only Congress.

Second, however one judges the conceptual possibility of precedential meanings, Justices of the Supreme Court—from the very beginning of the nation—have openly and notoriously maintained that T2 precedents can sometimes excuse them from their obligations to adhere to T1 constitutional meanings. Indeed, I can put the proposition more strongly. Judicial recognition of precedent as establishing the legally valid and binding law of the United States has been a central, widely accepted feature of our constitutional practice almost from the beginning.[35] Even critics of judicial reliance on nonoriginalist precedent acknowledge that "the idea that '[t]he judicial Power' establishes precedents as binding law, obligatory in future cases," began to take root no later than the early nineteenth century.[36] So far as I am aware, no Justice up through and including those currently sitting has persistently questioned the legitimacy of the doctrine of stare decisis—which holds, roughly speaking, that the Court should stand by its T2 precedents—or failed to apply it in some cases.[37]

Indeed, all current and recent Justices, including the self-proclaimed originalist Justices Scalia and Clarence Thomas, have specifically and self-consciously accepted the authority of past judicial precedents that could not themselves have been justified under strict originalist principles. For example, those two Justices joined an opinion that relied on precedent to subject federal affirmative action programs to strict judicial scrutiny in *Adarand Constructors, Inc. v. Pena*, notwithstanding the total absence of any evidence that the pertinent constitutional provision, the Due Process Clause of the Fifth Amendment, which was ratified in 1791, was originally understood to bar racially discriminatory legislation.[38] Equally tellingly, all of the current and recent Justices, again including the originalists, have apparently converged in their unwillingness to hear cases that would force them to revisit a number of past decisions that some scholars think would be difficult if not impossible to justify based on T1 constitutional meanings.[39] These include decisions establishing that paper money is constitutional, as is Social Security; that the Equal Protection Clause bars race discrimination in the public schools; and that Congress has broad power under the Commerce Clause to regulate the national economy.

Conflicts of Legitimate Authorities

We come now to the question whether Justices of the Supreme Court, looking backward to the authorities whose decisions they are bound to respect, can encounter conflicts of authority.[40] In addressing it, we should pause briefly over a conceptual issue. By definition, a legitimate authority is a decision or a decision maker with the capacity to alter normative obligations. In order to achieve this effect, the directive of a legitimate authority must not only give reasons for action to those who are subject to its authority but also bar them from giving weight to some contrary reasons that they otherwise would have had.[41] Nevertheless, an authority's dictate or pronouncement need not, as a conceptual matter, rule out reliance on all possible contrary reasons. For example, a military officer's command to do X may preclude a soldier from weighing reasons suggesting that doing X would be unwise or imprudent, but not that doing X would constitute a crime against humanity. Similarly, a statute mandating a harsh criminal penalty will preclude a sentencing judge from weighing reasons indicating that the penalty would be undesirable as a policy matter, but not that it would violate the Constitution.

These cases of course present no difficult or interesting conflicts of authority because, in both instances, one authority has a clear lexical priority over the other. There would similarly be no interesting conflict if either T_1 or T_2 meanings had lexical priority over the other in constitutional cases in the Supreme Court, so that no need to choose between them could arise. But no such lexical priority exists.[42] As a result, conflict, or at least the appearance of conflict, is endemic to the Court's modern role.

Although Madison said he expected practice and precedent to fix the meaning of the Constitution, precedent can actually have the opposite effect in the Supreme Court. As precedent and practice accumulate, they offer eligible foundations for modern Court decisions: the Court can point to T_2 precedents and identify them as binding authorities. At the same time, the Court insists—and nearly all others concur—that it is always open to the Court to appeal to the ultimate authority of the Constitution, as measured by its T_1 meaning: if the Court thinks it important to reject practice or precedent in order to base a decision directly on first principles or original meaning (or meanings), it has the prerogative to do so. The Court thus says, again and again, that adherence to precedent occurs as a matter of "policy," not unyielding constitutional mandate, and that its decisions whether to reassess or overturn its own precedents reflect "prudential and pragmatic considerations."[43]

As it is with judicial precedents, so it appears to be with liquidation, historical gloss, and tradition. In *Vermont Agency of Natural Resources v. United States ex rel Stevens*, the Supreme Court relied on long-standing historical practice to hold that Congress could validly confer "standing" on private plaintiffs to sue on behalf of the government when they believe that the government has paid out money to people who made false claims against it.[44] In the very same case, however, the Justices ruled that historical practice did not necessarily resolve another constitutional question, involving whether allowing private litigants to represent the United States might impermissibly interfere with the president's responsibility under Article II to enforce the laws of the United States.[45] In reserving that question, the Court gave no hint of how it would settle any possible conflict between T1 and T2 authority. In *Immigration and Naturalization Service v. Chadha*, the Court dismissed historical practice as substantially beside the point in invalidating a statute that authorized either house of Congress to exercise a "legislative veto" over action by an administrative agency.[46] Although Congress had enacted more than two hundred legislative veto provisions over a span of five decades, typically with presidential acquiescence, the Court rejected legislative vetoes as incompatible with the Framers' design. But the Court seems no more consistently committed to the idea that T1 meaning always prevails over T2 congressional and executive practice than it does in the parallel case of judicial precedent. Similarly, although the Court sometimes says that tradition settles matters, it sometimes denies that tradition binds its hands—as, for example, in its recent decision holding that the constitutional right to marriage embraces same-sex unions.[47]

Recognition of alternative sources of T2 authority, which can authorize but apparently seldom mandate deviations from the Constitution's T1 meaning if a majority of the Justices believe deviation to be unwarranted, increasingly creates situations in which the Supreme Court, when looking backward at authorities that either bind it or alter its obligations, needs to exercise normative judgment of some kind. In the face of conflict, the Court can, and must, decide which potential source of authority prevails.

As we consider this situation, however, the puzzle about legitimate judicial authority deepens. On the one hand, no one doubts the importance of backward-looking legitimacy claims and historical authority. On the other hand, we can have multiple rival contenders to provide the legitimately controlling answer to constitutional questions. Under these circumstances, some of the considerations that any one source of legitimate authority would have ruled out if it were the only authority in the picture—such as considerations involving what the Court would have thought best or wisest as an independent matter—may become pertinent. But we should not rush to reach conclusions.

In asking what the Justices do or ought to do, we should recall the Janus-faced aspect of the concept of moral legitimacy as it bears on adjudication by the Supreme Court. The Court must not only acknowledge and respect the dictates of preexisting legitimate authorities, most centrally including the Constitution. The Justices must also so conduct themselves as to establish and maintain their own legitimate authority and the legitimate authority of the Court's decisions as tested, in part, by forward-looking considerations of substantive justice and procedural fairness.

Taken in the terms in which I have thus formulated it, the challenge before the Supreme Court is a hugely daunting one. We might now think it no wonder that charges of judicial illegitimacy could erupt so frequently, often across ideological lines that reflect differing visions of what backward- and forward-looking obligations, substantive justice, and procedural fairness all require.

Before considering how the Court ought to go forward, however, we need to examine another piece of the emerging puzzle. So far I have spoken only sketchily about the nature, foundations, and varieties of law in the Supreme Court. This is the subject to which I shall turn next. Among our questions will be whether, and, if so, how, law might guide or determine choices among competing senses of constitutional meaning and rival sources of T_1 and T_2 authority in constitutional adjudication.

4

Law in the Supreme Court

Jurisprudential Foundations

THIS CHAPTER EXPLORES the nature and foundations of law in reasonably contestable cases in the Supreme Court. Where do the legal norms that apply to the Court come from, and how do they acquire their legitimate authority? These questions apply fully as much to the Constitution as to second-order norms of constitutional interpretation.

In addressing this topic, I begin with—but only in order to debunk—a picture of law and legitimacy in the Supreme Court that many people find intuitively compelling. According to this model, the Constitution was lawfully adopted and, having been lawfully adopted, applies in the ways in which the Framers understood or expected it to apply, unless and until the American people lawfully amend it. (The amendment process laid out in Article V normally requires votes by two-thirds majorities in both houses of Congress and ratification by three-fourths of the states.[1] Due to the extreme difficulty of this process—under which just thirteen states, potentially constituting less than 5 percent of the population, could block an amendment—formal amendment has rarely occurred.) Today, no major scholar may endorse the model of the Constitution as the Framers' lawful and therefore binding commands in all of the particulars in which I shall present it. Nevertheless, decades of experience with students leave me convinced that this way of thinking exerts a continuing grip on many minds.

Views that identify legitimate constitutional authority with the dictates of those who wrote and lawfully ratified the Constitution reflect a number of misunderstandings, some hidden in unarticulated premises. But we can start by noticing the shakiness of the intuitive model's historical assumptions. On that front, it is doubtful that the Constitution actually was adopted lawfully under the law as it stood in 1787 and 1788.[2] The Articles of Confederation that previously linked the states permitted changes in their terms only by the unanimous agreement of the states, voting in Congress. In seeking approval of the Constitution drafted by the Constitutional Convention, the Convention's delegates ignored this stricture. They vested responsibility for approving or disapproving their handiwork directly in the people of the thirteen states, voting in state ratifying conventions, and provided in Article VII that the new Constitution would take effect if as few as nine states approved. The Constitutional Convention's decision to seek ratification by conventions, rather than by state legislatures, posed especially deep difficulties under prior law. Each of the states had its own structure of government, functioning under a state constitution, and many of the state constitutions contemplated that the states could be bound only by the votes of their legislatures. In bypassing the state legislatures and seeking approval from delegates to conventions, the process of the Constitution's ratification arguably violated the law of many if not most states.[3]

It is also very arguable that the Thirteenth and Fourteenth Amendments were not lawfully ratified under the standards for constitutional amendment that Article V sets out. Ratification of the Thirteenth Amendment, which abolished slavery, depended on the approval of a number of Southern legislatures then subject to military Reconstruction.[4] Whether those legislatures could consent to a constitutional amendment on behalf of their states seems questionable. However one judges that issue, ratification of the Fourteenth Amendment, which includes the Equal Protection Clause, occurred only as a result of manifest coercion.[5] After ten Southern states had rejected the Fourteenth Amendment, Congress insisted that they must ratify it as a condition of regaining their representation in Congress.[6] Given the compulsion, some argue that the Fourteenth Amendment's "rat-ification" failed to meet constitutional standards.

In discussing the lawfulness of the Constitution's ratification, I have inserted the words "arguable" and "arguably" at several points. Constitutional scholars have made clever cases supporting the law-fulness of both the Constitution's ratification and the processes that produced the Thirteenth and Fourteenth Amendments.[7] For present purposes, however, we have no need to dig deeper into legal techni-calities involving the remote past. Even without doing so, we can recognize that the difficulty with predicating the Constitution's current authority on its lawful ratification hundreds of years ago is not just historical but also both practical and conceptual. Merely contemplating that the entire Constitution might be adjudged in-valid based on the terms of the Articles of Confederation or state law in the eighteenth century, or that the current validity of the Thir-teenth and Fourteenth Amendments depends on the outcome of debates about events during Reconstruction, should bring out the crucial point: nothing of practical, legal consequence hinges on the historical arguments.

The ultimate measure of legality in our legal system—as in any other—inheres in currently accepted standards for identifying past events as possessing legal authority. In 1787 and 1788, it was ques-tionable whether the prescribed process for ratifying the Constitu-tion was legally legitimate. In the minds of some, the doubtful legality bore on whether the draft Constitution, if adopted, could succeed in establishing a legally and sociologically legitimate gov-ernment. Significantly, however, the answer to those questions did not come through decisions by the Supreme Court or any other tri-bunal. It came from widespread public acceptance of the new Constitution as legally valid by the American people and their chosen political officials. Correspondingly, what ultimately matters today—legally as well as practically—is that nearly everyone con-tinues to accept the Constitution, including the Thirteenth and Fourteenth Amendments, as valid, binding law.[8]

A thought experiment will further illustrate the point that the foundations of constitutional legality inhere in current practices of accepting past actions and decisions as legally authoritative. Imagine that another revolution, analogous to the one that began in 1776, were to occur in the United States. The Constitution would lose its status as law if enough people ceased to accept it as a legitimate authority, just as the British Parliament and King ceased to be legitimate legal authorities for the colonies when the colonists threw off their rule, whether legally or illegally. This result would occur even if we assume that the current Constitution was validly ratified under preexisting law. The validity of the Constitution's ratification under preexisting law is neither a necessary nor a sufficient condition for its legal authority today or in the future. Sociological legitimacy with relevant constituencies—a concept defined in Chapter 1—ultimately plays the determinative role.

As is generally true with sociological legitimacy, the Constitution did not enjoy unanimous acceptance in 1788. Nor does it possess legitimacy in the Weberian sense—meaning a belief that it ought to be obeyed—in everyone's eyes today. To point only to the most urgent ground for resistance in 1788, a Constitution that contemplated the race-based bondage of some (nearly 20 percent of the population, according to the 1790 census) could not plausibly have enjoyed unanimous acceptance. Nevertheless, when enough people embraced the Constitution as the operative framework of government, there was no need for further questioning whether its ratification satisfied prior law. Its sociological legitimacy gave it legal legitimacy, at least in a minimal sense.[9]

This blunt statement about the relation of the Constitution's legal legitimacy to its sociological legitimacy deliberately skirts many complexities. In particular, in asserting that the Constitution enjoys legal legitimacy because it is "accepted," I mean to elide, for now, the questions (to which I shall return) of exactly what needs to be accepted and by whom for the Constitution to enjoy its lawful status. In his jurisprudential classic *The Concept of Law*, H. L. A. Hart suggested that for a legal system to exist, government officials must embrace shared legal norms—such as those embodied in the Constitution—as providing reasons for action and grounds for criticism and self-criticism.[10] "The ordinary citizen," he wrote, "manifests his acceptance largely by acquiescence."[11]

Once the Constitution is accepted as legally valid, an additional basis for assessing claims of legal validity and legitimacy obviously exists. The legal legitimacy of governmental actions will typically depend on their conformity with constitutional norms. As is illustrated by the Constitution itself, however, not all legally valid authority needs to be or even could be derived from more ultimate, purely legal norms. If embrace and acceptance confer legal validity on the Constitution, they might also confer legal validity on norms that supplement, or qualify, or even partially displace the written Constitution.[12] For example, we can imagine that the Thirteenth and Fourteenth Amendments would be legally valid, due to the fundamental and presently unshakable status of their acceptance, even if they were not otherwise validly enacted within the terms of Article V. In other words, both public officials and overwhelming majorities of the public might agree that the fundamental law of the United States consists of the original written Constitution, of all amendments subsequently enacted pursuant to Article V, and of the Thirteenth and Fourteenth Amendments, regardless of whether their enactments satisfied Article V.

It may seem unsettling to trace the foundations of our constitutional order to nothing more solid than a vague, potentially amorphous, and irreducibly contingent phenomenon of sociological acceptance. But if it is unsettling to recognize that legal validity and legitimacy can depend on sociological legitimacy, so recognizing can also provide inspiration. It highlights the role and responsibility of each successive generation, including our own, in maintaining and possibly reshaping the constitutional order. Our acceptance may be active or sheeplike, but we cannot plead that the Framers rule us tyrannically from the grave. Even if we think that we as individuals have no choice as a practical matter but to go on with the Constitution that the Framers left us, we should direct our complaints, if we have them, more at contemporary Americans who uphold the constitutional order than at those who established it.

A Practice-Based Theory of Law

By insisting that the foundations of our constitutional order lie in sociological phenomena of acceptance, I endorse the basic tenets of a practice-based theory of law in the sense of "practice" in which philosophers sometimes use that term. So employed, it refers to activities that are constituted by the convergent or overlapping understandings, expectations, and intentions of multiple participants.[13] Chess is a practice in this sense, as is baseball. So are promising, speaking English, and joke telling.

Philosophers often say that practices have a necessary connection with, or are constituted by, rules.[14] The rules of chess constitute the game of chess. The rules of baseball give a point to the hitting and throwing of balls that would otherwise be unintelligible. Sometimes, as with chess and baseball, the constitutive rules of practices are clearly set out in propositional form. In other practices, the pertinent "rules" are rules only in the sense made famous by the philosopher Ludwig Wittgenstein: the term marks the existence of a shared and often tacit understanding among some relevant group concerning how to "go on" in ways that will be acknowledged by other members of the group as appropriate or correct.[15] What makes a remark a joke—or not a joke? Within a community, there is likely to be substantial convergence in judgment, and if I am asked to tell a joke, then I follow the rules of joke telling insofar as I conduct myself in accordance with shared if tacit norms that count as "rules" in the relevant sense. In doing so, I must hold myself open to the possibility that I have failed to conform to the standards that I set out to satisfy: maybe my intended joke failed utterly, reflecting a lack of true understanding of the practice in which I meant to engage.

American constitutional law is a practice in this sense, constituted by the shared understandings, expectations, and intentions of those who accept the constitutional order and participate in constitutional argument and adjudicative practices. It is crucial to recognize, moreover, that the relevant understandings and expectations go far beyond knowledge of the linguistic meanings of the Constitution's words and the history of its drafting and ratification. To take a relatively simple example—which I shall actually oversimplify in order to avoid becoming hopelessly bogged down—let us imagine that someone asks me whether a state law that forbids flag burning or nude dancing is constitutionally valid. Although the Constitution written in 1787 and formally amended since then undoubtedly furnishes a touchstone, I cannot reliably appraise the challenged law's legal status and effects without also knowing a good deal about widely shared rules, practices, precedents, and assumptions that bear on proper constitutional interpretation in the present day. Among the relevant assumptions and precedents would be these:

Although the First Amendment says that "Congress shall make no law . . . abridging the freedom of speech," the Supreme Court has held, and nearly everyone accepts, that the Due Process Clause of the Fourteenth Amendment, which was ratified in 1868, "incorporates" the First Amendment (along with most other provisions of the Bill of Rights) and thus makes it applicable against states.[16] As a result, state laws are subject to scrutiny under the First Amendment, even though the First Amendment does not say so. If someone else were to object that the Fourteenth Amendment is not a valid part of the Constitution because its purported ratification was coerced, I need to know that virtually no one will take this argument seriously. Almost everybody will think that history has settled the matter. It also matters that nearly everyone, centrally including the Supreme Court, now understands that the First Amendment guarantee of freedom of speech extends to some forms of "expressive conduct," not just to pure speech; that the Court has rendered specific rulings that flag burning is a form of expression the prohibition of which triggers the most demanding form of judicial scrutiny but that a prohibition against nude dancing can be justified pursuant to less exacting standards; and that nearly everyone accepts, as the Supreme Court insists, that rulings by the Justices bind lower courts.[17] It might also be relevant, however—as nearly all informed participants in constitutional practice would agree—that the Justices were narrowly divided in their decisions about the protected or unprotected status of flag burning and nude dancing and that the Court itself could imaginably reconsider its rulings in a future case.[18] As I said previously, moreover, these recitations barely scratch the surface. Nearly all lawyers and judges have attended law schools in which a central aspect of the educational mission involves "distinguishing cases" and other techniques of legal reasoning.

The significance of these points about the nature and elements of American legal practice runs deep. Insofar as constitutional adjudication is a practice, situated in the broader practice of American law, the most fundamental governing rules—including those supplying the ultimate criteria for determining what the Constitution means or requires—are necessarily rooted in social facts involving the behaviors, expectations, and attitudes of participants in those practices. The intentions of past generations, and even the purportedly plain meaning of the constitutional text, matter only insofar as currently prevailing norms make them relevant. Think again of the First Amendment, which today binds both the states and the president, even though it "plainly" begins with the words "*Congress* shall make no law."

Moreover, if the foundations of our constitutional order lie in acceptance, acceptance is not limited to the written Constitution. It could not be. We also need shared assumptions about the nature of proper legal interpretation. The Constitution does not, and could not, contain adequately determinate rules for the process of constitutional interpretation. Even if the Constitution attempted to provide such rules, as it mostly does not, questions could always arise about how those rules should be interpreted.[19] Rules for the interpretation of constitutional rules might then seem necessary, but they could not be sufficient: a naïvely puzzled or a skeptical person could always ask what rules of interpretation to use in interpreting the interpretive rules. At some point, we would need to end the regress through reliance on shared understandings that are more tacit and foundational. At the limit, shared understandings of this kind may ground our capacities to communicate through language in the first place. Insofar as they exist, such understandings are necessarily external to the Constitution and to formal rules of legal interpretation.

In the most widely embraced practice theory of law, Professor Hart referred to the criteria that officials and especially judges apply in identifying what the law is and means—including, for example, many of those that I invoked earlier in discussing the constitutionality of state prohibitions against flag burning and nude dancing—as "rules of recognition" that he suggested could be traced to a master "rule of recognition."[20] His basic idea involved the convergence of judicial and other officials in recognizing what is law and what is not and what the law requires.

Although accepting the basic Hartian idea that the foundations of law lie in acceptance, we should elaborate on (and perhaps partially qualify) the Hartian picture in several ways. First, we should recognize—as Hart himself came to do—that the concept of a "rule," as it functions in the technical idea of a rule of recognition, can easily prove more misleading than illuminating.[21] We would do better to speak of practices of recognition.[22] As Hart himself later made explicit, he did not mean to imply that judges and legal officials who practiced or applied rules of recognition could necessarily state the rule or rules to which they conformed or that they would necessarily agree with each other's attempts at articulation.[23] Rather, in the formulation of a source that Hart cited approvingly, "the test of whether a man's actions are the application of a rule is . . . whether it makes sense to distinguish between a right and a wrong way of doing things in connection with what he does."[24]

Second, in describing American constitutional law as a practice that is constituted by the shared assumptions and understandings of those who participate in it, we should recognize that American constitutional law is a relatively fluid and open practice and that, in particular, it opens at a number of points into the domains of moral, political, and prudential judgment. Practices can be more or less open or closed.[25] In relatively closed practices, such as chess or baseball, the constitutive rules can be stated more or less exhaustively, they are more or less fixed, and they are highly determinate. In open practices, by contrast, it will be less possible, even in principle, to furnish a comprehensive list of the pertinent rules or standards, which may evolve over time. And if decision making within a relatively open practice invites the exercise of moral or political judgment, then issues arising within the practice will, to that extent, understandably occasion ideologically related controversy.

Any descriptively plausible account of American constitutional practice must acknowledge its partial openness to or reliance on moral and political criteria of sound decision making.[26] No other credible way exists to account for the extent of ideologically based division between judicial liberals and conservatives that our practice exhibits—for example, about whether the Constitution includes or should be interpreted to include abortion rights, or about whether Congress can validly require people who do not want health insurance to buy it anyway. In some cases, knowing how to "go on" within the practice may include knowing how and when to incorporate moral and political judgment into otherwise indeterminate processes of constitutional analysis—even though we have to expect that the resulting conclusions will prove controversial. If so, it is possible for the Justices of the Supreme Court to share practices of recognition or criteria of legal validity, and for them further to agree that they must make practical judgments in resolving otherwise disputable cases, without agreeing on the outcomes of such cases.

Third, we need to recognize that the practices of Supreme Court Justices in ascertaining what the Constitution means or requires are nested among the recognition practices of other officials.[27] This nestedness manifests itself in various respects. Ordinarily, other officials accept that the dictates of the Justices authoritatively determine what the law is. At the very least, officials usually feel obliged to obey. But there may be extreme cases in which other officials would not accede to the Justices' rulings. I shall pursue this theme further in Chapter 5. Although the issues here are complex, we should not assume that the Justices' practices of recognition are or could be sealed off from the practices of other relevant constituencies.

Fourth, although the Supreme Court's most fundamental interpretive standards and practices tend to be relatively fixed, interpretive norms, understandings, and expectations can shift over time.[28] As becomes obvious every time a vacancy on the Supreme Court emerges, presidents and senators have their own rough-and-ready standards for determining what the Constitution means or requires, and they routinely seek—through their nominations and confirmation votes—to alter the Court's practices and standards, at least at the margins. As history demonstrates, shifts in the balance of power on the Court can have profound effects in unsettling and then sometimes resettling norms of interpretive practice. Transformation has happened before. It could happen again. This is a phenomenon that any practice-based theory of law, and in particular of constitutional law in the Supreme Court, must explain, rather than deny.[29] The consequences can be huge.

Law, Argument, and Disagreement

Looking at the foundations of constitutional law as potentially shifting and as subject to dispute in some cases, we might easily fall into either of two errors. First, we might think that American constitutional law is not really law at all in any meaningful sense, or at least that there is no real constitutional law in the Supreme Court. In order to appraise this possibility, we need to clarify its presuppositions and entailments. No sensible person has ever thought that all of the "rules" of constitutional law could be written down, or that they brook no disagreement, as we might imagine to be the case with the rules of chess. If we want to know whether there is law in the Supreme Court, the question is not whether the Justices sometimes have competing views of what the law requires but whether there is enough convergent agreement to support the conclusion that the Justices feel bound by, and seek to obey and enforce, legal rules in the relevant sense: Do they recognize, endeavor to comply with, and seek to hold each other to norms of proper conduct that define their and others' legal duties? Available evidence warrants an affirmative conclusion.

Given the nature of the Supreme Court's docket, we should feel no surprise that the Justices divide frequently when it comes time to decide the cases that they agree to hear. Disagreement is virtually inevitable in light of what political scientists call "the selection effect." Under modern statutes, the Supreme Court has almost complete discretion in deciding which cases to review from among the more than eight thousand per year that parties ask them to hear.[30] But the Justices' principal job is to resolve hard cases about which reasonable people disagree. With the Justices' docket made up of the legally hardest and most divisive cases, their frequent divisions in those cases do not support the conclusion that no law governs the Supreme Court. Insofar as many if not most legal matters are concerned, there is no reason to doubt that the Justices are as law bound and as agreed about what the law requires as are the rest of us.

One indicator of the relevance of law in the Supreme Court emerges from the Justices' evident convergence of judgment in the myriad of cases that they choose not to hear and, perhaps more importantly, in the numberless possible cases that no one ever would think to bring. With regard to these cases, there is every reason to believe that the Justices recognize what the law requires and behave accordingly. By all appearances, the Justices, just like the rest of us, know without needing even to think about it that elections for president must occur every four years and that all of the powers that we associate with the presidency accrue to the winner. They similarly agree unanimously that nearly all of the laws enacted by Congress and the state legislatures are constitutionally valid. Sophisticated constitutional analysts though they are, the Justices take it for granted as much as the rest of us that speed limits on the highways do not violate anyone's constitutional rights. They know they lack constitutional grounds to reject most if not all of the laws that they disagree with. They might think taxes either too high or too low without imagining that the statutes they dislike are constitutionally defective. In short, for the most part, the Justices concur about how best to go on. In most actual and hypothetical cases—including the numberless "easy" cases that never get brought because their outcome would be beyond serious dispute—there will be no question concerning what the applicable constitutional rules, standards, or practices of recognition require.[31]

The Justices' practice in selecting cases also reveals a good deal. In exercising their discretion concerning which cases to review, the current Court invariably chooses fewer than one hundred per year, even though the Justices could, and in the past sometimes did, elect to decide many more. For the most part, the lower courts are not confused about the constitutional rules that they must apply, and the Justices evidently agree that the lower courts have identified the applicable rules or tests correctly. Seeing no reason to intervene in the vast majority of cases, the Justices normally agree to review only issues of exceptional importance or those about which lower courts have come to divergent conclusions.[32]

The scope of agreement among the Justices grows especially noteworthy when we recognize that many of the issues on which they concur unanimously today once provoked strident disagreement. These include such issues as whether the Constitution bars race discrimination in the public schools, whether Congress can validly establish a Social Security system, and whether paper money is constitutional in light of a provision of Article I that empowers Congress to "coin" money but makes no reference to paper currency. At one point in the past, the Court's precedents either established or suggested negative answers to all of these questions.[33] Today, the relevant precedents give affirmative answers from which not a single Justice has signaled any disposition to dissent.

Even when the Justices agree to hear a case, moreover, close and angry divisions mark the exception, not the norm. From the 1940s to the present, the Justices have decided an average of approximately 40 percent of their cases by unanimous vote.[34]

A second error into which we might fall is that of thinking that where agreement among the Justices ends, the law—as defined in practice-based terms rooted in acceptance—necessarily runs out. This need not be so. As I emphasized previously, the Justices can share standards that call for the exercise of moral or practical judgment in some cases yet disagree about what good judgment requires. In addition, we should not discount the possibility of simpler forms of error in correctly identifying and applying substantive and interpretive rules. To put the same point only slightly differently, only the truly fundamental or ground-level rules, standards, or practices of recognition depend for their validity on the sheer sociological fact of their acceptance. Disagreement about less fundamental matters may sometimes result from legal mistakes, including by the Justices.

Think of *Plessy v. Ferguson*, the notorious 1896 case in which the Supreme Court held by eight to one that state-mandated segregation in public transportation (and, by implication, in public education) did not offend the Equal Protection Clause.[35] At the time, it appears that nearly everyone regarded the case as an easy one, rightly decided by the Justices.[36] The sole dissenting Justice, John Marshall Harlan, stood as an outlier at the time of the case's decision. Today, nearly everyone thinks that Harlan was right and that the opposing consensus was wrong, based on rules of recognition that applied to the case even at the time of its decision.[37] As psychologists recurrently demonstrate, a variety of cognitive biases, often reinforced by socially entrenched expectations, can lead to demonstrable mistakes in reasoning, including in legal analysis.[38] Today, nearly everyone can see

the fallacies of the *Plessy* majority's credulous denial that "the enforced separation of the two races stamps the colored race with a
badge of inferiority," followed immediately by its explanation that "if
this be so, it is . . . solely because the colored race chooses to put that
construction upon it."[39] As Charles Black memorably wrote, at this
point in the Court's opinion, "the curves of callousness and stupidity
intersect at their respective maxima."[40] Put less memorably, the Justices' rationale for decision was utterly indefensible.

The realization that the Justices can err in the application of legal
norms binding on them may give us a quasi-paradoxical picture of
the rules, standards, or practices of recognition that apply in the
Supreme Court. But the picture is only quasi-paradoxical, not entirely so. From a purely sociological point of view, there is no escape
from the dependence of all claims of legal validity and legitimacy on
sociologically dominant understandings and expectations. For
many purposes, the correct answer to the question whether statutes requiring racial segregation were legally valid in the United
States in the immediate aftermath of *Plessy v. Ferguson* would be yes.
But when we adopt a legal perspective or point of view, the deepest
assumption of our constitutional arguments, embraced by all who
argue in good faith about what the Constitution means or requires,
is that a majority or even all of the Justices can make mistakes both
about how best to formulate the norms of our constitutional order
and about how those norms apply to particular cases.

Practice-Based Rules in the Supreme Court

If we accept that legal standards apply in the Supreme Court, and
that the Justices have meaningful disagreements when they differ
about what the Constitution requires—that it is not just a matter of
their making up the rules for themselves as they go along—then it
becomes our challenge to identify some of the most pertinent,
practice-based rules or standards of recognition. In embarking on
this task, we should have realistic expectations. On the one hand, we
should expect to be able to account for the very wide-ranging agreement among the Justices that manifestly exists. Across a vast range
of cases, they converge in their judgment about what the Constitu-

tion requires or permits. On the other hand, we must expect the applicable rules or standards to permit reasonable disagreement in their applications to some issues. As I have emphasized, reasonable disagreement in constitutional law is a phenomenon to be explained, not elided or denied. In the apt formulation of the legal philosopher Ronald M. Dworkin, American constitutional law is a deeply "argumentative" practice.[41] Relatedly, we must be prepared to accept, for now-familiar reasons, that the applicable rules or standards at least permit, and possibly require, the Justices to resolve reasonable interpretive uncertainties based on partly normative criteria. (Chapter 7 will consider the possibility, which I put aside for now, that the Justices might be Cynical Realists who conduct their arguments in bad faith.)

Throughout, we must aim to identify what the Justices do from a sense of obligation, not mere habit or convenience. Historical practices or decisions that triggered sustained criticism from the legal profession, and from which the Court's subsequent retreat might signal the learning of a lesson, are also relevant.[42]

In setting out to identify what counts as "going on" in accordance with the constitutive standards of constitutional adjudication in the Supreme Court, I must proceed selectively. Those who have tried to make lists of legally valid "canons of interpretation" have compiled scores or even hundreds of entries.[43] My aim here is similar to theirs in one way: it is to give relatively explicit formulation to widely shared tacit understandings. The validity of the proposed, articulated rules must be tested against practice and against others' efforts to excavate the implicit norms to which practice conforms. In comparison with those who have compiled lists of interpretive canons, however, my aspiration here is more nearly architectonic: I hope to distill only a relative few of the implicit rules or standards of constitutional practice as they apply in the Supreme Court, with the aim of identifying some of those that have the greatest organizing, predictive, and explanatory power. Others would undoubtedly produce different, possibly better, lists. But their improvements would not demonstrate the utter failure of my effort. My relatively modest aim is to determine whether, and, if so, to chart roughly how, "it makes sense to distinguish between a right and a wrong way of doing things in connection with" constitutional adjudication by the Justices of the Supreme Court.[44]

Any of my proposed formulations could, in principle, be challenged on the ground that it fails to conform to a putatively more fundamental rule. In my view, the challenges of this kind ought to fail. To explain why would require a deep immersion in controversial matters. Here, my hope is that many of those who might differ with me on some of those controversies will agree, nevertheless, that I have offered good approximations of seven relatively fundamental rules practiced by the Supreme Court that are not inconsistent with even more fundamental rules of constitutional practice that are also validated by acceptance. Proceeding in this somewhat rough-and-ready way, I shall make no pretense of assigning my distilled rules of Supreme Court practice either lexical priorities or comparative weights.

With all of these caveats, here are seven relatively architectonic rules of constitutional practice that constitute law binding in the Supreme Court:

First, the Justices must acknowledge the paramount authority of the Constitution in all cases. The Supreme Court's authority derives from the Constitution. By nearly unanimous consensus, the Justices' rulings must permit explanation as mandated by or consistent with the meaning of the Constitution and the authority that the Constitution assigns to the Court. I know of no case in which the Justices have ever suggested that they could reach a decision contrary to the Constitution's requirements.

Although the rule that assigns paramount authority to the Constitution is truly fundamental, we should not overestimate its rigidity. In ways that previous chapters have signaled, the Constitution requires interpretation.

Second, although the Justices must treat the Constitution as a legitimate and binding authority, they must sometimes choose from among multiple candidates to furnish the Constitution's most legally salient meaning in a particular case, as described in Chapter 2. Significantly, these candidates can include reasonable meanings—when, for example, the Court reads categorical language as having implied exceptions for cases involving "compelling" state interests—and precedential meanings. As I noted in Chapter 3, every Justice in

Supreme Court history appears to have assumed a power and obligation to adhere to some prior Court decisions that he or she believed to have been initially erroneous.

Some think that a preference for precedential meaning over original meaning is inconsistent with the idea of written constitutionalism.[45] But it is not. As the Justices' practices of recognition implicitly recognize, if the Constitution is law because it is accepted as such, we need to ask if there are other legal norms that are valid for the same reason. Second-order rules of interpretation—not all of which can be derived from the Constitution itself—are prime candidates to achieve legal validity based on the sociological phenomenon of their acceptance or their coherence with other widely accepted norms.

Third, the Justices should maintain reasonable stability in constitutional doctrine, even when the doctrine—as judged by criteria unrelated to interests in stability—is less than optimal by their lights.[46] To begin with a well-known example, a majority of the Justices who were sitting on the Supreme Court in 2000 would almost surely have liked to rewrite the *Miranda* warning, or even eliminate it, if they could have begun constitutional adjudication anew.[47] But of course they could not. So acknowledging, a strong majority affirmed *Miranda*'s continuing validity in *Dickerson v. United States*, "whether or not we would agree with *Miranda*'s reasoning and its resulting rule, were we addressing the issue in the first instance."[48]

The same point holds even more powerfully for some Justices who may believe that the country and the Supreme Court took a wrong turn, decades ago, when it began to accept the constitutional permissibility of vast federal welfare and regulatory bureaucracies that the Founding generation could never possibly have contemplated. The normative pressure to adhere to past decisions becomes especially great when large portions of the public have come to rely on the programs or policies that such decisions validated. (Think of the chaos that would ensue if the Supreme Court were to hold today that paper money or Social Security is unconstitutional.)[49]

Fourth, the Justices have an obligation not only to maintain stability insofar as it exists but also to give weight in their decision making to an interest in establishing law that gives reasonably clear guidance for the future. In one manifestation of this obligation, the Justices sometimes compromise their personal views about what would be constitutionally best in order to agree on majority opinions that create clear, settled law. As a matter of second best, a decisive, readily comprehensible, and tolerable resolution of a constitutional issue is often preferable to a state of continuing confusion among the lower courts and the population more generally about what the Constitution requires or permits.

The Justices have further acknowledged an obligation to make reasonable efforts to achieve legal clarity by crafting or constructing a number of relatively determinate doctrines to implement vague constitutional language.[50] In the 1960s and 1970s, for example, the Justices devised the now-familiar strict scrutiny test under which statutes that discriminate on the basis of race or religion will be deemed invalid unless "necessary to promote a compelling governmental interest."[51] The Court has crafted, and adhered to, a number of comparable tests to enforce the First Amendment guarantee of free speech, the Due Process Clause, and many other constitutional provisions.[52]

Fifth, although an important standard calls for the Justices to keep the law reasonably clear and settled, the obligation to maintain stable understandings does not hold when sufficiently powerful legal or moral considerations call for a different course. Although the Justices obviously regard it as more important for many issues to be resolved than for them to be decided correctly, all agree that some prior errors should be corrected, some decisions overruled, and some doctrines revamped (even if they disagree concerning which ones). In talking about when the Supreme Court will overrule its own precedents, the Justices often recite a multifactor test (a representative formulation of which is quoted in the endnotes) that relies heavily on such mundane considerations as whether a decision has proved unworkable in practice and whether more recent cases have undermined its premises.[53]

We should take the test that the Court recites with a grain of salt. If read literally, it may obscure the central consideration, which involves the egregiousness of the alleged error—as measured in both moral and legal terms—as well as the costs of correcting it. *Brown v.*

Board of Education is now an unshakable precedent, even though many believe that it deviated from the best account of the original public meaning of the Equal Protection Clause, because *Brown*'s technical legal error—if it committed one—advanced rather than retarded substantive moral justice. Even if the Court's decisions upholding Social Security could be shown legally erroneous as an original matter, the costs of invalidating it would be too great. By contrast, *Roe v. Wade* will remain controversial and potentially vulnerable to overruling as long as some Justices and a substantial segment of the American public believe that abortion is murder.

Sixth, the capacity of what Chapter 3 described as T2 authorities to control outcomes depends on forward- as well as backward-looking considerations. Roughly speaking, I would say that in cases in which the T2 historical settlement of an issue by practice or precedent is reasonably just and practical, Justices normally will and ought to accept it even if the best evidence of the original public meaning points to a contrary conclusion. By contrast, if a T2 authority produces a result that is not reasonably just, and if evidence of T1 meaning points to a better outcome as measured by forward-looking criteria, then the Justices will and should reconsider the question of the T2 authority's constitutional validity.

Seventh, and more generally, the Justices should resolve doubts about proper interpretations and priorities of authority in light of both backward- and forward-looking legitimacy concerns. To put the point only slightly differently, the rules or standards of recognition that apply in the Supreme Court authorize and sometimes require the Justices to make partly moral judgments about which authorities to treat as controlling, consistent with the premise that precedential or interpreted meaning is a permissible sense of constitutional meaning. In cases of reasonable moral disagreement, we need to expect that the Justices may disagree morally.

If the foregoing sketch is even approximately correct, then the rules or standards of recognition that apply in the Supreme Court establish a framework for normative decision and, in some instances, for normative "bargaining" among the Justices.[54] In many disputed cases, the Justices must decide how best to go on in light of reasonable disagreements and sometimes competing desiderata. Once again, however, it would be a mistake to regard the framework within which the Justices operate as entirely malleable. If tempted by that conclusion, we should think back to the very broad set of issues concerning which the Justices agree unanimously in their judgments.

On any particular point or at any particular time, the unanimity may be contingent, for reasons that I have explained. Applying the partly open-ended standards of recognition that I have sketched, a new Justice might conclude that the Court should unsettle a matter that all Justices previously agreed should be regarded as settled. In the early years after Justice William Rehnquist joined the Supreme Court in 1972, he frequently filed solitary dissents, adopting positions that others found outlandish.[55] Eventually, largely as a result of new appointments, the Court moved substantially in his direction.[56] Justice Antonin Scalia sometimes played a similar role and achieved a similar effect.[57] Today, Justice Clarence Thomas stakes out deliberately iconoclastic positions on some issues.[58] Overall, however, shared assumptions and expectations predominate. If one examines the totality of the Justices' decisions—including their patterns of criticizing other Justices for reaching contrary conclusions—it is hard not to acknowledge that the Justices attempt both to adhere to and to enforce shared norms of recognition, even if they disagree about how those sometimes indeterminate norms are best formulated, interpreted, or specified. For Justices who accept that such norms exist and who seek to identify and conform to them, those norms, in turn, help to make the idea of law that is binding in the Supreme Court not only intelligible but also functionally important.

Transitional Clarifications

I should conclude with three points of clarification concerning the limits of the argument that I have offered in this chapter. First, in emphasizing the nature and importance of law in the Supreme Court, I in no way mean to deny the human, psychological dimension of the Justices' decision making. The Justices are people, like the rest of us. Quirks of personality, resentments, and jealousies may matter to their legal analysis in some cases or on some points.

A Justice's race or gender may affect his or her judgment in subtle or not-so-subtle ways. The same may be true of religion. In the history of the Supreme Court, some Justices have famously disliked, resented, or even hated one another.[59] It is by no means unimaginable that jealousies and dislikes affected the positions that some adopted.

Beyond matters of personal affection and disaffection, the Justices need to engage actively with each other's opinions. Among other things, it is their job to try to find common ground in blending continuity with change in legal doctrine and in formulating tests to be applied by lower courts and other officials.[60] Accordingly, what a Justice ought to do will depend in part on the accident of what her changing cast of colleagues thinks at any particular time.

But this, again, is not to say that the Justices are or ought to be politicians in robes, always ready to compromise to pick up a needed vote. To take just one example, in the year that I spent as a Supreme Court law clerk in 1981–1982, I never observed even a single incident of vote trading among the Justices. More systematic and historical studies corroborate strict adherence to the norm that I observed.[61] However tempting it might have been for a Justice who cared greatly about the outcome in case A but little about case B to have swapped votes with another Justice whose preferences were reversed, institutional norms flatly forbade such conduct. As I have emphasized, constitutional adjudication in the Supreme Court is a practice with distinctive rules and standards.

Second, although I have focused on law and constitutional adjudication in the Supreme Court, much of my analysis—both in this chapter and throughout the book—applies to lower courts as well. Many Western democracies vest responsibility for all constitutional adjudication in a single constitutional court. In the United States, nearly all constitutional litigation begins in lower courts.[62] Like the Supreme Court, lower courts must recognize the Constitution as paramount law and also must interpret it. In doing so, moreover, lower court judges face both backward- and forward-looking demands of legally and morally legitimate decision making that are similar to those that exist in the Supreme Court. Nevertheless, there is one signal difference, which has led me to focus both this chapter and the book predominantly on the Supreme Court. Unlike the

Supreme Court, all lower courts must accept the Supreme Court's prior rulings as categorically binding on them, however erroneous they believe those rulings to be. To offer just one vivid example, if *Roe v. Wade* were ever to be overturned, only the Supreme Court could effect the overruling. Because the Supreme Court can overrule or modify its precedents if it chooses to do so, it has a partially distinctive role in declaring, developing, and revising the constitutional law of the United States.

Third, in arguing that legal norms apply in the Supreme Court, and that they structure and sometimes determine the Justices' decision making, I have not yet responded directly to skeptical critics who maintain that, for all practical purposes, the Justices stand above the law, even if the law theoretically binds them. A familiar version of that position posits that in the absence of coercive enforcement mechanisms, no real law exists. Absent an enforcer, the argument continues, the notion of law in the Supreme Court is the functional equivalent of tennis without a net. Chapter 5 takes up issues involving the actual and possible enforcement of the Justices' legal obligations.

5

Constitutional Constraints

CHAPTER 4 TALKED about law in the Supreme Court, but it did not discuss in any depth the problem of how that law might be enforced. Charles Evans Hughes, who would later serve as Chief Justice of the United States, once remarked that "the Constitution is what the judges say it is."[1] If there is no way to enforce the Constitution against the Justices, and if they are thus practically unconstrained, then talk of rules of recognition or other law that theoretically applies to them may seem naïve.[2] This chapter therefore takes up the topic of constitutional constraints on governmental officials, signally including the Justices of the Supreme Court.

In thinking about the constraints to which the Justices are subject, I shall generally follow an approach that James Madison suggested in *The Federalist No. 51*, which discusses the need to supplement constitutional norms—or standards to which officials ought to conform in recognition of the Constitution's legitimate authority—with constraints arising from checks imposed by others.[3] I refer to the latter as "external constraints," the former as "normative constraints."[4] I consider external constraints before describing and appraising normative constraints, largely because a number of observers question whether "merely" normative constraints could have any practical potency in restraining the Justices.

First, however, we need to explore what it means for the Constitution to "constrain" the Justices. This is not so easy a question as one might think. Approaching it, we might be tempted by skeptical questions about how words on paper or "parchment barriers" could ever constrain anyone. Upon analysis, however, the thought that the Constitution might fail to constrain the Justices, and thus leave them free to say that the Constitution means whatever they might wish, proves practically unimaginable. To be a Justice of the Supreme Court is to serve in an institution that is constituted by the Constitution and, as a result, almost necessarily constrained by constitutional rules and by other institutions—including Congress, the president, and the electorate—that the Constitution also creates and empowers.[5] To be a Justice is different from being president or a member of Congress. If the Justices sought to take over the functions of presidents or Congress, or if they ignored or denied the president's or Congress's lawful powers, they would bump immediately into a myriad of practical and political, as well as legal, impediments. When we grasp this obvious point, we may fear that the question whether the Constitution constrains the Justices has somehow slipped away from us, even though there must surely be something to it.

In order to think about whether the Constitution meaningfully constrains Supreme Court Justices, we need to consider the relationship between constitutional rules, including rules of recognition, on the one hand, and the Justices' goals and motivations, on the other hand.[6] The Justices undoubtedly possess some goals that have little or nothing to do with law and that might even run contrary to it. For example, they might like to become richer and more famous or to advance their political preferences. Focused on concerns of this kind, we might imagine that a central function of the Constitution is to constrain the Justices by stopping them from doing what they would want to do in the absence of constitutional obstacles.

There is undoubtedly a nugget of truth here. We will need to come back to it. We will go wrong at the outset, however, if we imagine that the Constitution most fundamentally constrains the Justices in the same way that laws against murder constrain those who would otherwise commit homicides. In the absence of laws forbidding murder, people would have the same power to threaten others that they have now. By contrast, in the absence of constitutional constraints on Supreme Court Justices, we would not have constitutionally unconstrained Justices but rather no officials whom we could call Justices at all.

The reason involves the conceptual linkage between constitutional constraint and constitutional empowerment. As part of the fundamental law of the United States, the Constitution does not merely regulate what the government and its officials can do. Its even more essential function is to constitute the government and its most basic institutions. In order to think clearly about the role of the Constitution in our legal system, we therefore need to recognize the conceptual connections between constituting and constraining.[7]

Considering the powers of the Supreme Court with this connection in mind, we can see that the Constitution constrains the Justices most elementally by helping create the context—including that of a government with three branches, one of them being the judiciary—in which questions of constraint and even some questions of motivation arise.[8] Just as the president cannot rule state laws unconstitutional or sentence people to jail for having committed tax fraud, the Justices cannot set interest rates or establish national defense policies. If we ask why, the answer is that to be a Justice, as to be the president, is to have certain recognized and lawful powers but not others. By constituting the offices of president and Supreme Court Justice, the Constitution helps establish widely accepted understandings of what presidents and Justices can (and cannot) lawfully, and thus authoritatively, do.

An analogy may drive home the point. Asking whether the Constitution constrains Justices of the Supreme Court is like asking whether the rules of baseball constrain the umpire from giving one team four strikes per batter or four outs per inning. A person who stood behind home plate and decreed that a batter was entitled to four strikes or that an inning was not over until one team had recorded four outs would have stepped outside the role of an umpire in a baseball game as defined by broadly shared understandings of the rules that make baseball baseball.

Even if so, a cynic might say, the crucial question with respect to the Supreme Court is whether the Justices could effect a comparable power grab and get away with it. Indeed, some claim that the Justices have. But their arguments do not hold water. With the analogy in mind of an umpire who flouts the rules of baseball, we could run a comparable thought experiment in the field of constitutional law: What would happen if the Justices of the Supreme Court, by a vote of five to four, simply ordered banks to raise or lower their interest rates (outside the context of a plausible legal argument that some law required them to do so) or ordered the army to invade Iran? Although the question is hard to take seriously, it points us in the right direction by acknowledging that what I described in Chapter 4 as the "rules of recognition" practiced by the Justices in adjudicating constitutional cases do not exist in a vacuum. Even if the Justices were otherwise tempted to deviate from widely recognized constitutional norms, they would be constrained by *others'* rules or practices of recognition in distinguishing legitimate from illegitimate claims of judicial power. In a very real sense, other officials and the public can, and sometimes do, enforce the Constitution against the Justices of the Supreme Court. Or at least other officials and the public would be available to do so if the Justices sufficiently overstepped their widely recognized powers under the Constitution.

At this point, the relentless cynic might retort that the only checks against judicial power are "political," not "constitutional." But we could say the same about checks on Congress and the president. The only way that the Constitution can constrain any officials of any branch is to constitute an interlocking set of institutions with distinctive powers, with the authority to identify when other officials have overstepped their roles, and with the capacity to check, resist, or sanction attempted abuses of power. Just as a "president" who dissolved Congress, suspended the power of the courts to exercise judicial review, and ruled by decree would not be a president in the constitutional sense of the term but a tyrant who had overthrown the Constitution, a "Supreme Court" that purported to exercise unbounded powers—if we could even imagine it—would not be a constitutionally legitimate Court. And if we count presidents as constitutionally constrained because the courts hold them to account for violating the Constitution, we should view the Supreme Court as constitutionally constrained when other constitutionally established and empowered institutions stand ready to respond if the Court should too dramatically exceed its lawful powers.

External Constraints

The mechanisms through which other officials and the public can enforce the Constitution against the Justices are of course not perfect. As much as the Justices, other officials might err in their judgments about what the Constitution requires or forbids. Other officials might purport to "enforce" the Constitution against the Justices when the Justices were correct and the other officials wrong in their constitutional judgments. (In so observing, I take the measure of correctness and of wrongness to come from the perspective of a perfectly informed and reasonable observer who seeks to identify and abide by what all good-faith participants in constitutional practice assume to be the shared, substantive, and methodological norms that ground our legal order. I further assume that those norms may permit or require the exercise of moral judgment in some cases.) There is no escaping the risk of human fallibility. Nonetheless, a variety of possible constraining and enforcement mechanisms exists.

Concurrent agreement requirements. In considering constraints on the Justices of the Supreme Court, it is easy to forget that the Court comprises nine Justices, each of whom is constrained individually by the need to secure the agreement of at least four colleagues in order to render legally efficacious judgments.[9] If a Justice's colleagues believed that he or she routinely violated constitutional or institutional norms, they could limit or even eliminate that Justice's influence in the Court's collective deliberations. They could, for example, refuse to join any opinions that the offending Justice wrote. Eight Justices took an even more extreme step late in the tenure of Justice William O. Douglas, after a stroke had left him mentally enfeebled and erratic. During his last year on the Court, Douglas's colleagues agreed to order a reargument the following year in any case in which they divided four to four and in which Douglas otherwise would have had the deciding vote.[10] As these and other examples attest, the need to procure the support or cooperation of others to act efficaciously functions as a constraint on the Justices individually.

Sanctions. The Constitution empowers Congress and the president to impose sanctions on the Supreme Court and its Justices if they deviate from what Congress and the president take to be the Constitution's dictates. The Constitution insulates the Supreme Court, as it does all federal judges, against certain kinds of sanctions. Article III provides that the Justices cannot be removed from office during good behavior and forbids Congress to reduce their salaries.[11] All judges, the Justices included, also enjoy immunity from suits for civil damages based on their official acts.[12] Despite these safeguards of judicial independence, the Constitution provides for some sanctions against Supreme Court Justices. Most formally and conspicuously, Justices can be impeached and removed from office for "high Crimes and Misdemeanors."[13] They are also subject to the criminal law, including its prohibitions against bribery and extortion.

Beyond the sanctions available against Supreme Court Justices, the Constitution creates mechanisms for the imposition of institutional sanctions directed at the Court as a whole. The Constitution permits Congress to withdraw cases from the Court's jurisdiction to hear appeals from lower court decisions—the source of virtually all of the important cases that come to the Court, from *Brown v. Board of Education*, to *Roe v. Wade*, to disputes about gay marriage and Obamacare. Although commentators debate the outer limits of congressional power, Article III specifically establishes that the Court's appellate jurisdiction is subject to "such Exceptions . . . as the Congress shall make."[14]

If so minded, Congress and the president could also "pack" the Court and thereby not only reduce the power of incumbent Justices but also diminish the Court's prestige. Over the course of American history, the number of seats on the Supreme Court has been as low as five and as high as ten. Nothing in the Constitution prohibits Congress from making the Court even larger. One would expect the Justices to regard Court packing as a sanction and to wish to avoid it. In 1937, President Franklin Roosevelt notoriously proposed to increase the size of the Court for the obvious purpose of avoiding the invalidation of New Deal legislation that he thought the Court should uphold.[15] Roosevelt's proposal failed after one or possibly two of the Justices, under threat, effected what commentators swiftly dubbed "the switch in time that saved the nine" by upholding legislation that previously appeared vulnerable.[16] If the Court had not shifted course and if the Court-packing plan had succeeded, nearly all would have viewed Congress as having sanctioned the Court for its perceived constitutional obduracy in threatening the New Deal, including the Social Security Act.

Insofar as threats of sanctions function as a constraint on judicial action, their directive force could sometimes create a tension with applicable normative constraints: the Justices might feel externally constrained to adopt positions that they think constitutionally erroneous. This possibility—which exemplifies the age-old dilemma of who should guard the guardians—is an unhappy one. It is also inescapable. Any scheme of constraints necessarily risks fallibility in the constraining institutions that it employs.

Nullification. Perhaps the most practically important constraint on the Justices emerges from the prospect that some decisions they might imaginably render would be treated as nullities or otherwise prove inefficacious.[17] To repeat earlier examples, a judicial directive purporting to raise or lower interest rates solely for policy reasons or to invade Iran would not be recognized as legally authoritative.[18]

This conclusion may appear trivial because the examples are far-fetched, but the contrary is more nearly true. Although the point is easily overlooked when the Supreme Court renders controversial decisions in high-stakes cases, the Court's docket typically includes few of the issues that most Americans regard as most pressing.[19] Matters of war and peace, economic boom and bust, and priorities in the provision of public services seldom come within the province of judicial decision making. In light of familiar assumptions that unchecked power tends to expand,[20] we might ask why this is so. Part of the answer lies in the Justices' awareness of external constraints, centrally including that of nullification of judicial orders by the political branches.

As a historical matter, the prospect of judicial pronouncements being treated as nullities or otherwise proving inefficacious—if the Justices overstepped what others take to be the constitutional limits of legitimate judicial power—is hardly hypothetical.[21] Three celebrated examples stand out.

First, in a crucially important showdown between a Federalist-dominated Supreme Court and the administration of the newly installed Democratic-Republican President Thomas Jefferson, the Court, led by the legendary Chief Justice John Marshall, backed down.[22] The showdown occurred early in U.S. history, after the Federalists—who had dominated the federal government up to that point—were swept out of office in the 1800 elections. In the aftermath of that defeat, the outgoing, lame-duck Federalists sought to entrench Federalist power in the judicial branch by creating sixteen new lower court judgeships, which the outgoing president, John Adams, quickly filled with the "advice and consent" of the Senate. Adams also used the lame-duck period to appoint Marshall, who had served previously as his secretary of state, as Chief Justice.

Upon taking office, Jefferson's congressional allies eliminated the sixteen judgeships that the outgoing Federalists had created and filled. Over the course of U.S. history, nearly all commentators have agreed that Congress's action in doing so violated the guarantee of Article III that federal judges shall hold their offices during "good Behaviour."[23] Beyond any shadow of doubt, sixteen judges lost their offices without anyone's alleging or proving that they had misbehaved in any way. President Jefferson and his Secretary of State James Madison also refused to deliver "commissions" to a few people whom Adams had appointed to minor federal offices but who had not yet received the requisite confirming documents. When lawsuits challenged the various actions of the Jeffersonians on legal and constitutional grounds, the ascendant Democratic-Republicans threatened defiance and possible judicial impeachments if the Supreme Court sought to thwart their rollbacks of what they viewed as partisan overreach by outgoing Federalists.

In the face of the threats, the Supreme Court largely (but not entirely) acquiesced. In *Stuart v. Laird*, the Justices declined even to consider whether a Jeffersonian Congress had violated the Constitution by abolishing the sixteen federal judgeships that the Federalists had so recently created and filled. Ignoring that issue, the Court instead ruled cryptically that another provision of the 1802 Judiciary Act, which forced the Justices to take over the ousted judges' functions—by, in effect, acting as lower court judges in the periods between the Court's formal sessions—was consistent with prior practice and therefore constitutionally permissible.[24]

In the more celebrated companion case of *Marbury v. Madison*, the Court also took pains to dodge a credible threat of defiance.[25] *Marbury* is often hailed as the foundation stone of judicial review because it was the first case in which the Court ever held a federal statute to be unconstitutional. The Court did so, however, in a complex chain of reasoning at the end of which it ruled against a Federalist challenger and in favor of the Jefferson administration: the Court held that it lacked jurisdiction to enter an order directing Secretary of State Madison to install the disappointed Federalist William Marbury as a minor federal officeholder. In its historical context, *Marbury*—especially when it is read in conjunction with *Stuart v. Laird*—can be understood as having initiated a "prudential" tradition in which the Supreme Court has almost always avoided issuing opinions that the president—with the support of the public—would have defied or refused to enforce.[26] It is often forgotten that if Madison had not won the case of *Marbury v. Madison*, then Jefferson and Madison would have defied a ruling in favor of Marbury, and Chief Justice Marshall might well have been impeached.[27]

Second, in a case filed during the early days of the Civil War, Abraham Lincoln oversaw and defended the defiance by Union military officers of a ruling by Chief Justice Roger B. Taney in *Ex parte Merryman*.[28] Taney claimed the power to free an alleged Confederate collaborator in the state of Maryland, where the Union army had effectively imposed martial law and detained him without trial. In the context of wartime emergency, Lincoln later explained, he thought it his duty not to accede. Both then and now, public opinion has largely supported Lincoln's judgment.[29]

A third example may come from the World War II case of *Ex parte Quirin*, in which the Court upheld executive branch authority to try alleged Nazi saboteurs who had been captured in the United States—one of whom was an American citizen—before a military tribunal rather than a civilian court.[30] While the case was pending, President Franklin Roosevelt made it known to the Justices that if they ruled for the petitioners, he would order military trials and summary executions to proceed anyway.[31] In the wartime circumstances, military personnel would almost certainly have obeyed presidential orders to ignore a judicial ruling—a consideration that may well have affected the Court's decision to uphold the constitutionality of military trials. Given the circumstances, the Justices announced their ruling in *Quirin* almost immediately after the argument in the case, but initially without any accompanying written opinion. The Court issued an opinion explaining its reasoning some months later, after the petitioners had already been tried and executed by the military.[32]

The Court may also have framed its famous order that local school boards should enforce the rights recognized in *Brown v. Board of Education* "with all deliberate speed," rather than posthaste, partly because it knew that a mandate of immediate desegregation might have proved inefficacious.[33] Many now believe that the Court miscalculated in *Brown*. The framing of its mandate may have done more to invite than to defuse resistance. But the basic point still holds: because the Supreme Court's powers depend on compliance by others, others' potential unwillingness to comply enforces what are, for all practical purposes, constitutional constraints on the Justices' authority.

Although my characterizing of other officials' capacities to resist the Supreme Court as "constitutional constraints" may seem linguistically or conceptually unfamiliar today, Madison, among other members of the Founding generation, avowedly embraced this constraining strategy. Under the Constitution, he wrote, "ambition must be made to counteract ambition."[34] He accordingly praised the constitutional policy of "divid[ing] and arrang[ing] the several offices in such a manner as that each may be a check on the other."[35] If judicial power to check other branches counts as a constitutional constraint—as almost everyone concurs that it does—then I believe that other branches' powers to check the Court deserve the same label. The only way in which the Constitution can constrain the Court "externally" is by setting up other institutions with checking and balancing capacities, which other institutions and officials sometimes exercise.

The Politically Constructed Bounds of Judicial Power

Looking at the constraints to which the Supreme Court is subject, political scientists sometimes assert that the Justices function within "politically constructed" bounds.[36] We should concur. The Constitution quite clearly contemplates that the Supreme Court can rule on constitutional issues in the cases that come before it. In the early years of American history, however, many thoughtful and informed Americans—notably including Jefferson—subscribed to a theory of "departmentalism."[37] Departmentalists held that each branch of the federal government—Congress and the president as much as the judiciary—has an obligation to interpret the Constitution for itself. On the departmentalist view, other branches had to take the Supreme Court's rulings into account but did not necessarily need to comply with them. In departmentalist thinking, the one domain in which the judiciary undoubtedly reigned supreme was that of the criminal law: all agreed that other branches could not imprison someone without a judicial trial (at least outside circumstances of war or similar emergency).

Despite the currency that departmentalism once enjoyed, the predominantly prevailing modern view is that nonjudicial officials normally must treat judicial pronouncements as legally binding on them. The best explanation of how the Supreme Court could have acquired and maintained this trumping power is that, with respect to the kinds of issues on which the courts speak authoritatively, elected officials generally prefer that courts, and especially the Supreme Court, should have the last word, provided that judicial decisions remain within the bounds of political and practical tolerability.[38] By maintaining an independent judiciary, risk-averse political leaders forgo some opportunities to exercise authority while they hold office in order to prevent their political adversaries from gaining unbounded power when the adversaries triumph at the polls. Politicians may also find it to their electoral advantage to leave a range of contentious issues for judicial decision. Disaffected citizens can then blame the Supreme Court, not elected officials, for their disappointments.[39]

In the United States today, the Supreme Court can authoritatively resolve constitutional issues within an impressively broad policy space. For example, almost no one questions the Court's mandate to determine the constitutionality of affirmative action programs, gun control legislation, or restrictions on political campaign contributions, however much critics may dislike the conclusions that the Court reaches. But the Court would almost as clearly step outside its bounds if it identified constitutional questions entitling it to the last word on what, if any, stimulus policies the government should employ in the face of a sagging economy, what marginal tax rates ought to be, or whether the United States should take a more accommodating or a more hostile stance toward China. To take other examples that once were more live, the Court would stray outside the politically acceptable space for judicial review if it were to hold, today, that Social Security or paper money is unconstitutional.[40]

In the practically unimaginable event that the Court were to mandate an outcome that would plunge millions into poverty or the economy into chaos, or to upset settled social and political expectations with no plausible basis in the Constitution's text or history for doing so, its egregiously disruptive decision almost surely would not stick. The Court can make, and has made, highly unpopular decisions. But it has not so far created havoc or issued rulings that lack any plausible constitutional foundation. If the Justices were to do so, the only question would involve the precise mechanism by which the Court's intolerable ruling would be denied effect—whether, for example, by executive and congressional defiance, a statutory denial of jurisdiction to any court to enforce the decision, impeachments of Justices who joined the majority opinion, Court packing, or some combination of these or similar responses.

In claiming that judicial review by the Supreme Court functions within a politically constructed domain, we should distinguish, as political scientists have not always done, between harder and softer versions of the political construction thesis. The harder version, which I have emphasized so far, holds that political officials, with the public's approbation, would dismiss some otherwise imaginable Supreme Court rulings as ultra vires and refuse to treat them as authoritative. The softer version maintains that Court decisions or patterns of Court decisions that provoke sufficiently broad and enduring public outrage will not survive in the long run even if they do not trigger immediate defiance. Over time, the voters will elect presidents who oppose the politically intolerable decisions. Those presidents then will nominate, and the Senate will confirm, Justices who will undermine or overrule those decisions.

As a result, as both historians and political scientists have emphasized, the Supreme Court's overall pattern of decisions on issues of significant public consequence has never strayed very far for very long from mainstream public opinion.[41] The New Deal offers perhaps history's most famous example of a collision between a majority of the Supreme Court and aroused political majorities. President Roosevelt's Court-packing plan failed in the Senate. But it is superficial to think of the Court-packing vote as a turning point in constitutional history. Roosevelt had a constitutional vision of expansive governmental power—adequate to tame the business cycle, ensure all who were willing to work a living wage, and provide a social safety net for the elderly and disabled. He not only sold his policy prescriptions to large majorities of the American people but also persuaded them that the Constitution, when properly interpreted, posed no obstacle to his preferred policies. Over the course of more than three presidential terms, Roosevelt ultimately got to appoint eight Justices to the Supreme Court, even without the aid of Court packing.[42] By the time of his death in 1945, the Supreme Court fairly could have been called "the Roosevelt Court." The old regime—defined by a commitment to enforce limits on government's regulatory and redistributive powers—was out. A new regime—defined by a set of constitutional assumptions that accepted sweeping economic regulation and redistributive programs such as Social Security—had taken its place and would reign largely unchallenged for roughly the following fifty years. During that period, policies and programs that once would have been constitutionally unacceptable were, by nearly consensus understanding, constitutionally permissible.

Over the half century or so in which Roosevelt's views about the reach of federal regulatory powers held nearly unchallenged predominance, the Supreme Court never wholly escaped turmoil. But its confrontations with public opinion—and its testing of the political constructed bounds within which the Justices function—came mostly in disputes about individual rights and liberties. Post–New Deal controversy swirled with famous frequency under the Warren Court, which began with the appointment of Earl Warren as Chief Justice in 1953. The Warren era may well have marked the only time in the nation's history when the Supreme Court pursued an aggressively liberal agenda in its decision making.[43] In addition to issuing its landmark school-desegregation ruling in *Brown v. Board of Education*, the Warren Court expanded free speech rights, including those of suspected subversives, and recognized a series of new constitutional protections for criminal suspects, including rights to counsel and *Miranda* warnings.[44]

The 1968 presidential election marked the end of the Warren era. During the latter half of the 1960s, as crime rates spiked and court-ordered busing to enforce the desegregation mandate became deeply unpopular, a shift occurred in the politically constructed bounds within which the Supreme Court operates. In the 1968 presidential campaign, the Republican nominee, Richard Nixon, took clear aim at the Warren Court's decisions, especially those that had expanded the rights of criminal suspects.[45] If elected, Nixon promised, he would appoint "law and order" Justices with a "strict constructionist" philosophy. Nixon's appeal struck a resonant chord. He won. By 1972 he had appointed four new Justices, and the Court predictably moved to the right.[46]

At the time of any particular judicial decision, the strength and durability of the kind of anticipated public outrage that matters to the softer version of the political construction thesis may be difficult, perhaps impossible, to quantify accurately. Backlash may dissipate. Public attitudes can be fickle, public attention fleeting. In addition, the Supreme Court possesses enough institutional capital that it can render some decisions that are broadly unpopular without undermining its practical authority.[47] That said, at a deep level, the thesis that the Supreme Court operates within politically constructed bounds seems inescapably correct. If large political majorities dislike the course that the Supreme Court has charted, electorally accountable presidents will use their powers of appointment to install Justices who will chart a new course, much as Roosevelt and Nixon did.

A readily imaginable response to the thesis that the Supreme Court operates within politically constructed bounds, which has analogues in other possible objections to my arguments in this chapter that I have noted previously, might be to acknowledge the thesis's truth but to deny that it has anything to do with law or with the way that the law could be enforced against a wayward or willful Court. If the Supreme Court is constrained, some would say, it is by politics, not by law. But if we are asking how the Constitution—which is a species

of law—constrains the Court, the distinction between legal and political constraints can easily prove misleading, for the Constitution
relies on political actors to constrain and sanction unlawful judicial
overreaching. We routinely look to the courts as expositors of the
law and count on the Supreme Court to enforce unpopular constitutional rights. And it is surely true that Congress, the president, or
the public might use brute political power to frustrate the proper
enforcement of the Constitution by a conscientious Supreme Court.
But in charting how constitutional law works, and indeed in identifying the Constitution's design, we should recall that theorists since
Madison have ascribed to the Constitution itself the strategy of leaving
no power unchecked and of setting ambition against ambition.

There is also a deeper, subtler point, involving the necessary foundations of law in practices of acceptance. In writing about law in the
Supreme Court, I have mostly focused on law as refracted through
and determined by the recognition practices of the Justices. But those
practices, as this chapter has recognized, are indissolubly interconnected with the practices of other officials and ultimately of the
public. Nonjudicial officials and the public normally follow rules or
practices of recognition under which they accept the Supreme Court's
dictates as authoritative but subject to exceptions when they believe
that the Court has egregiously or dangerously overstepped its constitutional mandate. Insofar as we are talking about possible interpretations of the Constitution of the United States, we should
therefore recognize that an interpretation by the Supreme Court can
count as law in one functionally important sense only if it lies within
the "hard" outer limits of politically acceptability. As we have seen, il-
lustrations come from Jefferson and Madison threatening defiance
of Chief Justice Marshall, Lincoln refusing to honor a judicial order
during the Civil War, and Roosevelt insisting that he would execute
suspected Nazi saboteurs regardless of what the Justices might say.

Apart from that jurisprudential point, we should recognize that
for external constraints on the Supreme Court to be effective, the
Justices need not respond to them self-consciously. For example, I
have suggested that external constraints would stop the Justices
from declaring Social Security unconstitutional or ordering the
military to invade Iran. But it is almost unimaginable that a Justice

would need even to think about external restraints in considering whether to pursue one of these courses. As one political scientist puts it, the Justices' thoughts, inclinations, and even their "ostensibly political preferences have themselves been constituted in part by legal ideas, and those legal ideas, in turn, have been derived in large part from ongoing debates in the broader political system."[48]

When we acknowledge that the Supreme Court operates within politically constructed bounds, there is no escaping the reality, also emphasized in earlier chapters, that the underpinnings of constitutional law lie in the potentially shifting terrain of sociological fact. Crucial importance attaches to the assumptions and expectations of the Justices who sit on the Court at any particular time. But the Justices, in turn, are almost necessarily responsive to the attitudes and expectations of other officials and, ultimately, the American public.

Normative Constraints on the Justices

Although I have emphasized that the Justices of the Supreme Court are subject to external constraints, I do not mean to overstate them. The political space within which the Justices interpret the Constitution is often capacious. There is a broad and widespread disposition to accede to Supreme Court rulings. And many of the most important rules of recognition operating in the Supreme Court—as Chapter 4 emphasized—are very vague or underdeterminate.

Under these circumstances, we need to ask whether it is a plausible hypothesis that the Justices take their purely normative obligations seriously. Do we have reason to believe that they strive to obey the Constitution and other surrounding legal norms out of a felt obligation to obey the law? Or, alternatively, could we more accurately view them as strategic political actors who care only about what they can get away with inside the politically constructed outer boundaries of their practical authority?

Although I cannot conclusively demonstrate the point, I believe that the Justices understand themselves as subject to legal obligations as well as political constraints and that they take their legal obligations seriously. As with many empirical matters, the issue seems to me to be one of degree, perhaps most urgently involving how relatively motivationally efficacious legal norms are for Justices who can get away with breaching them on particular occasions when the temptation to do so may be great. I shall return to this question in Chapter 7. For now, my question is more general and less pointed, involving whether legal norms exert any significant constraining influence on the Justices, even if the Justices may sometimes yield to other pressures.

In addressing that admittedly fuzzy question, we should begin by recognizing that norms can sometimes be very effective in controlling human behavior. It is easy to cite instances in which people incur grave risks and losses, and even accept death, in order to adhere to religious and moral norms. It seems almost equally plain that some people take their legal obligations comparably seriously, perhaps in part because they believe that they have moral obligations to obey the law, as Chapter 1 argued that the Justices normally do. As Jon Elster has pointed out, the practice of explaining behavior by appeal to norms would presumably cease if people, based on their own experiences, did not find norm-based accounts credible.[49]

If we credit the idea that people sometimes internalize norms and strive to comply with them, the Justices of the Supreme Court look like highly plausible candidates to take their normative obligations seriously. Law presents itself as a normative system. The realms of discourse that surround the Court abound in appeals to legal norms. Parties to Supreme Court litigation—including the wealthiest and most sophisticated corporations—spend large sums of money on elite lawyers, whose briefs to the Court typically consist entirely of legal-norm-based argumentation.[50] In writing their opinions, the Justices themselves cite legal norms. Dissenting Justices criticize their colleagues for alleged deviations from legal norms, as if their charges ought to sting. These criticisms are highly characteristic of the ways in which members of norm-governed communities enforce their mutually recognized obligations.[51] It is possible that the Justices are rank hypocrites—a possibility to which I shall return in Chapter 7—but hardly inevitable that they would be.

The most sophisticated challenge to the view that the Justices regard themselves as law bound and seek to meet their legal obligations comes from political scientists. The most norm skeptical of the political science accounts is called "the attitudinal model." It postulates that Supreme Court Justices consistently vote to decide cases in ways that directly reflect their ideological values.[52] As the leading proponents of the attitudinal model pithily summarize their causal theory, "[William] Rehnquist vote[d] the way he [did] because he [was] extremely conservative; [Thurgood] Marshall voted the way he did because he [was] extremely liberal."[53]

In assessing the challenge that the attitudinal model poses, we should insistently reject the dichotomous assumption that the Justices' moral and political views must either play no role in their decision making, on the one hand, or that they must always dominate all other considerations, on the other. As Chapter 4 emphasized, many of the cases that come before the Supreme Court are understandably controversial. The Court's cases frequently involve multiple contending candidates to furnish the original meaning of constitutional language. In many cases, moreover, there are plausible, contending claims that alternative sources of T2 authority—including judicial precedent, historical practice, and tradition—control the outcome. In balancing competing considerations of backward-looking and forward-looking legitimacy, the Justices' political judgments concerning what would be best for the future necessarily come into play.

If we assume, realistically, that the Justices' moral and political views will inescapably influence their decisions in some kinds of cases, but also remain open to the possibility that legal norms might sometimes exercise an independent importance, we should recall that the Justices reach unanimous judgments in many cases—in 62 percent during the 2013 Term, for example.[54] Although the outcomes in clear cases do not by themselves prove that the Justices' decisions result from a sense of normative obligation, rather than a response to external constraints or strategic calculations, unanimous decisions signal the existence of rules of recognition that would generate a sense of obligation among those who take legal obligations seriously.

A study by political scientist Thomas M. Keck more directly supports the suggestion that the Justices frequently seek to identify and adhere to constitutional norms as an alternative to voting in accordance with their naked ideological preferences.[55] Based on an examination of the coalitions of Justices that invalidated fifty-three federal laws between 1980 and 2004, Keck concludes that more than 70 percent had a bipartisan composition and that "more than [60 percent] . . . [were] inconsistent with a model of policy-motivated judging, either because they were joined by both liberal and conservative [J]ustices or because they reached results that are difficult to place in ideological space."[56]

Cases in which the Justices divide along what plainly look to be ideological lines obviously present different issues, but ones that are far more complex than "Realists" of a cynical stripe often acknowledge. As Chapter 4 argued, considerations of moral or practical desirability are not always external to law or incompatible alternatives to legal reasons for decision in constitutional cases. Sometimes the rules of recognition that apply in the Supreme Court direct the Justices to resolve reasonable legal doubts in the ways that would be morally or prudentially best.

If this view of the Justices' normative obligations is correct, it generates the initially counterintuitive conclusion—which Professor Ronald Dworkin long pressed—that conscientious Justices who diverge in their normative views might actually feel normatively constrained to reach divergent conclusions in reasonably disputable cases.[57] For example, if the Justices must decide what would be legally best in the loose sense that I have described, some Justices may feel duty bound to uphold a claim of constitutional right in an abortion or affirmative action case, while other Justices, who have different criteria for identifying what is best, may feel obliged to deny that same claim. However one judges this proposition, Dworkin clearly seems right about this much: from reasonable disagreement among the Justices, even when it reflects ideological division, one cannot infer that the Justices do not feel normatively constrained by the Constitution and applicable interpretive norms to decide as they do.

A Refocus

Because this chapter has ranged rather broadly, I should conclude by refocusing its argument. In this chapter, I have asked whether the Justices of the Supreme Court are meaningfully constrained by the

Constitution. The answer, I have concluded, is yes. But in order to grasp the full import of the conclusion, we may need to adjust our views of what law is—as I argued in Chapter 4—and of how it constrains. In particular, we need to acknowledge that what the law is depends on what relevant groups or constituencies understand the law to be at a fundamental level. Of equal importance, we have to recognize that enforcement of the Constitution against the Justices of the Supreme Court typically depends on mechanisms other than judicial trial and proof. Some of those mechanisms involve the externally constraining attitudes and actions of nonjudicial officials and the American public. Some are internal to the thought processes of conscientious Justices—and we have reason to believe that some and maybe most of the Justices are indeed conscientious, even if they are not perfectly conscientious all of the time. I shall return to this theme in Chapter 7.

6

Constitutional Theory and Its Relation to Constitutional Practice

PRIOR CHAPTERS HAVE argued that the Justices of the Supreme Court are meaningfully bound by law, but that the relevant legal authorities are often indeterminate. If so, questions arise concerning how the Justices ought to resolve indeterminacies and how the rest of us should assess their performance in doing so. The most straightforward question involves what the Justices would need to do to settle constitutional issues correctly (or as an ideal judge with perfect factual knowledge and flawless practical judgment would decide them). A closely related question returns us to the issue of judicial legitimacy in the Supreme Court: In a world in which no one has perfect factual knowledge and in which we must anticipate and respect legal and moral disagreement, how do we mark the boundaries of legitimate judicial decision making? And how, in doing so, do we give due recognition to the dual status of legitimacy as a minimal demand and an ideal?

Prescriptive constitutional theories—including originalism and multiple varieties of living constitutionalism—draw their point from questions such as these. They seek to prescribe how the Justices of the Supreme Court should resolve the cases that they confront. Equally important, the proponents of such theories advance arguments to explain why their approaches would advance, establish, or ensure judicial legitimacy.

This chapter seeks not so much to resolve the existing debate among constitutional theorists as to transform and partly transcend it. According to the standard model that I shall critique, the Justices of the Supreme Court would ideally adopt a constitutional theory before ascending to the bench for the first time. The Justices then would apply that theory consistently to decide the cases that come before them. Uncompromising fidelity to a preselected theory would preclude unprincipled, outcome-driven adjudication in which the Justices experience no real methodological discipline and vote for whatever results they think attractive or find ideologically congenial.

Unfortunately, there are two problems with the approach that the standard model endorses. First, all of the leading, extant constitutional theories are highly substantially indeterminate. They leave their adherents with many choices and, thus, many opportunities for result-driven decision making. Second, insofar as we could imagine a Justice developing a rigorously determinate theory prior to confrontation with actual, challenging, often unforeseen kinds of cases, a previously formulated, rigidly algorithmic theory might prove procrustean. To put the point somewhat more dramatically, it might yield intolerably unjust or practically disastrous outcomes in some cases.

In order to meet the resulting challenges to the possibility of legally and morally legitimate decision making in the Supreme Court, we need an approach that integrates constitutional theorizing more indissolubly into the practice of identifying the proper outcomes of concrete cases while preserving enough bite to ensure meaningful consistency and good faith in constitutional argumentation. More particularly, we need a model in which the Justices—in common with the rest of us—work out their constitutional theories in the process of arguing about testing cases.

According to the Reflective Equilibrium Theory that I propose in this chapter, the Justices should approach the occasions of constitutional decision making with a provisional commitment to interpretive methodological principles. In doing so, however, they should anticipate that new, unforeseen cases will sometimes require them to formulate those principles more specifically in order to resolve the questions at issue. They should also contemplate that hard cases may occasionally test their principles. When the Justices' provisional, quasi-intuitive judgments about just and legitimate results conflict with their prior methodological commitments, they should normally adjust their views about how cases ought to be resolved. But sometimes their efforts to achieve a reflective equilibrium between their judgments involving defensible principles and just or legitimate results may cause them to reconsider and revise their previously articulated methodological theories.

Although this proposed reflective equilibrium approach may seem radical, it is well grounded in certain aspects of existing practice. As between the alternatives of excessive flaccidity and untenable rigidity in interpretive methodologies, it offers a partial middle ground. But it does so not so much by entering the debate among proponents of the best-known constitutional theories as by partly shifting the question from what our first-order constitutional theories ought to be to how we should go about developing our constitutional theories. That shift of focus will enable sharpened thinking about how Supreme Court decision making could best promote legal and moral legitimacy while simultaneously exemplifying an ideal of constitutional argument in good faith.

Desiderata of Morally Legitimate Decision Making in the Supreme Court

To clarify the challenge to which constitutional theories respond, we should pause for a brief recap. As Chapter 1 emphasized, legitimate decision making by the Supreme Court has backward-looking and forward-looking aspects. The Court derives its legitimate authority from that of the Constitution and the legal system as a whole. Accordingly, the Court's moral legitimacy depends on its adherence to law. At a minimum, the Justices must strive conscientiously to identify what past authorities have established and to apply the law that those authorities have created. When the Justices look backward, however, they may often perceive multiple candidates to furnish the T_1 meaning of constitutional language. Insofar as the original meaning is indeterminate, various T_2 authorities may become legally pertinent. Indeed, T_2 precedential meaning can sometimes emerge as an independent candidate to supply the Constitution's meaning. And when multiple authorities compete with one another, applicable rules of recognition may supply no clear standards of priority.

When legal rules of recognition are vague or indeterminate, the demands of moral legitimacy look to the future. The Justices must decide the cases before them in such a way as to establish their own decisions as legitimate authorities. In order to do so, the Justices must make normative judgments concerning what would be best, fairest, or most legitimacy enhancing. Indeterminacy does not license decision based on whim or caprice.

In deciding cases within their jurisdiction, the Justices speak in the name of the Constitution and the legal system as a whole. Insofar as their reasons for decision are moral ones, they should be moral reasons of a kind appropriate to the Justices' public function and representative capacity. Moral legitimacy imports respect-worthiness. Insofar as legitimacy is a political virtue distinct from moral correctness, part of its distinctness inheres in its relationship to the values of those from whom a political regime asks respect and obedience. As an approximation, the ideal of moral legitimacy in judicial decision making therefore requires the Justices to rely only on reasons that reasonable citizens would acknowledge as enjoying the status of reasons—as distinguished from idiosyncratic, partisan, or narrowly theistic concerns—even if they might reach different ultimate judgments.

Much more could be said about the kinds of reasons on which legitimacy-seeking Justices of the Supreme Court could, and could not, rely. Different political philosophers have sought to capture the appropriate restrictions in different ways.[1] Without pretending to have offered a wholly adequate formula, I wish only to affirm that constitutional decision makers who must base their decisions partly on moral values must recognize restrictions on the range of moral values to which they can legitimately appeal.

When we take simultaneous account of the backward- and forward-looking aspects of the challenge that the Supreme Court must meet in order to render legally and morally legitimate constitutional decisions, four desiderata stand out. I use the term "desiderata," rather than "requirements," because—as Chapter 1 argued—moral legitimacy is often a matter of degree.

First, the Justices must employ reliable methods for ascertaining historical facts that bear on what past legitimate authorities have established. Insofar as historical facts matter, the Justices must seek evidence from reliable sources, test its validity, and fairly appraise its probative value.

Second, the Justices must make reasonable judgments in determining the legal significance of historical facts and of the prior, T1 and T2 decisions of legitimate authorities. At a minimum, these judgments must accord with prevailing legal rules or practices of recognition, as reasonably interpreted. Again, however, we must expect that the relevant rules or practices will sometimes require judgment in their application to contested cases in the Supreme Court. To count as reasonable, the Justices' appraisals of various considerations' legal weight must not only rely on reasons that accord with relevant precedents and other legally legitimate authorities but also take due account of forward-looking legal implications. In cases of reasonable doubt, the Justices should, for example, reason in light of the premises that workable and sensible interpretations should be preferred to unworkable and undesirable ones.

Third, the Justices must make reasonable moral judgments in resolving open questions and creating law for the future. Moral reasonableness is a contestable concept that I shall unpack later in this chapter. It is distinct from moral correctness. It is also a less demanding criterion in one sense: decisions can be morally reasonable without being morally correct. In another sense, however, the demand for reasonableness, which implies respect for and sometimes an accommodation of the values of others, alters the standards for gauging legal correctness.[2] For one thing, correctness in judicial decisions requires reasonableness in respecting and sometimes accommodating the values of those with diverse views. In addition, the ideal of moral reasonableness in judicial decision making includes considerations involving the fair allocation of political power. Accordingly, it might sometimes be morally unreasonable for courts to mandate results that legislatures should view as morally imperative to achieve. (Perhaps legislatures should adopt socialist or, alternatively, libertarian policies. Even if so, it would typically be morally unreasonable for courts to dictate either.)

Fourth, legitimacy in Supreme Court decision making requires good faith in argumentation and consistency in the application of legal norms. The significance of good faith emerges when we recognize that the Justices typically support their conclusions by offering arguments that rely on methodological premises. These premises may involve such matters as the authority of original meanings, the proper kind of evidence to consider in identifying original meanings, the senses of "meaning" that the notion of "original meaning" can encompass, the possibility and means of effective "liquidation" of the meaning of previously indeterminate constitutional terms through practice, and the weight or authority of judicial precedent when it deviates from one or another kind of original meaning.

In appealing to a methodological premise in one case, a Justice—just like any of the rest of us who engage in constitutional argument—implicitly affirms his or her commitment to abide by that same premise in future cases, whatever conclusion it might yield, unless the future cases are legally and morally distinguishable. Consistency along this dimension is a minimal requirement of reasoning and arguing in good faith.[3] And good faith in argument is vital in law, as it is in life more generally. As I emphasized in the Introduction, we would be exasperated with a conversational partner who unabashedly and unaccountably relied on a premise in one case that she had scornfully dismissed in discussing another case, or who cavalierly rejected a premise on which she had previously depended. When someone feels no obligation of consistency, argument becomes pointless. Reason holds no sway.

If there are places in which it is essential for reason to govern decision making, the Supreme Court numbers among them. The Justices' core mission involves the provision of reasoned justice under law. Given the role of the Supreme Court in our system, we should be deeply troubled when the Justices argue in a sophistical, faithless way. The reasoning of a Supreme Court Justice who insisted in one case that constitutional legitimacy requires adherence to the original meaning of constitutional language but who derided originalist arguments as simply beside the point in another would deservedly engender suspicion and possibly contempt, not respect.

This analysis implies that legitimacy in constitutional decision making in the Supreme Court has an individual, process-based aspect. We care whether the Justices, individually, are methodologically consistent and principled in their decision making. When the Justices adhere consistently to reasonable positions, we can respect their decisions, even if we think that both their methodological commitments and their substantive conclusions are ultimately mistaken. By contrast, we cannot respect relentlessly outcome-driven jurists whose avowed methodological premises vary from one case to the next as they seek to justify whatever position they find most politically or ideologically attractive.

It would be better in some ways (though not in others, I shall argue) if we could demand methodological consistency from the Supreme Court as an institution. It is imaginable that the Justices could establish and abide by clear rules for determining, for example, which of the possible senses of original public meaning should prevail under which circumstances; how to evaluate whether an original meaning (in one of its senses) is sufficiently determinate to control particular outcomes without reliance on other sources of T_2 authority; how to specify and assign relative priorities to liquidated meanings, historical glosses, tradition, and judicial precedent; precisely when, if ever, precedential meaning could displace original meaning; and what values Justices could permissibly rely on or not rely on in resolving otherwise underdetermined issues.

Interestingly, however, the Court has seldom attempted to lay down rules establishing binding interpretive methodologies.[4] For example, the Court has never tried to decide as a general matter, by majority vote, when original meanings do and do not control. Insofar as the Justices disagree on methodological issues that are not resolved by existing rules of recognition, they appear to respect the entitlement of each to go his or her own way. Although the Court has not explained its practice in this regard, decisions to adopt binding methodological rules and to enforce them in all future cases could prove hugely consequential because of their unforeseen and possibly unforeseeable implications across a boundless range of issues. In light of the stakes and the limitations of human foresight, achieving agreement among a majority of the Justices on particular, reasonably determinate methodological principles might prove hopelessly difficult if not flatly impossible. All things considered, it may be realistically impossible to demand that a multimember institution dealing with such diverse and complex substantive issues as the Supreme Court confronts, involving the sometimes intermingled considerations of backward- and forward-looking legitimacy, should work out and consistently rely on any reasonably determinate set of methodological principles for resolving hard cases. Nevertheless, we should not excuse individual Justices from obligations of arguing in good faith as they proceed from one case to the next.[5] Even if not all nine Justices are in accord concerning proper interpretive premises, individual Justices should not argue sophistically.

A Brief Survey of Leading Constitutional Theories

Prescriptive constitutional theories, such as originalism and various forms of living constitutionalism, acknowledge the necessity of methodological premises or commitments in constitutional argument and seek to specify the criteria of decision that the Justices should, or at least legitimately can, apply. In the capacious sense in which I shall use the term, constitutional theories may be either explicitly articulated or tacit. Originalism is an explicit theory. By contrast, someone would have an implicit theory if she disavowed highly general methodological commitments and maintained that the Justices should sometimes adhere to the original meaning of constitutional language, but not always, and that they should sometimes permit constitutional doctrine to pursue a course of evolutionary development. A practitioner of this eclectic approach would presumably deny the appropriateness of deciding on whim but instead claim a tacit understanding or knowledge of which approach to pursue in which cases. Some judges and lawyers who disdain "academic" theories proudly endorse this approach.[6]

Both express and tacit constitutional theories perform two offices. First, they pick out norms—including rules of recognition—capable of binding the Supreme Court. All plausible theories would thus agree that the Constitution is law binding on the Supreme Court but that John Rawls's *A Theory of Justice* is not. A second function of prescriptive constitutional theories is to furnish standards for resolving constitutional issues that the constitutive norms of the American legal system otherwise leave underdetermined. Although constitutional theories in my capacious sense can be tacit, unarticulated, or eclectic, my definition excludes the possibility that any participant in constitutional debate could have no constitutional theory or methodology at all. If someone were to say, "My methodology is just to follow the law," we should recognize that claim as being mistaken, misleading, or possibly in bad faith. It is untenable to maintain that foundational rules of practice uniquely determine the correctness of a single methodological approach that is adequately determinate to resolve all hard cases.[7] Interpretive theories guide or determine decision making that requires the exercise of normative judgment at either a general or a case-by-case level. Correspondingly, the embrace of an interpretive methodology requires defense on partly normative grounds.

The appropriate criteria for selecting a constitutional theory are, of course, potentially as controversial as the theories under debate. Nevertheless, any adequate defense must address issues of morally as well as legally legitimate judicial authority. For now, suffice it to say that different theories' strategies for achieving legitimacy in Supreme Court decision making vary greatly, as a brief survey will attest.

Brevity is in order because we, like the Justices, should not imagine that we could simply choose a theory and thereafter rely on it as a guarantor of legitimacy in constitutional interpretation. If I am correct that we need to develop, refine, and adjust our constitutional theories in the process of thinking and arguing about hard constitutional cases, the familiar, traditional theories can offer provisional starting points, but no more.

Originalist theories, which have often dominated constitutional debates since the 1980s (even though most Supreme Court Justices and most commentators have not embraced originalism), speak to concerns about judicial legitimacy with special directness. Originalism is a theory, or perhaps more accurately a family of theories, defined by some version of what Professor Lawrence B. Solum calls the "fixation" and "constraint" principles.[8] These hold, respectively, that a constitutional provision's meaning was fixed at the time of its ratification and that original meaning must function as an important constraint on Supreme Court decision making. Emphasizing the status of the Constitution as the paramount legitimate authority within the American legal order, originalists believe that adherence to the fixation and constraint principles is at least necessary, and often sufficient, for decision making by the Supreme Court to be both legitimate and correct.

Apart from the fixation and constraint principles, originalists disagree among themselves about many matters, including the nature of the historical phenomena that fix constitutional meaning.[9] As Chapter 2 noted, some emphasize evidence bearing on the Framers' intentions, others the "original understanding" or "original public meaning" of constitutional language. Originalists also disagree about whether constitutional "meaning" always suffices to dictate the outcome of constitutional cases. Some say yes. Others believe that judges must sometimes engage in "construction" to reach determinate conclusions when constitutional language is vague or ambiguous.[10] Originalists further divide about whether courts should ever decide constitutional cases based on precedents that deviate from the Constitution's original (and fixed) meaning.

Nonoriginalist or "living constitutionalist" theories come in even more diverse varieties than their originalist rivals. A traditional theory of deference or judicial restraint holds that courts should invalidate statutes only in cases of plain unconstitutionality, reflecting a "clear mistake" by Congress or a state legislature concerning what the Constitution will permit.[11] Adherents of this approach rely on a theory of judicial legitimacy that emphasizes the legal and moral significance of decision making by democratically accountable lawmakers. Absent a clear mistake by the legislature, they affirm that judges' views should yield to those of more politically accountable institutions.[12]

Much more influential today is the "common law" method of constitutional adjudication that Professor David A. Strauss has championed.[13] Well into the nineteenth century, Congress and the state legislatures still had enacted comparatively few statutes, and the most basic law—called the common law—was developed by judges on the basis of custom and reason. In deciding cases at common law, judges begin with the rules as formulated in prior cases, but they also enjoy some flexibility to adapt those rules as circumstances change or as custom and reason require.[14]

According to common-law constitutional theorists, Supreme Court Justices should employ a comparably flexible approach in deciding constitutional issues. They should generally begin with the text of the written Constitution, with which any interpretation must at least be reconciled.[15] And they should often treat the original constitutional meaning as relevant and sometimes should accept it as decisive. But under the common-law approach, judges and especially Justices should also give weight to previous judicial decisions, including those that depart from original constitutional understandings. They also should take express account of what is fair, reasonable, workable, and desirable under modern circumstances.[16]

Professor Strauss defends the legitimacy of a common-law-like approach on mixed grounds of substantive justice and democratic fairness. A flexible, evolving approach to constitutional interpretation is necessary to maintain the workability and reasonable justice of our constitutional order under evolving social conditions, he argues.[17] Strauss also maintains that common-law-like interpretation allows evolving public sentiments to influence the content of constitutional law and thus provides much-needed accommodation of norms of democratic fairness.[18] In his view, originalism would unfairly privilege the views of people who lived long ago over the judgments of those living today.

In another leading contribution to debate about constitutional theory, Professor Philip Bobbitt has identified a number of "modalities" of constitutional interpretation, including historical, textual, structural, prudential, and doctrinal argument.[19] Different modalities of constitutional analysis may sometimes point toward different conclusions. For example, historical argument might support the conclusion that the Equal Protection Clause allows discrimination against women, but doctrinal argument, based on the holdings of modern Supreme Court cases, would call for a different result. In the face of such conflict, Bobbitt maintains that interpreters should choose based on "conscience."[20]

In Bobbitt's view, norms of legitimacy in constitutional interpretation are internal to constitutional practice: in essence, familiar and accepted practices define American constitutional law as we know it and require no distinctively moral justification (any more than the umpire in a baseball game needs to defend allowing each team three outs per inning). Nevertheless, Bobbitt's theory offers a meaningful criterion of legal legitimacy: to reach decisions that are legally legitimate, the Justices must apply the standards of legal reasoning that define at least one of the recognized modalities of constitutional analysis (such as historical, textual, or doctrinal argument).

Other versions of living constitutionalism call for Justices to identify the best "moral reading" of the Constitution or to engage in "pragmatic" decision making.[21] Theories of this stripe ground the Supreme Court's moral legitimacy in norms of good or just constitutional governance.

Despite a rising flood of constitutional theorizing in scholarly books and articles, a number of skeptics—including prominent political scientists and judges—debunk debates about interpretive methodology as an academic pretension that bears no meaningful relation to what courts do or ought to do.[22] But the skeptics should not put us off our inquiry. Whether they recognize it or not, the skeptics propose to put aside, as irrelevant to any practical point, all discussion of the legal and moral legitimacy of constitutional decision making in the Supreme Court. They maintain that the Justices have, and should have, no worries about legitimacy in the legal or moral senses of that term. This stance ought to rankle. Even if the Justices do not care about the scope of their legitimate authority, they should. Citizens should care, too, whether the Justices routinely proceed in breach of the public's trust in their claims to be legitimate authorities whose entitlement to respect or obedience depends on their satisfaction of legal and moral criteria, including respect for prior legitimate authorities.

Leading Theories' Limitations

Having briefly surveyed the field of prominent prescriptive constitutional theories, we could now ask which furnishes the most promising path to legal and moral legitimacy in Supreme Court decision making. To do so, however, would reinforce a traditional, two-step approach that asks the Justices—like the rest of us—to choose a theory and then, resolutely if not mechanistically, proceed to apply it. But the view that theory should come first and practice second is misguided. To see why, and to begin to grasp how constitutional theory could best address issues of legally and morally legitimate decision making in the Supreme Court, we can profitably begin by focusing on just two of the desiderata that I listed earlier: (a) reasonable judgment in ascertaining the legal significance of historical facts and past legitimate authorities for current cases and (b) good faith and methodological consistency in constitutional argumentation.

If we assess constitutional theories with these two criteria in mind, the analysis offered in Chapters 2, 3, and 4—which detailed the nearly boundless range and complexity of the linguistic, historical, legal, and moral judgments that the Supreme Court must make—points to an unmistakable yet striking conclusion: no off-the-rack version of the leading constitutional theories, including those that I just sketched, is determinate enough to guarantee case-by-case methodological consistency, and thus to ensure good faith in constitutional argumentation, in hard cases. As an aspect of the quest for legal and moral legitimacy, constitutional theorizing needs to blend with constitutional practice and struggle with important, testing cases.

In illustration of this point, I offer the case of originalism. As will become clear later, I do not regard the indeterminacy of what I loosely call off-the-rack versions of originalism as a fair ground for rejecting a generally originalist approach to constitutional law (although it is not the approach that I favor). Here I single out originalism solely to illustrate a general point about the varieties of constitutional theory that I have canvassed: we cannot simply choose one of them and be done with constitutional theorizing thereafter. Originalism furnishes the best test case for introducing this claim not because it is less determinate than other theories but because some originalists (not all) cite relative determinacy as among their theories' leading virtues.[23] In describing how originalists respond to ambiguities or indeterminacies involving the original public meaning of constitutional language, and in critically assessing those responses, any generalization will fail to reflect all nuanced differences among originalists and their theories. Although I shall strive for a happy medium between too much and too little differentiation and detail, no perfect balance exists.

In light of potential ambiguity or vagueness in the idea of an original public meaning, as explained in Chapter 2, one route open to originalists would be to stipulate that original public meaning should always be specified as the original contextual meaning of constitutional language. Having so stipulated, originalists could then aim for even more determinacy by defining the original contextual meaning partly by reference to the shared presuppositions of speakers and listeners concerning applications and nonapplications. In an apparent exemplification of this position, to which Chapter 2 alluded, the avowedly originalist Justice Antonin Scalia, in interpreting "cruel" in the Eighth Amendment's prohibition against cruel and unusual punishments, equated the original and controlling meaning with "the existing [that is, "enacting"] society's assessment of what is cruel."[24]

Many originalists, however, decline to bind themselves in this way. Much constitutional language guarantees rights that correspond closely to moral rights.[25] When contemporary understandings of moral rights diverge from those prevailing at the time of a provision's enactment, originalists may feel a strain about whether to adhere to original contextual meaning—as framed by the shared presuppositions of speakers and listeners, including anticipated applications and nonapplications—or instead to adopt either original semantic meaning or moral conceptual meaning as the sense appropriate to the determination of legal meaning. Indeed, when interpreting the First Amendment, Justice Scalia largely ignored historical evidence that the Founding generation held a narrow view of the Constitution's guarantee of "the freedom of speech."[26] Without substantial methodological explanation, he maintained that the amendment's language mandates protection of all forms of human communication absent specific proof of a "tradition" allowing a particular category of speech to be regulated.[27] Other originalists insist that the meaning of the Equal Protection Clause requires nondiscriminatory treatment of women or racial minorities, even if most people did not so understand it at the time of its ratification in 1868.[28]

For originalists who more rigorously insist that the shared presuppositions of the Founding generation, including widely expected applications and nonapplications, frame and limit constitutional meaning, a similar need for choice arises when historical inquiry discloses disagreement concerning a provision's proper applications. Chapter 3 took note of the celebrated disagreement between Thomas Jefferson and Alexander Hamilton (and their respective followers) concerning whether Article I authorized Congress to create a Bank of the United States.[29] Founding-era Justices also divided about whether Article III and an implementing jurisdictional statute had divested the states of the "sovereign immunity" from being sued that they had enjoyed before the Constitution's ratification.[30] In another dispute, this one rife with partisan overtones, Federalists and Republicans differed in their judgments concerning whether Congress's 1798 enactment of the Alien and Sedition Acts, which forbade criticism of the president, violated the First Amendment guarantee of the freedom of speech.[31]

Acknowledging that purely historical and linguistic inquiries cannot make determinate what was historically and linguistically indeterminate, an increasing number of originalists embrace a distinction—which Chapter 2 discussed when exploring the relationship between linguistic and legal meanings—between constitutional interpretation, on the one hand, and constitutional "construction," on the other.[32] When linguistic meaning is vague, originalists of this stripe recognize the necessity of contestable judgments in constructing a determinate doctrinal framework. This seems to me the most cogent and honest position for a public-meaning originalist to adopt. No less an authority than James Madison described the Constitution as vague in many respects.[33] Nevertheless, judicial "constructions" require a reliance on normative judgment that some originalists have often disdained.

In a further retreat from pretensions to determinacy, many originalists also accept that interpreted meaning, rather than the original public meaning, can define legal meaning in some cases.[34] Some originalists make this concession only grudgingly: Justice Scalia called it an exception to, rather than a part of, his constitutional theory.[35] Other originalists seek to explain how respect for stare decisis—or adherence to even erroneous precedents—reflects original legal practice or otherwise accords with originalist princi-ples.[36] For example, many originalists appeal to precedent, rather than original semantic or contextually defined and limited meaning, as their basis for accepting that the Due Process Clause of the Fourteenth Amendment incorporates nearly all of the Bill of Rights and thus makes constitutional restraints that initially applied only to the fed-eral government applicable against the states.[37] Others appear to reason similarly in holding that the due process guarantee of the Fifth Amendment forbids race discrimination by the federal government.[38] Once again, originalism of the kind that accepts the authority of interpreted meaning in some cases but not in others requires se-lections among candidates to define constitutional meaning for which many if not most versions of originalism offer little guidance.

The relative indeterminacy of leading constitutional theories, and their resulting incapacity to guarantee realization of important desiderata of legitimate judicial decision making, has an ironic conse-quence—at least when we think about legitimacy as a sociological, as distinguished from a moral, concept. The relative indeterminacy or malleability of leading theories invites derisive allegations of argu-mentative bad faith when their champions purport to apply them yet find ways to reach ideologically congenial conclusions in a high per-centage of cases. "Hermeneutic suspicion" abounds.[39] Political sci-entists advance an "attitudinal model" of Supreme Court decision making that relatively accurately predicts outcomes on the basis of judicial ideology, wholly without regard to methodological consid-erations.[40] Partisans on all sides recurrently argue that those who dis-agree with them are not only wrong but unprincipled, and that they reach whatever conclusions they like, unrestrained by the theories or methodologies to which they have purported to bind themselves.

In response to this unhappy state of affairs, we might consider whether it would be better if constitutional theories could be revised to make them more determinate in application. Many people believe that more advance commitments are better because they reduce the opportunity for result-oriented adjudication of particular cases. Be-fore embracing this conclusion, however, we should think carefully about the forward-looking aspect of judicial legitimacy, which in-cludes considerations of moral attractiveness and practical wisdom.

In considering the wisdom of making unyielding methodological commitments in advance of deliberations about particular, and possibly urgently important, cases, we can once again use originalism as a test case. Let us now imagine that the current indeterminacies in originalist theories could be purged and that a new version of originalism would dictate one right answer to all possible constitutional questions with algorithmic precision. It is of course impossible fully to assess the desirability of a categorically determinate version of originalism without knowing exactly what would be programmed into it. In my view, however, the very ambition of developing a perfectly determinate constitutional theory should strike us as misguided—indeed, as terrifyingly so.

Justice Scalia reportedly once said, "I am an originalist, but I am not a nut."[41] The implied contrast reveals much. A more stringently determinate form of originalism than Scalia practiced would risk practically and morally disastrous outcomes. Some critics believe that honest and rigid originalist analysis would dictate that paper money and Social Security are unconstitutional, the Bill of Rights does not apply to the states, and *Brown v. Board of Education* was wrongly decided.[42] I do not mean to presuppose that rigorously pursued originalist inquiries would necessarily yield these conclusions. Perhaps they would not. My point is simply that the stakes are too high to take the risk by making an advance, let-the-chips-fall-where-they-may commitment to any originalist constitutional theory that promised algorithmic determinacy.

Although earnest in my embrace of this argument, I must immediately acknowledge a ground for ambivalence, reflecting the importance of principled consistency and good-faith argumentation to moral legitimacy in judicial decision making. In expressing skepticism about advance, unyielding commitments to methodological premises, I may appear to have grasped one horn of a dilemma without taking due note of the other. Although wary of excessive methodological rigidity, I have also argued that participants in constitutional debate necessarily make commitments through their appeal to particular interpretive premises in particular cases. And for those who argue in good faith, I have maintained, the invocation of an interpretive premise implies an endorsement of its validity and constitutes a pledge to adhere to it in future cases. To see the force of this fundamental but intuitively obvious point, consider the case of Justice Stephen Breyer, who often has expressed wariness of unyielding doctrinal and methodological frameworks.[43] Although disavowing the embrace of any overarching and determinate theory, Breyer inevitably makes methodological commitments through the positions that he adopts in the decision of cases. In *NLRB v. Noel Canning*, for example, he acknowledged that a clear original meaning—if there were one—would authoritatively determine the scope of presidential power under the Recess Appointments Clause in the absence of an on-point judicial precedent, regardless of any long-standing presidential practice that might have developed since T1.[44] One would expect him to honor that commitment, and indeed to generalize from it, in subsequent cases.

One way or another, it may thus appear that legitimate constitutional adjudication by the Supreme Court requires unyielding adherence to methodological commitments made in advance of cases to which the Justices must apply them. And if such commitments need to be made anyway, should we not prefer a theory that binds the Court's hands sooner, rather than later, as a check against case-by-case efforts by the Justices to realize their raw, outcome-based preferences?

A Better Approach: Reflective Equilibrium Theory

Before embracing the conclusion that the demands of judicial legitimacy present a dilemma as applied to constitutional adjudication in the Supreme Court, we should take a step back. In particular, we should reflect on the relationship between prescriptive constitutional theories and our case-by-case judgments of constitutional correctness, reasonableness, and legal and moral legitimacy. Prescriptive constitutional theories offer methodologies or guidelines for reaching correct or legitimate decisions in individual cases. But our judgments concerning the merits of constitutional theories are not, and could not be, wholly independent of the results that they yield. We have case-specific intuitions about good and acceptable outcomes because we know that constitutional law is interconnected with substantive morality in a variety of complex ways.[45]

At the same time, our judgments about particular cases are sensitive to our judgments about proper decision-making methodology within our practice as we currently understand it. This sensitivity necessarily exists if we take the idea of legally and morally legitimate judicial power seriously. Even if we are socialists or libertarians, if we know anything about constitutional law, we know that it has enough partial autonomy to foreclose the conclusion that the Constitution dictates socialist or libertarian conclusions to every issue of public policy. Considerations involving constitutional text, precedent, and interpretive integrity intrude. Constitutional reasoning and argument require methodological premises, including ones for determining what past authorities have resolved, and those premises may sometimes point us toward surprising or unwanted results.

In thinking about how case-specific intuitions and general methodological premises relate to one another as aspects of constitutional interpretation—especially but not exclusively in the Supreme Court—we can profitably consider an analogy drawn from moral and political philosophy. As most famously elaborated by Rawls in *A Theory of Justice*, moral reasoning involves a two-way traffic between our provisional judgments about particular cases and our overarching moral principles.[46] In cases of initial inconsistency between case-specific judgments and our moral principles, Rawls posits that adjustment can occur on either end. We seek to conform our judgments to general moral principles. At the same time, however, we formulate, assess, and reassess our principles partly in reference to the conclusions that they would generate. In Rawls's terminology, our efforts to bring our case-specific judgments into alignment with our principles, and vice versa, involve a quest for "reflective equilibrium."[47] As conceived by Rawls, a reflective equilibrium approach to moral judgment can be, and typically is, dynamic rather than static. Any occasion for moral judgment can provoke reconsideration of what our overarching principles ought to be and of whether we have previously formulated them correctly.[48]

Rumination on the role of reflective equilibrium in Rawlsian moral and political theory yields potentially important insights for constitutional law—a point that Mitchell N. Berman has also recognized.[49] In constitutional law as in morality, we should aim at principled consistency, and we should want our Justices to decide cases with that aim in view. Nevertheless, the reflective equilibrium model helps to persuade me that we should not think it requisite or necessarily even desirable to begin our quest for principled consistency with a full set of unbending principles or wholly fixed methodological premises. In constitutional law as in morals, we do better to develop our commitments on a partially rolling basis, with concrete cases—concerning which we may already have quasi-intuitive judgments of correctness—in mind. When previously unanticipated cases arise, the reflective equilibrium model suggests that the Justices, along with the rest of us who participate in constitutional arguments in good faith, should feel not only free but obliged to reconsider previous methodological commitments if the implications would prove disturbing. In the resulting reconsideration, we should not assume that prior methodological commitments should always yield to case-specific intuitions or judgments of constitutional correctness. Rather, we should reflect critically on both our substantive judgments and our methodological premises, without prejudging where the adjustment needed to achieve overall consistency should occur.

Admittedly, the analogy of constitutional argument to moral and political theory is not perfect. In the domain of moral and political philosophy, the quest for reflective equilibrium involves a simultaneous assessment of considered judgments in particular cases and general substantive principles that would systematize and explain those judgments.[50] By contrast, in commending the use of a reflective equilibrium approach to constitutional analysis, I imagine a back-and-forth traffic that most centrally involves substantive constitutional judgments and methodological or interpretive principles.

Nevertheless, an overriding commonality exists. In constitutional law as in moral and political philosophy, we need principles or premises to guide and discipline our case-by-case judgments, but we necessarily rely on case-by-case judgments to test the tenability of proposed theories. There is no Archimedean perspective, however much we might crave one. Under these circumstances, reflective equilibrium has emerged as perhaps the most common methodology among modern-day moral philosophers.[51] In law, we similarly test theories based on their implications for cases, whether or not we are happy to acknowledge that we do so. In Michael W. McConnell's much-quoted illustration, "Such is the moral authority of *Brown* [*v. Board of Education*] that if any particular theory does not produce the conclusion that *Brown* was correctly decided, the theory is seriously discredited."[52] This formulation may be slightly too strong. Even if so, the hyperbole helps to drive home the insight that nearly all of us use our judgments about outcomes in cases—to which we may be more or less committed—in testing proposed constitutional theories.

In applying Reflective Equilibrium Theory to concrete constitutional cases, we should have a relatively strong presumption in favor of adhering to methodological premises that we have endorsed in the past. Sometimes, however, previously embraced premises may fail to resolve some of the issues that I sketched in Chapters 2, 3, and 4. If so, we will need to refine our interpretive approaches. Through this process, we can expect our theories or methodologies to become more dense and determinate, even if more complex, over time. Sometimes, moreover, new cases may provoke a rethinking of previously accepted methodological premises. If and when we revise our methodological premises, no breach of the obligation of good-faith argumentation about constitutional cases necessarily occurs. We can say, and should say without apology, that we now believe our prior judgments to have been mistaken. No more in constitutional law than in the domain of morality should an ideal of principled consistency require us to persist in what we conscientiously believe to be past errors, especially when issues of legal and moral legitimacy are at stake.

Consider the following hypothetical case. A Justice has long maintained that the Supreme Court should always adhere to either the original contextual or the traditionally understood meaning of constitutional language. Then a case comes along that provokes a Justice to rethink these views—as it appears that some of the Justices actually may have done in *Brown v. Board of Education*.[53] If the Justice now believes that the correct interpretation of the Constitution forbids racial segregation in the public schools, even though that conclusion deviates from traditional understandings, then a view of legitimate decision making that would require that Justice to adhere to methodological premises that she now believes to be mistaken must itself be mistaken.

In so saying, I do not mean to provide a justification for judicial "flip-flops," as judges change their positions on claims of appropriate methodology solely to justify a substantively preferred outcome in a particular case.[54] To the contrary, shifts of methodological stance are proper insofar, but only insofar, as they result from a reconsideration that leads to a genuine revision in judgment and commitment concerning the issue in question. A demand for publicity or candor in acknowledging a change of methodological view, and the reasons for it, would provide a significant safeguard against abuse.[55] In law as in life more generally, we expect our conversational partners to hold themselves to the same standards of arguing in good faith to which most of us (I believe) try to hold ourselves. Surely the ideal of arguing in good faith does not preclude acknowledgment of prior error.

As my imagined variation on some Justices' thinking about *Brown v. Board of Education* suggests, originalism can provide an illustration of how Reflective Equilibrium Theory—which, once again, is a second-order theory and does not preclude the possibility that some form of originalism might be the best first-order theory—would work in practice. Although no off-the-rack version of originalist theory resolves all of the questions that arise in constitutional practice, it is easy to imagine an originalist viewing new, testing cases as occasions to ask and answer such questions as, Exactly what sort of originalist am I? and How would someone who adheres to the central, general tenets that appear to link originalists best resolve an issue of this kind? With those questions on the table, an originalist might, for example, gradually specify the circumstances, if any, under which the literal or semantic meaning of a constitutional provision should count as its relevant original meaning, despite evidence of a different or narrower original contextual meaning, as framed by shared presuppositions and anticipated applications. She might similarly work out answers to such questions as when, if ever, precedential or interpreted meaning, or evidence of a historical tradition, should prevail over contrary evidence of original contextual meaning; when original meaning is sufficiently vague or indeterminate for historical liquidations or glosses to possess controlling authority; and whether, when, and, if so, how courts should go about constitutional construction or implementation in cases involving vague original meaning. A nonoriginalist similarly could, and should, develop, elaborate, or revise her methodological premises from time to time if reflection on new cases persuaded her to do so.

The widespread adoption of Reflective Equilibrium Theory would undoubtedly require significant revisions in our existing constitutional practice, but it should occasion no troubling disruptions. My central contention is that constitutional theorists have too often misunderstood the relationship between constitutional theory and the necessarily case-by-case practice of constitutional adjudication. And in doing so, they have misled us about the criteria of legal and moral legitimacy in constitutional adjudication in the Supreme Court.

Descriptively, Reflective Equilibrium Theory either fits with or makes sense of a variety of crucial data points that emerged in Chapters 2, 3, and 4 and enables good-faith participants in constitutional argument to proceed sensibly in light of them. Those data points include all of the following:

- Interpreters' normative values exert a significant influence on their constitutional judgments. To insist otherwise is to blink reality.
- For those who engage in constitutional argument, the embrace of theoretical or methodological premises occurs, like it or not. Participants in constitutional argument necessarily take positions about which arguments are good and which are bad. In doing so, they presuppose the validity or invalidity of interpretive theories, methodologies, or premises.
- Constitutional practice routinely generates issues that leading constitutional theories fail to resolve and, what is more, that no human theory designer could plausibly have anticipated. As a result, the emergence of unforeseen categories of cases can almost self-evidently put strain on and provoke reconsideration of previously articulated methodological premises.
- For reasons involving the legitimacy of judicial authority, constitutional decision making appropriately has a forward-looking aspect, concerned with the establishment of just rules for the future, as well as a more widely recognized

backward-looking aspect, rooted in an obligation to respect the legitimate authority of decision makers to lay down rules binding on the future. Both of these kinds of legitimacy-based concerns bear on assessments of appropriate outcomes in many contestable cases and also on judgments with respect to soundly defensible interpretive premises or methodologies.

- There is no reason to think that advance settlement of all methodological questions would always be better than case-by-case decision making. Normative legitimacy claims are too complex and tangled for all of the issues that have arisen in the past and will arise in the future to permit sensible resolution on a once-and-for-all basis.

In an era of hermeneutic suspicion, Reflective Equilibrium Theory also encourages interpretive charity:[56] it invites us to view our coparticipants in constitutional argument as proceeding in good faith, even when they embrace methodological positions that initially surprise us in support of conclusions that they obviously find ideologically congenial. Chapter 7 will return to this theme.

For now, I would emphasize that the arguments supporting Reflective Equilibrium Theory yield a startlingly counterintuitive conclusion. Nearly everyone seems to believe that although prescriptive constitutional theories require normative defenses, rule-of-law principles and standards of judicial legitimacy forbid anyone who has embraced a theory from adjusting it on a case-by-case basis thereafter. That view is mistaken and counterproductive. As Reflective Equilibrium Theory highlights, commitments to interpretive methodologies are and ought to be revisable, though subject to the demands and discipline of good faith in constitutional argument.

Accommodating Further Complexities

If all of the Justices of the Supreme Court adopted Reflective Equilibrium Theory in the form in which I have so far described it, would their doing so suffice to guarantee the moral legitimacy of their decisions? The answer is not necessarily. The first approximation of the theory that I have discussed so far seeks principally to address and accommodate just two of the four desiderata of legally and morally legitimate judicial decision making that I introduced earlier in this chapter: reasonable judgment in ascertaining the legal significance of historical facts and past legitimate authorities for current cases, and good faith and reasonable consistency in constitutional argumentation. Two further desiderata remain. The Justices, I have insisted, must employ reliable methods for ascertaining historical facts that bear on what past legitimate authorities have established, and they must make reasonable moral judgments in resolving open questions and creating law for the future.

The first of these remaining desiderata is relatively simple to accommodate. Anyone who adopts Reflective Equilibrium Theory should also employ reliable methods of historical inquiry. Doing so may prove easier said than done. As historians recognize even if constitutional lawyers sometimes do not, good history is hard to do. In principle, however, the need is incontrovertible. Judicial decisions should not rest on false historical premises.

The desideratum involving reasonable moral judgment introduces several elements of complexity. To begin with, "reasonableness" is a concept with a significant, vague, and contestable moral dimension. As defined by leading philosophers, reasonableness requires a disposition to consider the interests and views of others in seeking to reach conclusions that others ought to respect.[57] Rawls, for example, defines reasonableness in contrast with rationality, which involves instrumental intelligence in the pursuit of goals. In the philosophical sense of reasonableness on which my argument depends, "knowing that people are reasonable where others are concerned, we know that they are willing to govern their conduct by a principle from which they and others can reason in common; and reasonable people take into account the consequences of their actions on others' well-being."[58]

Given that anchoring claim, we can rule out the defining beliefs of Nazis and terrorists as unreasonable. More generally, we should expect fewer disagreements about what is reasonable than about what is morally optimal or correct. Most of us have no difficulty in recognizing some views with which we disagree as reasonable ones. Reasonable moral disagreement among those who manifestly care about the interests of others is a familiar fact of life. But this judgment about the reasonableness of others' views itself rests on partly moral foundations.[59] Reasonableness is not a statistical average of existing views.[60] Nor can moral reasonableness be defined by social consensus. Slavery would be morally unreasonable even if nearly everyone in a particular society, including some or even all of the slaves, thought otherwise.

But—and this is an important "but"—insofar as a conception of reasonableness anchors an ideal of morally legitimate government, assessments of reasonableness cannot be wholly oblivious to what actual people think. Ideal legitimacy would involve justifications for the exercise of governmental power that pass muster before the tribunal of each person's understanding. Short of the ideal, lawmakers, including judges, should still aspire to justify their rulings in terms that those subject to their decisions can actually respect, though subject to sometimes contestable limits.

Against this background, we can see that judgments of moral reasonableness matter to constitutional law in the Supreme Court in two related but subtly different ways. First, we can ask whether others' constitutional judgments, including those of the Court, are reasonable ones. In the case of the Court, unreasonable judgments suffer a moral legitimacy deficit, even if the Justices who reached those judgments hold substantive and methodological views that are in reflective equilibrium. (The substantive and methodological views of Nazi judges might be in reflective equilibrium but still be unreasonable.) Second, we can ask how reasonableness in the accommodation of others' views bears on the question of how we should think about, or the Justices ought to decide, particular cases.

In introducing Reflective Equilibrium Theory, I have so far emphasized the possibility of a process of mutual consideration and reconsideration that involves only two elements—case-specific intuitions and methodological premises. But the quest for reflective equilibrium in constitutional deliberations can, and should, reach across a broader range of considerations, including appraisals of moral reasonableness. In *Political Liberalism* and elsewhere, Rawls distinguished between narrow reflective equilibrium, which imagined the simultaneous assessment and sometimes the adjustment of just two variables, and "wide" reflective equilibrium, which potentially encompasses many more.[61] As a second-order theory of constitutional decision making, Reflective Equilibrium Theory can and should treat the specification of the notion of reasonable moral judgment in resolving disputable cases as potentially involving adjustment as part of a quest for wide reflective equilibrium. The "liberal principle of legitimacy," as Rawls terms it, demands justifications for the exercise of judicial power that all reasonable people could be expected to respect "in the light of principles and ideals acceptable to their common human reason."[62] But there is no pre-fixed standard for gauging compliance with that ideal. Efforts by the Justices of the Supreme Court to reach the kind of moral judgments necessary to the legitimate exercise of their office also might include reference to and possible reformulations of ideals of substantive justice, procedural fairness in the allocation of lawmaking power, and the rule of law.[63]

One further complexity also deserves attention. The Supreme Court is a multimember body. By long tradition, it functions by majority rule, with Justices often joining in opinions written by others but then characterized as "the opinion of the Court." As noted earlier, the production of majority opinions often requires accommodation and compromise.[64] Although I have emphasized the importance to judicial legitimacy of the Justices' arguing in good faith, and have maintained that they assume commitments of methodological consistency from one case to the next, opinions "of the Court" introduce a large complication. Does a Justice breach her obligation to argue in good faith if she joins an opinion that includes arguments that she believes weak or that depend on premises that she would not endorse?

Judicial opinions have multiple dimensions. Apart from who wins and who loses, an opinion will state a rule of decision, which may be either narrow or broad. If, for example, a Court opinion holds that a statute that singles out gays and lesbians for disfavored treatment is unconstitutional, it can do so on either narrow or broad grounds. It could focus on highly distinctive features of the challenged law, leaving doubts about whether other statutes that disadvantage gays and lesbians might be permissible nevertheless, or it could mark all statutes that treat gays and gay couples differently from heterosexuals and heterosexual couples as categorically invalid. Intermediate options may also exist. Partially distinct from their substantive conclusions, judicial opinions also have a methodological dimension, identifying the authorities that the Court regards as mandating or justifying its conclusion. As I have emphasized, the identification of pertinent authorities inescapably rests on methodological assumptions about such matters as the relevant sense of original constitutional meaning, the capacity of subsequent authorities (including judicial precedents) to clarify or precisify vague language, and the circumstances, if any, under which "precedential meaning" can displace original meaning.[65]

With respect to all of these matters, a Justice reasons in good faith as long as what she writes or joins is consistent with her actual substantive and methodological beliefs, even if her actual beliefs would permit her to go further or say more. The Justices may often have good reasons to say less than all that they believe—for example, about the scope of gays' rights not to be discriminated against—in order achieve "opinions of the Court" on which a majority can agree. The Anglo-American tradition of case-by-case adjudication also embodies the plausible assumption that the facts of actual cases, when they arise, may improve judicial thinking by illuminating unanticipated issues and clarifying stakes. If so, there are times when Justices should hesitate to commit themselves definitively even to some positions that they currently believe to be correct.

Harder questions arise when the pressures of collegiality on a multimember Court call for a Justice to write or join opinions that include arguments whose validity she questions. Imagine she believes that there are good arguments for the result that the Court reaches and the rule of decision that it announces, but she disagrees with some aspects of the Court's reasoning. (To make the issue seem slightly more concrete, many observers believe that *Brown v. Board of Education* was rightly decided but not persuasively reasoned.)[66] If others do not see wholly eye to eye with a Justice in a situation of this kind, she faces a choice whether to join her colleagues in making a majority or whether to write for herself alone. In acknowledging the problems that cases of this kind present, we should recall that consistency and good faith in argumentation are one desideratum of judicial legitimacy in the moral sense, but not the only one. At some point, we may need to confront the question whether argumentation in good faith is an irreducible necessity of morally legitimate judicial decision making. First, however, we should more carefully consider or reconsider what judicial argumentation in good faith requires in the context of multimember courts through a process analogous to that of seeking wide reflective equilibrium. There may be some flexibility in specifying what good-faith argumentation by Justices requires.

Thinking in these terms, I would not insist categorically that Justices should not ever join Court opinions unless they are prepared to endorse the premises on which every line of argument depends. In my view, a Justice's obligation of good faith necessarily and minimally demands integrity in her own processes of reasoning to a conclusion: if she cannot justify an outcome consistently with methodological premises that she believes valid, then she cannot join an opinion that issues in that outcome. But when a Justice should feel obliged to register her methodological disagreements with a majority opinion would seem to me to depend on many variables, including the centrality of the premises with which a Justice takes issue to the rule of decision that an opinion announces. Without purporting to resolve all relevant complexities, I would simply emphasize that we must not demand more of the Justices than the nature of their role—which requires accommodation and compromise in order to achieve opinions "of the Court"— reasonably permits.

Looking Backward and Forward

In appraising the role of constitutional theories in promoting judicial legitimacy in the Supreme Court, we can usefully return to a now-familiar point: legitimacy in judicial decision making is, and needs to be, a less demanding standard than correctness. It cannot reasonably demand more than we can realistically expect human beings, reasoning in good faith, to deliver. When we take due note of the complexities that constitutional cases frequently present, and of the inadequacy of human foresight to anticipate all of them, we should recognize the need to balance adaptability with argumentative good faith through the embrace of Reflective Equilibrium

Theory. In light of the multifaceted, Janus-faced demands of legitimate judicial authority, we should be as open to applauding as to condemning when participants in constitutional debate—including Justices of the Supreme Court—are prepared to say openly that, upon further reflection triggered by the facts or imperatives of an unanticipated case, they have clarified or refined their methodological approaches or even changed their minds about an issue of interpretive methodology. Better than the familiar constitutional theories that it more nearly transcends than displaces, Reflective Equilibrium Theory captures the appropriate relationship between theory and case-by-case practice in the quest for moral and legal legitimacy in constitutional adjudication. Although Reflective Equilibrium Theory could not guarantee legitimacy in Supreme Court decision making, its embrace would help to put the Justices, like the rest of us, on a better footing.

7

Sociological, Legal, and Moral Legitimacy

Today and Tomorrow

IN PRIOR CHAPTERS of this book, concepts and conceptual ideals, centrally including those of law and legitimacy in hard cases in the Supreme Court, have occupied center stage. My motivations for inquiry have included puzzlement, a yearning for clarity, and a hope. My hope was that honest analysis would reveal that substantial moral legitimacy in constitutional adjudication—not just the most barely "minimal" kind that Chapter 1 distinguished from ideal legitimacy—is not only possible but actual in the Supreme Court's disposition of legally, culturally, and morally divisive cases. This chapter focuses on questions that express that hope: To what extent do we have legally and morally legitimate decision making in the Supreme Court today? And if the Court is failing to meet ideal or even minimal standards, how could we realistically hope to rectify the current legitimacy deficit?

Both of these questions have empirical dimensions, involving, respectively, the nature of the Court's current practices and the likelihood that the Justices could be pushed, pulled, or persuaded to change their ways for the better. I begin the inquiry into the legitimacy of decision making in the Supreme Court today with some observations concerning sociological legitimacy. As throughout the book, I am mostly concerned with moral legitimacy. As Chapter 1 emphasized, however, the moral legitimacy of the Court's decisions is interconnected with issues of legal and sociological legitimacy. Some degree of sociological legitimacy is crucial to the health, if not the existence, of a legal system. And in a minimally morally legitimate legal system (in the special sense in which Chapter 1 used that term), such as ours, moral legitimacy will often and perhaps typically depend on legal legitimacy.

Sociological Legitimacy

Political scientists routinely attempt to gauge the sociological legitimacy of the Supreme Court and its decisions. In doing so, some distinguish, as I have differentiated, between appraisals of particular decisions and the Court's overall institutional legitimacy, as measured by "diffuse support" from the public.[1] As recently as a few decades ago, political scientists found that overall confidence in the Court varied much less with particular decisions than many law professors had speculated.[2] In one striking example, confidence in the Court rebounded remarkably swiftly in the aftermath of *Bush v. Gore*, which many professors had predicted would do enduring damage to the Court's stature.

From 1972, when the Gallup organization began collecting relevant polling data, through *Bush v. Gore* and for a decade or more thereafter, public opinion surveys routinely registered support and approval ratings for the Supreme Court that vastly outstripped those for Congress and that most frequently ran ahead of those for the president.[3] More recent years, however, have seen a significant decline in measures of public respect for and confidence in the Court.[4] A 2015 Gallup poll found that only 45 percent of Americans approved of the way that the Court was doing its job, compared with 50 percent who disapproved.[5] When respondents were asked the similar but different question of "how much trust and confidence" they had "in the judicial branch headed by the Supreme Court," a slightly more encouraging 53 percent reported that they had either "a great deal" or "a fair amount," but that figure was the lowest that Gallup had ever recorded.[6] The comparable figures had been 75 percent in 2000 and 74 percent in September 2001, roughly nine months after *Bush v. Gore*.[7]

The negative trend line in public confidence in the Supreme Court should surprise no one. When ideologically charged issues come before the Court, politicians encourage skeptical, even cynical, attitudes by castigating judgments with which they disagree and by impugning the competence or character of Justices whom they believe decided wrongly. But it may not take much help from politicians to erode trust in the Supreme Court. Few Americans view the Justices as standing disinterestedly above the divisions that they undertake to resolve.[8] In embracing the Constitution as law, many Americans posit or assume a close alignment between constitutional norms and their substantive visions of good or just government.[9] As our politics grow increasingly polarized, it becomes harder for those on either side of the divide to credit the decency and good will of those on the other.

Examples of strong correlations between political ideology and beliefs about correct constitutional outcomes abound.[10] We see a nearly perfect match of ideological and constitutional views on both sides of the public debate about abortion. One camp ardently believes that the Constitution, properly interpreted, protects abortion rights. The other side is just as vehemently convinced that it does not. Members of the public have strongly held but conflicting views about whether the Second Amendment guarantees a right to possess guns for personal self-defense. In debates about the constitutionality of Obamacare, it sometimes appeared that everyone had an opinion, which almost unfailingly corresponded to whether he or she viewed compulsory national health insurance as a good or a bad policy idea. With respect to this last case, I speak from personal experience. On several occasions in recent years, taxi drivers, after having elicited that I am a law professor, lectured me on the constitutional invalidity of the Affordable Care Act.

In many ways it is healthy, even admirable, that in a nation in which applicable constitutional norms sometimes require Supreme Court Justices to exercise moral judgment, taxi drivers would lecture constitutional law professors about the proper outcomes of constitutional controversies. But if democratic constitutional interpretation can be a good thing, there also is a risk of excess.

In the United States today, the conjunction of democracy in constitutional interpretation with sharp ideological division in politics has produced, or at least threatens to generate, serious grounds for forward-looking worry about the legitimacy of constitutional adjudication by the Supreme Court, at least in the sociological and ultimately in the moral sense.[11] In a society in which the ideological gulfs are too wide, perceived illegitimacy in Supreme Court decision making may become as familiar a fact of life as reasonable disagreement is in politically and culturally healthier societies. When we believe others' moral views to be not just mistaken but unreasonable, we will almost inevitably conclude that judicial decisions that reflect those views—with the reflection occurring at the porous intersection between legal and moral decision making in the Supreme Court—are unworthy of respect. And if we develop moral outlooks that leave too little common ground for us to comprehend and respect the positions of those who disagree with us, then the aspiration of a liberal theory of moral legitimacy—which is to root justifications for the exercise of political power in ideals and principles reasonably acceptable to all—may prove impossible to realize or even approximate.[12] A regime can be minimally morally legitimate even if many of its citizens do not regard it as morally legitimate. But considerations of moral legitimacy in the forward-looking sense make it relevant whether our political institutions, centrally including the Court, conduct themselves in a way that not only should but will command broad respect. Our political institutions, including the Court, bear at least some responsibility for the health of our political culture. All else equal, judicial decisions are better if they promote trust and respect than if they do not.

If we ask whether there is a way to check the descent into increasing perceptions of illegitimacy in Supreme Court decision making, the question has no obvious answer. With regard to the most contentious issues, partisans on both sides believe that *not* to rule in their favor would be not only wrong but also legally and morally illegitimate. Some hold that the Court would fall into legal and moral illegitimacy if it overruled *Roe v. Wade;* others believe that the Court will remain mired in illegitimacy until it renounces *Roe* as inexcusable error. Depending on one's point of view, considerations of legal and moral legitimacy either required or forbade the invalidation of Obamacare. On issue after issue, so it goes. In the culture wars, it often seems that no neutral ground exists.

To arrive at a politically and sociologically better state of affairs will take adjustments from many, and maybe all, of us. The next two sections of this chapter will offer brief remarks about adjustments that I would hope to see from, respectively, the Justices of the Supreme Court and from presidents and Senators in determining who will serve as Justices. Although these two sections will highlight considerations of sociological legitimacy—involving the Court's stature in the public mind—we should remember throughout that enhanced sociological legitimacy is morally relevant insofar as it seems necessary to sustain a climate of mutual respect among citizens and of recognition by citizens of the government's right to rule, both generally and in particular ways.

The Case for Greater "Judicial Restraint"

As Chapters 4 and 5 emphasized, constitutional law in the Supreme Court is inevitably sensitive to and in many ways tends to reflect our national politics. Nevertheless, constitutional law is partly (even though not wholly) autonomous from politics. It is not merely a mirror, incapable of effecting improvements. The Justices have life tenure. They have important responsibilities for the future health of our constitutional order.

In my view, it would be a good start for the Justices to exhibit greater restraint in overturning state and especially federal legislation than they have in recent decades. "Judicial restraint" is a chameleonlike term that means different things in different contexts.[13] Here I equate judicial restraint with a reluctance to reject as unconstitutional legislation that Congress or the state legislatures have presumably adjudged to be constitutionally valid at the time when they enacted it. Congress and the state legislatures have claims to moral or political legitimacy that arise from their democratic accountability.[14]

In proposing more judicial deference to Congress and the state legislatures, I certainly do not mean to imply that the Supreme Court should never overturn popularly enacted legislation. To the contrary, the Constitution charges the Justices with a responsibility sometimes to do so. The best justification for judicial review relies on the assumption that it is normally worse, both morally and legally, for individual rights to be violated than for them to be overprotected.[15] If

Congress or a state legislature errs on the side of underprotection by enacting laws that infringe individual rights, judicial review functions as a valuable check (even if the Court sometimes errs on the side of overenforcement by recognizing claims of right that ought to fail). Significantly, however, neither this nor any other argument in favor of judicial review establishes precisely how exacting judicial review ought to be. In an earlier era, the Justices frequently observed "the rule of clear mistake."[16] Under that rule, the Justices would presume that legislators had found the legislation that they enacted to be constitutionally permissible and would hold such legislation unconstitutional only if the legislature had made a "clear mistake" in constitutional reasoning.

Current doctrine exhibits both less deference and more variability. Under leading modern tests, the Supreme Court sometimes asks whether challenged legislation is "necessary" to promote a "compelling" governmental interest.[17] In other cases, the Justices take a more restrained approach by assessing, for example, whether legislation is rationally related to any merely "legitimate" governmental interests.[18] Even when nominally applying "strict" judicial scrutiny, however, the Court sometimes proves more and sometimes less willing to accede to governmental claims of practical imperative.[19] Under these circumstances, an increase in judicial restraint in invalidating legislation would not require a large-scale abandonment of existing doctrinal structures. Nevertheless, a change of tone or mood would mark a healthy contrast with what some recent commentators have viewed as an increasingly ascendant Supreme Court suspicion of, if not sometimes an outright contempt for, Congress.[20]

Arguments for judicial restraint that appeal to considerations of democratic legitimacy have a long pedigree.[21] Most often, such arguments have won the support of political constituencies that thought they would fare better in democratic politics than in the Supreme Court. During the so-called *Lochner* era, when the Court recurrently invalidated legislation designed to protect vulnerable groups from economic exploitation by powerful corporations, liberals called for judicial restraint.[22] During the tenure of the liberal Warren Court in the 1950s and 1960s, the political valence shifted, and conservatives became the champions of restraint. More recently, as conservatives have embraced judicial enforcement of libertarian conceptions of the Constitution's original meaning—for example, in opposing a federal mandate to purchase health insurance—liberals have again begun to argue for judicial restraint.[23] Or at least they tend so to argue in cases in which conservatives attack environmental and economic regulatory legislation, such as Obamacare, on constitutional grounds.

As these shifts of position may illustrate, "judicial restraint" makes sense as the clarion cry of those who face a hostile Supreme Court, but why should those with five votes in the Court—including Justices who are part of a relatively stable majority voting coalition—forbear from exercising their power? It may seem a chump's game for those on either side to forgo exploiting their advantage to the greatest possible extent unless they are convinced that those on the other side will also exhibit restraint when they possess five votes.

In my view, the Justices sitting on the Court right now—who are relatively evenly divided ideologically—should attempt to move us onto the better footing that I have urged for the reasons that I have advanced: it would be better for the Justices to defer more often to the constitutional judgments of institutions with generally greater democratic legitimacy than the federal courts possess. It would also be desirable for the Justices to model a greater respect for reasonable but divergent points of view than they frequently exhibit. For the Justices to adjust their practices in relevant respects would of course require reciprocity and good faith. One cannot reasonably expect restraint from the left but not the right, or vice versa. But it is not unreasonable to demand good faith from the Justices, all of whom sometimes profess their commitments to judicial restraint. Over the long term, a genuine norm of restraint would not necessarily or predictably favor one ideology over another.

In their own minds, the Justices probably do not regard themselves (individually) as lacking due restraint in their votes to invalidate legislation. From their perspective, every invalidation for which they vote likely seems well justified, legally as well as morally, regardless of whether the issue involves gun control, campaign finance restrictions, the death penalty, or gay marriage.[24] Nevertheless, the Justices are smart and manifestly capable of intellectual discipline. Insofar as they believe in judicial restraint, they should practice it more consistently.

Two points of clarification are immediately in order. First, we should not mistake what today passes for "moderation" for restraint. Some of history's most celebrated moderate or "swing" Justices have shown very little restraint in the sense in which I have used the term. Anthony Kennedy furnishes a case in point. In newspaper headlines, Kennedy is a judicial moderate who most often votes with the conservatives but occasionally joins the liberals.[25] As such, he is easily seen as the Court's center of gravity. But that description would be misleading. It would be more accurate to say that Kennedy swings from what liberals deride as conservative judicial activism in one case to what conservatives castigate as liberal judicial activism in another.

In *Citizens United v. Federal Election Commission*,[26] for example, Kennedy wrote for a bare five-to-four majority in devastating the congressionally enacted scheme of campaign finance regulation. Kennedy also stood among the four Justices who would have held the central provisions of the Affordable Care Act unconstitutional.[27] Swinging to the other side, Justice Kennedy has written for liberal majorities in invalidating laws that restricted legally recognized marriage to one man and one woman.[28]

Second, I do not favor eviscerating the role of the Supreme Court, just limiting it, especially with regard to high-visibility issues that have riveted but continue to divide politically accountable institutions. The Court should play a more active role with respect to many low-visibility issues, especially of procedural justice, with which the public and often the legislature have not engaged attentively. In addition, there is no avoiding an important judicial role in statutory interpretation. Deference is often impossible in statutory cases. With Congress having spoken, the only issue in statutory interpretation disputes concerns the meaning of what Congress said.

Cases involving claims of minority rights pose the most testing challenges for principles of judicial restraint. If the Supreme Court had adhered to a strictly deferential approach, it likely would have upheld school segregation in *Brown v. Board of Education*.[29] Yet few today would attack the Court's stance in *Brown*—certainly not I. Similarly, many believe that the Court shamefully shirked its responsibilities by failing to invalidate a wartime policy under which the government held tens of thousands of Japanese Americans in relocation camps during World War II.[30] Nor, in citing cases in which I believe that the Court recently has engaged in questionable liberal judicial activism, did I refer to decisions protecting gays against various forms of governmentally approved or mandated discrimination before the culminating, further-reaching decision establishing constitutional rights to same-sex marriage. Finally, and perhaps most importantly, I have not called for the abandonment of doctrinal structures that subject some kinds of legislation to strict judicial scrutiny, only for greater restraint in extending and applying existing frameworks.

In a captivatingly argued book entitled *Democracy and Distrust*, John Hart Ely labored to establish that judicial restraint by the Supreme Court should end at the point, but only at the point, where minority rights begin.[31] Most groups' interests are reasonably well protected through the political process, he maintained. Judicial review is especially important for minority groups that have traditionally been objects of prejudice and that, accordingly, suffer from an unfair handicap in the political arena. This view contains far more than a kernel of truth. In the final analysis, however, it is often difficult if not impossible to identify which minorities deserve special solicitude, and what in particular the courts should protect them from, without making substantive judgments.[32] In many cases, what appears to be prejudice from one set of eyes looks like a moral judgment from another. Consider the issue posed by laws that forbid transgender men and women from using the restrooms of their choice. In another example, people debate in evident good faith whether affirmative action benefits racial minorities or harms them in the long run. And if affirmative action helps African Americans but disadvantages Asians (as some argue), there is no choice but to consider substantive arguments about how constitutional law should respond. Nor does the purported lodestar of minority protection help much with abortion controversies. Some maintain that women, or pregnant women, should qualify as a minority deserving of judicial solicitude. Others contend that the relevant minority is not women but fetuses. As the conjunction of these examples may illustrate, judgments concerning which minorities deserve special judicial protection, and in which contexts, often have substantive dimensions and can prove as controversial and divisive as any other issues that come before the Supreme Court.

In the entire history of the Supreme Court of the United States, the most restrained or deferential Justice may well have been the legendary Yankee from Olympus, Oliver Wendell Holmes Jr. The Constitution, he insisted, "is made for people of fundamentally differing views."[33] Under the circumstances, it was not the job of the Justices to preempt political debate and compromise.[34] But even Holmes had what he called his "can't helps," or cases in which he could not stop himself from voting to invalidate legislation that he thought simply too odious in light of values that he could not disavow.[35] On this basis Holmes became a famous champion of free speech rights.[36]

Not disposed to criticize Holmes on this score, I would temper my general call for judicial restraint or deference with an acknowledgment that Justices appropriately adjust their standards for identifying new rights or invalidating legislation, at least at the margins, in legally hard cases that exhibit genuine moral urgency. Admittedly, moral urgency may sometimes be a question of deep dispute. For my own part, I would put many cases of antigay discrimination in this category, in contrast with complaints about mandates to purchase health care. Others of course will disagree. But it is impossible to imagine that good judging in the Supreme Court would not depend partly on good moral judgment, even if we disagree about what good moral judgment requires in particular cases. It seems plain to me, moreover, that a substantial fraction of the cases in which the Justices invalidate legislation present no claim of moral urgency whatsoever. In short, there is ample opportunity for the Justices to lower the average ideological temperature of Supreme Court litigation without, for example, disavowing the correctness of the ruling in *Brown*. The best mechanism for working out the substantive and methodological details of a more appropriately restrained approach to constitutional adjudication would be the Reflective Equilibrium Theory that Chapter 6 described.

To sum up, it would be possible to move the Court from a role at the center of a number of political debates to a role slightly closer to the margins. At first, the Justices' invocation of a maxim of restraint might be perceived as a covert way for the Justices simply to ally themselves with the winning side in political battles in Congress or the state legislatures. Over time, a pattern of restrained decisions might help to establish the Justices as disposed more generally to defer to legislative judgments, largely (though not entirely) without regard to which interests benefit from the deference in particular cases.

In recent years, the most conspicuous example of judicial restraint reaching across an evident ideological divide came from Chief Justice John Roberts, who broke ranks with his conservative brethren in voting to uphold penalties for failure to purchase health insurance under the Affordable Care Act.[37] In analogous displays, Justice Stephen Breyer has exhibited much more measured caution than other liberal Justices in response to claims that state action violates the Establishment Clause.[38] It would reflect better on recent tendencies in our practice of judicial review by the Supreme Court if I could point to more examples of evident judicial restraint across ideological lines in politically salient cases.

Changing Norms of Judicial Nomination and Confirmation

As the Supreme Court has come to play an increasingly prominent and ideologically inflected role in our constitutional scheme, presidents in making nominations to the Court and the Senate in confirmation votes have correspondingly viewed the appointment of Justices as matters of high political and sometimes partisan consequence. An unhealthy regime of scheming, posturing, and gamesmanship has resulted. It would be far better if presidents and Senators of both parties would agree on and abide by principles of moderation, here defined roughly by reference to legal and political centrism at any particular moment in our history. The strongest reasons once again sound in the register of political morality. All else equal, representatives of political extremes on the Supreme Court should not frustrate the operation of the political process by invalidating legislation adopted by institutions with greater political legitimacy. By design, the Court should exercise sober second thought concerning legislative decisions, but the sober second thought presumptively comes better from Justices with relatively mainstream values than from ideological outliers, nominated and confirmed to advance a politically polar agenda.

In light of these considerations, Senators should feel no obligation to confirm a politically immoderate nominee who is not, based on available evidence, prepared to practice what I have described as judicial restraint. Reciprocally, presidents should develop a practice—in expectation that their successors in office would adhere to it—of appointing only moderate and "restrained" Justices.[39]

In the current circumstances, movement to a general norm of moderation in Supreme Court nominations might appear impossible to imagine. Why would politically motivated presidents not always try to push the Court as far as possible in a preferred ideological direction? And why would Senators not always seek the maximum long-run political advantage in deciding which judicial nominees to support and oppose?

Although the principal reasons involve democratic theory and political fairness, it may also be worth pointing out that if a convention of moderation in judicial nominations could be established, it could operate in the long-term interest of both conservative and liberal political leaders. Over the sweep of time, there is no reason to believe that either presidents or the Court will more often be conservative than liberal, or vice versa. If not, a rule or convention of moderation would not predictably stop either party from exploiting a distinctive, natural, long-term advantage in being able to stock the Court with aggressive partisans.

To the contrary, a leading view among political scientists about why political leaders favor judicial review at all, rather than seeking systematically to undermine it, would suggest that a norm of moderation might leave everyone better off in the long run. According to political scientists, political leaders favor judicial review because of their aversion to risk. Leaders of all parties give up the capacity to reap some gains that they could otherwise achieve while in office (by, for example, rewarding their friends and punishing their enemies) in return for assurance that they themselves cannot be treated too badly when they are out.[40] If risk-averse political leaders favor judicial review as a hedge against partisan overreaching by their political opponents, they will gain even greater assurance if they can reasonably expect that the Supreme Court cannot be pushed too far in a partisan direction hostile to their interests.

An Appraisal of the Moral Legitimacy of Supreme Court Decision Making

Having talked about the sociological legitimacy of constitutional adjudication in the Supreme Court, and having offered some forward-looking prescriptions predicated on respect for democracy as an important source of moral legitimacy (though certainly not the only one), I come at last to an appraisal of the moral legitimacy of Supreme Court decision making. This appraisal requires a mix of factual assessment and value judgments. For a number of reasons that bear reviewing, matters are more complex than we might wish.

To begin with, we need to remember that moral legitimacy can exist along a spectrum. No one should think that we have what Chapter 1 characterized as ideal legitimacy. Our concern involves a standard with respect to which we can—with ideals in view—make appraisals of more or less. We should also remember that legitimacy is a different standard from correctness. Decisions can be legitimate though mistaken. Finally, we need to recall that appraisals of judicial legitimacy in the Supreme Court can have multiple components. These include consideration of whether the Justices employ reasonable and consistent decision making methodologies, exhibit fidelity to legitimate prior authorities, show morally good substantive judgment in establishing law for the future, and maintain a fair distribution of political authority among courts and other institutions.

Taking these desiderata in reverse order, I believe that the Court's relative lack of restraint—or refusal to give greater deference to the reasonable judgments of more democratically accountable institutions—raises significant issues about fairness in the allocation of political power within our political system, for reasons that I have suggested already. To put the conclusion bluntly, the Justices exert more authority to limit democratic decision making than they should. But the issue here calls for a modest recalibration, not a dramatic change of course. As Chapter 5 emphasized, the Supreme Court has essentially no role in many matters of high public salience, including the setting of tax rates, the establishment of fiscal priorities, and the conduct of foreign policy. My point applies primarily to the kinds of highly politically salient issues about which the Court tends to divide along ideological lines.

I also believe that a large fraction of the Supreme Court's decisions would pass minimal tests of substantive legal and moral reasonableness in establishing law for the future. It would serve no good purpose for me to engage in case-by-case discussion of the Court's most controversial decisions. I have grave qualms about some, as I expect nearly everyone does, but not about most. Each can judge for him- or herself. For my own part, I tend to view the vast bulk of the Court's judgments as reasonable ones, even when I disagree.

Consistent with the analysis of Chapters 4 and 5, I further believe that the Supreme Court largely stays within the outer boundaries set by applicable rules of recognition in its approach and adherence to prior authorities. This assessment will undoubtedly provoke disagreement from many (but not all) originalists, some of whom speak of the Constitution as being "in exile" following the vast expansion of the federal government since the New Deal and the proliferation of judicially enforceable rights since the Warren Court.[41] But if originalism is possibly "our law," in the words of a recent essay by a thoughtful originalist, any version of originalism that could plausibly claim that description would need to permit Supreme Court adherence to nonoriginalist precedent in some cases.[42] An originalist theory with pretensions of fitting current constitutional practice would also need to acknowledge multiple senses of the concept of original "meaning" and authorize creative judicial "precisification," "construction," or implementation of the Constitution in cases of original indeterminacy. Again, I shall not attempt to argue these points here, though they largely follow from Chapter 4's account of the nature of law in the Supreme Court.

In my view, the most difficult issues in appraising the moral legitimacy of Supreme Court decision making involve matters of procedural regularity and good faith in constitutional argument, as discussed in Chapter 6: Do the Justices apply reasonable interpretive frameworks and otherwise reason with principled consistency across cases? That is, within politically constructed bounds, and within the limits set by legal norms that define minimally tenable constitutional outcomes and arguments, do the Justices deliberate and argue in good faith in ideologically freighted cases? Or do judicial conservatives and liberals, as some believe, merely and perhaps cynically rely on the trappings of legal argumentation to conceal the true, sometimes legally insupportable, ideological bases for their decisions?

Although otherwise diverse, the most challenging Cynical Realists—who include prominent political scientists, some law professors, and the distinguished federal judge Richard Posner—rely on three premises, all of which should be familiar now, that I think impossible to deny persuasively. First, the Justices' moral, political, and ideological views exert an important influence on constitutional decision making in the Supreme Court. Second, the kinds of constitutional theories that commentators defend and with which Justices occasionally ally themselves lack sufficient determinacy to dictate clear outcomes in many cases. Third, it is easy to cite cases in which individual Justices appear to deviate from methodological premises that they have previously embraced. In one set of examples, critics charge that originalist Justices reach ideologically congenial conclusions that would be impossible to defend on narrowly originalist grounds.[43] In another set, Justices who affirm the importance of adherence to precedent in some cases seemingly cavalierly overrule or ignore relevant prior decisions in other cases.

These are formidable arguments. In considering whether to accept them, however, we should recall arguments from earlier chapters, especially Chapter 5, that would support different appraisals of the Justices' characteristic decision making. Ideology, we have seen, cannot explain all of the Justices' votes. The Justices converge in their judgments more often than not, especially if we expand the sample to include "easy" cases that they see no need for the Supreme Court even to review in depth. The Justices also argue about methodology with apparent sincerity, sometimes even passion. When they do so, they must expect their arguments to have resonance with the judges and lawyers who read their opinions, based on shared understandings of the requirements of good-faith legal argumentation. If anyone has assimilated and embraced the norms of good-faith legal argument, one might expect that it would be the Justices of the Supreme Court.

In light of these arguments, we should consider how the Cynical Realist view of Supreme Court decision making stacks up against plausible competitors. For present purposes, we can usefully focus on two rival models. One, which I shall call the Reflective Equilibrium Hypothesis, recasts the Reflective Equilibrium Theory, which Chapter 6 introduced as a prescriptive theory, as an empirical hypothesis about Supreme Court Justices' actual behavior. The other alternative to the Cynical Realists' position is the Fainthearted Commitments Hypothesis, which holds that the Justices generally apply consistent decision-making premises from one case to the next, but that they tend to deviate when necessary to reach what they regard as morally and practically desirable outcomes in high-stakes cases.

Among the rival candidates to describe or explain decision making in the Supreme Court, the Reflective Equilibrium Hypothesis is easily the most attractive as a matter of political morality and moral legitimacy: it posits that the Justices aim for consistency in their interpretive methodologies, but that they do so pursuant to the kind of intricate, gradually developing theory that Chapter 6 argued we all ought to hold. Eschewing too many, too rigid, advance commitments, the Justices—the Reflective Equilibrium Hypothesis would predict—refine and revise their methodological approaches on an ongoing basis, in ways that allow them to reach ideologically congenial results in a substantial fraction of, but not all, cases. According to the Reflective Equilibrium Hypothesis, the Justices' seeming case-by-case variations in their methodological approaches occur—when they do occur—not because they are cynical manipulators but because new cases alter their understandings of the field in which they operate. One would assume that the revised perspectives typically require minor alterations in, rather than major overhauls of, their interpretive premises.

When cast as a descriptive rather than a prescriptive theory, the Reflective Equilibrium Hypothesis claims to fit and explain most of the known, publicly observable facts that animate Cynical Realists. The Reflective Equilibrium Hypothesis probably also captures most of our personal experience of constitutional arguments with friends and colleagues. As a frequent participant in constitutional arguments, I would insist that I almost invariably attempt to argue in good faith and generally perceive my conversational partners as proceeding on the same basis—even though I have no doubt that ideology plays a large role in shaping the sometimes quite divergent conclusions that we reach. If others reason as I do, and if we change our methodological stances from time to time, I would like to believe that we do so not because we are cynical manipulators but because we experience new cases as prodding us to enrich our understandings of constitutional law and practice. It is possible, of course, that the Justices are a breed apart. But we may gain perspective—on both the Justices and ourselves—if we provisionally lump together all who engage seriously in constitutional argument.

If confronted with an all-or-nothing choice between the Reflective Equilibrium Hypothesis and the Cynical Realist conclusion that methodological argumentation in the Supreme Court is merely a sham, I, for one, would opt for the Reflective Equilibrium Hypothesis. My supporting argument would not take the form of an attempted empirical proof, for I do not believe that any could be made. My argument would instead depend on the principle of interpretive charity and would claim only that the Reflective Equilibrium Hypothesis fits the observable data, including those canvassed in Chapters 4 and 5, at least as well as Cynical Realism.

Before choosing, however, we should take the measure of the Fainthearted Commitments Hypothesis. Along a spectrum, the Fainthearted Commitments Hypothesis stands roughly midway between Cynical Realism and the Reflective Equilibrium Hypothesis: it holds that methodological arguments and prior methodological commitments matter to constitutional adjudication in the Supreme Court, but typically only for so long as the practical stakes remain relatively modest.[44] When the stakes grow large, and when a methodological theory would dictate results that a purported adherent deems seriously objectionable, nearly all of the Justices, this hypothesis continues, will conveniently ignore or wriggle sophistically out of their previously articulated interpretive methodological commitments. But the lapse will be only temporary. According to the Fainthearted Commitments Hypothesis, Justices who stray from their articulated principles in cases of high consequence will tend to return to those principles in subsequent cases. Indeed, they will continue in the future to embrace—and to denounce others for failing to meet—the standards from which they themselves occasionally deviate.

Some might cite *Bush v. Gore* as evidence that the Fainthearted Commitments Hypothesis offers the best descriptive account of the role of ostensible methodological commitments in constitutional adjudication in the Supreme Court. Others—evidencing hermeneutic suspicion and ready to allege bad faith—emphasize that purportedly originalist Justices' opinions holding that affirmative action violates the Constitution are difficult to square with their originalist commitments.[45] Yet others have accused Justice Kennedy, in opinions joined by the liberal Justices, of having abandoned a variety of prior methodological commitments in opinions recognizing rights of gays and same-sex couples to freedom from discrimination.[46] More examples will spring readily to nearly everyone's mind.

As between the Reflective Equilibrium Hypothesis and the Fainthearted Commitments Hypothesis, I would very much like to conclude that the former is the more plausible, or at least that it fits the observable facts as well. At the beginning of this chapter, I acknowledged a hope that analysis might affirm the moral legitimacy of Supreme Court decision making in a relatively robust, rather than an emphatically minimal, sense. If the Reflective Equilibrium Hypothesis were true, that hope would be substantially vindicated—if I am correct in my assessments concerning the quality of the Court's performance along other dimensions that matter to overall judicial legitimacy in the legal and moral senses. To my regret, however, the evidence does not warrant the conclusion that I had hoped to reach.

Two considerations lead me to conclude that the Fainthearted Commitments Hypothesis offers a better description of current Supreme Court practice than does the Reflective Equilibrium Hypothesis. First, it is easy to identify apparent "flip-flops" on methodological issues as Justices reach substantively congenial results in one highly salient case after another.[47] Second, the Reflective Equilibrium Hypothesis fails to capture either the rhetoric or the analytical structure of the mine-run of constitutional decisions by the

Supreme Court. Many opinions include no overt methodological argument. Nor can I point to many opinions that furnish explicit models of a reflective equilibrium approach. In particular, the Justices virtually never acknowledge changes of view about appropriate interpretive methodology.

With the Fainthearted Commitments Hypothesis thus looking more descriptively plausible to me than the Reflective Equilibrium Hypothesis, my overall conclusions about the legal and moral legitimacy of constitutional adjudication in the Supreme Court are mixed. On the positive side, the Cynical Realists' position seems to me to be at best unproven and probably false. On the negative side, current Supreme Court practice appears to include more than a few deviations from interpretive methodological regularity and argumentative good faith. It is impossible to be certain on this point. Perhaps the Justices whose decisions I have in mind could state complex but principled and plausible theories that would dissolve what appear from the outside to be inconsistencies. For the moment, I remain skeptical.

Another, admittedly speculative, conclusion is more hopeful. If the Fainthearted Commitments Hypothesis is roughly correct, we should think carefully about its relationship to the Reflective Equilibrium Hypothesis and to the avowedly normative Reflective Equilibrium Theory that I advanced in Chapter 6. If we assume for the moment that most Justices whose constitutional arguments entail methodological commitments will normally adhere to those commitments (to practice originalism or to adhere to precedent, for example) but recognize exceptions for extraordinary cases, we can also imagine that the Justices might employ a reflective equilibrium methodology in determining the threshold above which otherwise-applicable commitments cease to hold.[48] If they did so, the Reflective Equilibrium Hypothesis could potentially explain and subsume the Fainthearted Commitments Hypothesis. All that would be necessary to achieve this happy reconciliation would be for the Justices to embrace the Reflective Equilibrium Theory that Chapter 6 defended. And, as Chapter 6 argued, the Justices could conform their behavior to the prescriptions of Reflective Equilibrium Theory with relatively modest and imaginable changes in their current patterns of behavior, centrally including more candor concerning their methodological practices and a commitment to developing more fully elaborated interpretive approaches over time.

This recognition should inspire hope for the future. By making readily achievable improvements in their approach to constitutional decision making, the Justices could do a great deal to enhance the moral legitimacy of constitutional adjudication in the Supreme Court.

Toward a Better Tomorrow

It is troubling to think that the moral legitimacy of constitutional adjudication in the Supreme Court not only falls short of ideal standards but also exhibits persistent deficiencies with respect to procedural regularity and argumentative good faith. In a book about judicial review written more than fifty years ago, Professor Charles L. Black Jr. recounted the story of a foreigner who exclaimed upon entering the United States that it was "wonderful . . . to breathe the sweet air of legitimacy."[49] We can both understand and savor the story while also appreciating that the air of constitutional legitimacy consists of diverse elements and fragrances. It is by no means a perfect compound, and never has been, nor is it necessarily stable. The foundations of constitutional legitimacy, and of legal and moral legitimacy in constitutional adjudication by the Supreme Court, are easily misunderstood. They should not be idealized, nor taken for granted. The Justices can and should do better. So should the rest of us who bear responsibility for the legal, moral, and political climate in which the Justices perform their roles.

NOTES

ACKNOWLEDGMENTS

INDEX

Notes

Introduction

1. *E.g.*, Jeremy Waldron, *The Core of the Case against Judicial Review*, 115 YALE L.J. 1346 (2006). For a response, see Richard H. Fallon Jr., *The Core of an Uneasy Case* for *Judicial Review*, 121 HARV. L. REV. 1693 (2008).

2. Extrapolating from survey data, an article by distinguished professors in a leading law review recently asserted almost off-handedly that "about three-quarters of Americans believe that judges—U.S. Supreme Court Justices and lower court jurists alike—base their decisions on their 'personal political views.'" Dan M. Kahan, David Hoffman, Daniel Evans, Neal Devins, Eugene Lucci, & Katherine Cheng, *"Ideology" or "Situation Sense"? An Experimental Investigation of Motivated Reasoning and Professional Judgment*, 164 U. PA. L. REV. 349, 351 (2016).

3. According to data regularly published in the annual November Supreme Court issue of the *Harvard Law Review*, the Court's unanimity rates for the past six years have been as follows: 2010: 46.4 percent; 2011: 42.7 percent; 2012: 48.7 percent; 2013: 63.9 percent; 2014: 40.5 percent; and 2015: 47 percent.

4. James L. Gibson & Gregory A. Caldeira, *Has Legal Realism Damaged the Legitimacy of the U.S. Supreme Court?*, 45 LAW & SOC'Y REV. 195, 199 (2011); James L. Gibson & Michael J. Nelson, *Change in Institutional Support for the US Supreme Court: Is the Court's Legitimacy Imperiled by the Decisions It Makes?*, 80 PUB. OPINION Q. 622 (2016), http://poq.oxfordjournals.org/content/early/2016 /06/01/poq.nfw011.abstract. As I discuss in Chapter 7, other political scientists paint a somewhat more disturbing picture, based on what they regard as changes in traditional attitudes toward the Court.

5. 531 U.S. 98 (2000).

6. Alan M. Dershowitz, Supreme Injustice: How the High Court Hijacked Election 2000, at 174 (2001); John C. Yoo, *In Defense of the Court's Legitimacy*, 68 U. Chi. L. Rev. 775, 775 (2001).

7. Jeffrey Toobin, The Nine 177 (2007).

8. 410 U.S. 113 (1973).

9. *Id.* at 174 (Rehnquist, J., dissenting).

10. 135 S. Ct. 2584, 2627 (2015) (Scalia, J., dissenting).

11. 558 U.S. 310 (2010).

12. *Id.* at 319.

13. *Id.* at 395–96 (Stevens, J., concurring in part and dissenting in part).

14. *See* Reva Siegel, *The Supreme Court, 2012 Term—Foreword: Equality Divided*, 127 Harv. L. Rev. 1, 73 n.371 (2013) ("Even originalists are concerned about Justice Scalia's failure to offer any nominally originalist justification in striking down affirmative action."); Michael B. Rappaport, *Originalism and the Colorblind Constitution*, 89 Notre Dame L. Rev. 71, 73 (2013).

15. *See, e.g.*, Jed Rubenfeld, *Affirmative Action*, 107 Yale L.J. 428 (1997); Eric Schnapper, *Affirmative Action and the Legislative History of the Fourteenth Amendment*, 71 Va. L. Rev. 753 (1985). *But see* Michael B. Rappaport, *Originalism and the Colorblind Constitution*, 89 Notre Dame L. Rev. 71, 73 (2013).

16. *See* Jed Rubenfeld, *Affirmative Action*, 107 Yale L.J. 428, 431 (1997).

17. Lawrence v. Texas, 539 U.S. 558 (2003); Bowers v. Hardwick, 478 U.S. 186 (1986).

18. *Lawrence*, 539 U.S. at 578.

19. *Id.* at 586–87 (Scalia, J., dissenting).

20. Atkins v. Virginia, 536 U.S. 304 (2002); Roper v. Simmons, 543 U.S. 551 (2005).

21. *See, e.g.*, H. L. A. Hart, *Commands and Authoritative Legal Reasons, in* Essays on Bentham: Studies in Jurisprudence and Political Theory 243 (1982); Frederick Schauer, *Authority and Authorities*, 94 Va. L. Rev. 1931, 1939 (2008).

22. Cooper v. Aaron, 358 U.S. 1 (1958); Brown v. Bd. of Educ., 347 U.S. 483 (1954).

23. *Cooper*, 358 U.S. at 18.

24. 505 U.S. 833, 867 (1992).

25. The Fifth Amendment guarantees due process rights against the federal government and the Fourteenth Amendment against the states.

26. I agree with John Gardner that when judges purport to speak with the authority of the law, they implicitly claim that the law is morally binding, but not necessarily that the law is morally correct. *See* John Gardner, *How Law Claims, What Law Claims, in* Law as a Leap of Faith 125, 139–45 (2012). But when judges or Justices claim moral authority for decisions resolving questions that the preinterpretive law had previously left open, they must make stronger claims for the optimality of their decisions—though the optimality may be measured in terms of legitimacy, rather than pure substantive justice. As Chapter 1 will explain, the concept of moral legitimacy compounds considerations of pure substantive justice with sometimes competing ideals that call for fair, reasonably democratic allocations of decision-making power.

27. JOHN MAYNARD KEYNES, THE GENERAL THEORY OF EMPLOYMENT, INTEREST, AND MONEY 383 (Harcourt, Brace & World 1964) (1936).

28. Richard H. Fallon Jr., *The Meaning of Legal "Meaning" and Its Implications for Theories of Legal Interpretation*, 82 U. CHI. L. REV. 1235 (2015).

29. THE FEDERALIST No. 37, at 225 (James Madison) (Clinton Rossiter ed., 1961) ("All new laws, though penned with the greatest technical skill and passed on the fullest and most mature deliberation, are considered more or less obscure and equivocal, until their meaning be *liquidated* and ascertained by a series of particular discussions and adjudications."); THE FEDERALIST No. 22, at 146 (Alexander Hamilton) (Clinton Rossiter ed., 1961) ("Laws are a dead letter without courts to expound and define their true meaning and operation.").

30. *See* H. L. A. HART, THE CONCEPT OF LAW 61 (2d ed. 1994). By contrast, Hart said, "The ordinary citizen manifests his acceptance largely by acquiescence." *Id.*

31. *See* Juvenal, *Satire 6, in* JUVENAL AND PERSIUS 230, 266 (Jeffrey Henderson ed., Susanna Morton Braund trans., Loeb Classical Library 2004).

32. *See generally* JOHN RAWLS, A THEORY OF JUSTICE 20–22, 48–53 (1971).

1 Legitimacy and Judicial Authority

1. On the obligation-altering implications of legitimate authority, see, *e.g.*, H. L. A. HART, *Commands and Authoritative Legal Reasons, in* ESSAYS ON BENTHAM: STUDIES IN JURISPRUDENCE AND POLITICAL THEORY 243 (1982); Frederick Schauer, *Authority and Authorities*, 94 VA. L. REV. 1931, 1939 (2008).

2. 410 U.S. 113 (1973).

3. Green v. Cty. Sch. Bd., 391 U.S. 430, 437–38 (1968); Brown v. Bd. of Educ., 347 U.S. 483 (1954).

4. *See* John C. Yoo, *In Defense of the Court's Legitimacy*, 68 U. CHI. L. REV. 775, 775 (2001); Bush v. Gore, 531 U.S. 98 (2000).

5. *See, e.g.,* SEYMOUR MARTIN LIPSET, POLITICAL MAN: THE SOCIAL BASES OF POLITICS 77 (1960); Tom R. Tyler, *Procedural Justice, Legitimacy, and the Effective Rule of Law*, 30 CRIME & JUST. 283, 307 (2003).

6. *See generally* 1 MAX WEBER, ECONOMY AND SOCIETY 33–38 (Guenther Roth & Claus Wittich eds., Ephraim Fischoff et al. trans., Bedminster Press 1968) (1922) (distinguishing bases of legitimacy); *id.* at 215–16 (distinguishing among "pure types of legitimate domination"). For analysis of the diverse variety of senses in which Weber used the term "legitimacy," see Joseph Bensman, *Max Weber's Concept of Legitimacy: An Evaluation, in* CONFLICT AND CONTROL: CHALLENGE TO LEGITIMACY OF MODERN GOVERNMENTS 17 (Arthur J. Vidich & Ronald M. Glassman eds., 1979).

7. *Cf.* Ariel Edwards-Levy, *Most Americans Support Sending Kim Davis to Jail, Poll Shows*, HUFFINGTON POST (Sept. 9, 2015, 1:00 PM), http://www.huffingtonpost.com/entry/kim-davis-poll_us_55f04a65e4b002d5c0776f39 (poll showing that the majority of Americans believe a public official should obey the law irrespective of her sincerely held religious beliefs). For a more skeptical appraisal of how many Americans obey the law just because it is the law, see FREDERICK SCHAUER, THE FORCE OF LAW (2015).

8. *See* Tom R. Tyler, Why People Obey the Law 18–20 (1990).

9. *See, e.g.*, Randy E. Barnett, *Constitutional Legitimacy*, 103 Colum. L. Rev. 111, 111 (2003).

10. *See* Plato, *The Republic, in* Collected Dialogues 575 (Edith Hamilton & Huntington Cairns eds., Paul Shorey trans., Princeton Univ. Press 1980); Jean-Jacques Rousseau, The Social Contract 84–88 (Maurice Cranston trans., Penguin Books 1968) (1762); Robert Nozick, Anarchy, State, and Utopia 297–334 (1974).

11. Among contemporary theorists, A. John Simmons most prominently defends a theory with this implication. *See* A. John Simmons, *Justification and Legitimacy*, 109 Ethics 739, 769 (1999) ("I . . . believe that no existing states are legitimate."). Simmons believes that states in some circumstances can be justified in asserting coercive power even if they are not legitimate and thus cannot generate moral duties of obedience on the part of their citizens. Although Simmons traces his theory of legitimacy to John Locke, *see id.* at 745, others have interpreted Locke differently, as Simmons acknowledges.

12. *See, e.g.*, Jean-Jacques Rousseau, The Social Contract 152 (Maurice Cranston trans., Penguin Books 1968) (1762); The Federalist No. 22, at 152 (Alexander Hamilton) (Clinton Rossiter ed., 1961); George Klosko, *Reformist Consent and Political Obligation*, 39 Pol. Stud. 676, 676–77 (1991).

13. *See* Leslie Green, *Authority and Convention*, 35 Phil. Q. 329, 329 (1985).

14. *See, e.g.*, Nicole Roughan, Authorities: Conflicts, Cooperation, and Transnational Legal Theory 29–31 (2013).

15. *See* John Rawls, A Theory of Justice 11 (1971) (defining justice by reference to "the principles that free and rational persons . . . would accept in an initial position of equality"). In contrast with hypothetical consent theories, John Locke famously advanced an argument based on the concept of "tacit consent," under which mere residence in a country was understood to signal consent to its government and laws. *See* John Locke, Two Treatises of Government 392 (Peter Laslett ed., Cambridge Univ. Press, rev. ed. 1965) (1690); *see also* Jean-Jacques Rousseau, The Social Contract 153 (Maurice Cranston trans., Penguin Books 1968) (1762). But subsequent theorists generally reject this basis for political obligation. *See* George Klosko, *Reformist Consent and Political Obligation*, 39 Pol. Stud. 676, 677–78 (1991); Hanna Pitkin, *Obligation and Consent*, 59 Am. Pol. Sci. Rev. 990, 995 (1965).

16. John Rawls, Political Liberalism 217 (1993).

17. *Id.* (emphasis added).

18. *Id.* at 49 n.1 (citing W. M. Sibley, *The Rational Versus the Reasonable*, 62 Phil. Rev. 554, 560 (1953)); *see* T. M. Scanlon, What We Owe to Each Other 191–92 (1998) (suggesting that reasonableness involves "tak[ing] others' interests into account").

19. *See* U.S. Const. art. I, § 3.

20. *See* Michael J. Klarman, The Framers' Coup: The Making of the United States Constitution 182–205 (2016).

21. The question of the Constitution's moral legitimacy is irreducibly moral in nature, not capable of resolution through sociological or legal inquiry alone. Many believe that the Constitution possesses moral legitimacy today because

it was lawfully adopted by the Founding generation and subsequently amended through equally lawful processes. *See, e.g.,* Michael W. McConnell, *Textualism and the Dead Hand of the Past,* 66 Geo. Wash. L. Rev. 1127, 1131 (1998). But this line of thought is mistaken. First, for reasons discussed in Chapter 4, it is doubtful that the original Constitution actually was *lawfully* ratified. Second, even if the Constitution had been lawfully adopted, it would not provide a morally legitimate foundation for coercive action today unless coercion pursuant to it could be justified *morally.*

22. John Rawls, *Reply to Habermas,* 92 J. Phil. 132, 175 (1995).

23. Once again, some controversy exists about exactly which practical questions a theory of moral legitimacy ought to answer. *Cf.* Leslie Green, The Authority of the State 221–22 (1988) (noting that "the problem of political obligation" subsumes a "whole family of questions" and that different classic writers have in fact addressed different questions). In the view of some, the questions whether governments and their officials are morally justified in exercising coercive power and whether citizens have a duty to obey legal directives ultimately collapse into one another: citizens have a duty to obey the law only in those cases in which officials are morally justified in enforcing it, and vice versa. *See, e.g., id.* at 235. Others, however, insist that an answer to one of the questions does not necessarily entail an answer to the other. In their view, the government can have a moral "right to rule" without citizens having a moral duty to obey all lawful directives by the government. *See, e.g.,* M. B. E. Smith, *Is There a Prima Facie Obligation to Obey the Law?,* 82 Yale L.J. 950, 976 (1973); Christopher H. Wellman, *Liberalism, Samaritanism, and Political Legitimacy,* 25 Phil. & Pub. Aff. 211, 211–12 (1996).

24. *See* David Copp, *The Idea of a Legitimate State,* 28 Phil. & Pub. Aff. 3, 43–44 (1999); Joseph Raz, *On the Authority and Interpretation of Constitutions: Some Preliminaries, in* Constitutionalism: Philosophical Foundations 152, 173 (Larry Alexander ed., 1998).

25. *See, e.g.,* Jeremy Waldron, *The Core of the Case against Judicial Review,* 115 Yale L.J. 1346, 1387–89 (2006).

26. *See, e.g.,* Derrick Bell, And We Are Not Saved: The Elusive Quest for Racial Justice 49 (1987); Kimberlé Williams Crenshaw, *Race, Reform, and Retrenchment: Transformation and Legitimation in Antidiscrimination Law,* 101 Harv. L. Rev. 1331, 1336, 1379 (1988); Dorothy E. Roberts, *The Meaning of Blacks' Fidelity to the Constitution,* 65 Fordham L. Rev. 1761, 1761 (1997); *see also* Tommie Shelby, *Inequality, Integration, and Imperatives of Justice: A Review Essay,* 42 Phil. & Pub. Aff. 253, 285 (2014) (describing and responding to arguments that "the basic structure is deeply unjust and the burdens of injustice have fallen heavily and disproportionately on a stigmatized racial group" and thus that "it is entirely appropriate for that oppressed group to withhold some allegiance to the nation and to invest more in cultivating solidarity and mutual aid within the group, simply as a matter of self-defense and group survival").

27. *See* Ronald Dworkin, *Objectivity and Truth: You'd Better Believe It,* 25 Phil & Pub. Aff. 87, 92 (1996) (describing as "the view you and I and most other people have" the belief that "genocide in Bosnia is wrong, immoral, wicked, odious . . . [and] moreover, that our opinions are not just subjective

reactions to the idea of genocide, but opinions about its actual moral character. We think, in other words, that it is an objective matter—a matter of how things really are—that genocide is wrong.").

28. *See* David Copp, *The Idea of a Legitimate State*, 28 PHIL. & PUB. AFF. 3, 10 & n.11 (1999).

29. *See, e.g.*, KENT GREENAWALT, CONFLICTS OF LAW AND MORALITY 49 (1987).

30. For prominent defenses of philosophical anarchism, see A. JOHN SIMMONS, JUSTIFICATION AND LEGITIMACY: ESSAYS ON RIGHTS AND OBLIGATIONS 102–12 (2001); ROBERT PAUL WOLFF, IN DEFENSE OF ANARCHISM (3d ed. 1998).

31. *See* Gerald J. Postema, *Coordination and Convention at the Foundations of Law*, 11 J. LEGAL STUD. 165 (1982). *See generally* Richard H. McAdams, *A Focal Point Theory of Expressive Law*, 86 VA. L. REV. 1649 (2000) (explaining legal rules as focal points aimed at addressing coordination problems); Jules Coleman, *Authority and Reason, in* THE AUTONOMY OF LAW: ESSAYS ON LEGAL POSITIVISM 287, 301–05 (Robert P. George ed., 1996) (describing law's coordinating function in terms of both narrow self-interest and the broader demands of institutional design).

32. *See, e.g.*, Russell Hardin, *Why a Constitution?, in* THE FEDERALIST PAPERS AND THE NEW INSTITUTIONALISM 100 (Bernard Grofman & Donald Wittman eds., 1989).

33. I adopt this formulation and some aspects of its elaboration from Frank I. Michelman, *Ida's Way: Constructing the Respect-Worthy Governmental System*, 72 FORDHAM L. REV. 345 (2003); Frank I. Michelman, *Is the Constitution a Contract for Legitimacy?*, 8 REV. CONST. STUD. 101 (2003); Frank I. Michelman, *Justice as Fairness, Legitimacy, and the Question of Judicial Review: A Comment*, 72 FORDHAM L. REV. 1407 (2004).

34. On a charitable reading, Rawls's liberal theory of legitimacy aspires to satisfy all of the relevant desiderata. In his view, assessments of legitimacy appropriately include both substantive and procedural elements, and "a significant aspect of the idea of legitimacy is that it allows a certain leeway in how well sovereigns rule and how far they may be tolerated." John Rawls, *Reply to Habermas*, 92 J. PHIL. 132, 175 (1995).

35. The classic natural law claim that an unjust law is "no law at all" is traditionally ascribed to Saint Thomas Aquinas. *See* Philip Soper, *In Defense of Classical Natural Law in Legal Theory: Why Unjust Law Is No Law at All*, 20 CAN. J. L. & JURIS. 201, 201–3 (2007). For a modern expositor of this view, see Gustav Radbruch, *Statutory Lawlessness and Supra-statutory Law*, 26 OXFORD J. LEGAL STUD. 1, 7 (Bonnie Litschewski Paulson & Stanley L. Paulson trans., 2006) (1946).

36. *See* DAVID LYONS, ETHICS AND THE RULE OF LAW 202 (1984); Richard Re, *Promising the Constitution*, 110 NW. U. L. REV. 299, 302 (2016).

37. 347 U.S. 497 (1954).

38. Brown v. Bd. of Educ, 347 U.S. 483 (1954). As I noted in the Introduction, the Equal Protection Clause, which was ratified in the aftermath of the Civil War, provides that "*no State* shall . . . deny to any person within its juris-

diction the equal protection of the laws." U.S. Const. amend. XIV, § 1 (emphasis added).

39. Although the Court had said in *Korematsu v. United States*, 323 U.S. 214 (1944), that all race-based classifications are suspect, *Korematsu* had actually upheld a scheme of race-based internments of people of Japanese descent, including American citizens, during World War II. *See id.* at 224.

40. For a lucid and fair-minded view of competing positions with respect to this issue, see Curtis A. Bradley & Neil S. Siegel, *Constructed Constraint and the Constitutional Text*, 64 Duke L.J. 1213, 1247–51 (2015).

41. Michael J. Klarman, From Jim Crow to Civil Rights 292 (2004).

42. U.S. Const. art. V provides, "The Congress, whenever two thirds of both Houses shall deem it necessary, shall propose Amendments to this Constitution, or, on the Application of the Legislatures of two thirds of the several States, shall call a Convention for proposing Amendments, which, in either Case, shall be valid to all Intents and Purposes, as part of this Constitution, when ratified by the Legislatures of three fourths of the several States, or by Conventions in three fourths thereof, as the one or the other Mode of Ratification may be proposed by the Congress."

43. For Professor Dworkin's initial formulation of the thesis that all legal questions have one right answer, and for his initial characterization of his ideal judge Hercules, see Ronald M. Dworkin, *Hard Cases*, 88 Harv. L. Rev. 1057 (1975).

44. For discussions of reasonable disagreement and its relevance to constitutional and political theory, see, for example, Amy Gutmann & Dennis Thompson, Democracy and Disagreement 1 (1996); Christopher McMahon, Reasonable Disagreement: A Theory of Political Morality (2009); John Rawls, Political Liberalism 54–58 (1993); Cass R. Sunstein, Legal Reasoning and Political Conflict 35 (1996); and Jeremy Waldron, Law and Disagreement (1999).

45. My claim about the predominant usage is offered as a generalization and no more. In certain usages, "legitimate" is simply a synonym for "lawful" and "illegitimate" for unlawful. *See, e.g.*, Freytag v. Comm'r of Internal Revenue, 501 U.S. 868, 896 (1991) (Scalia, J., concurring in part and concurring in the judgment) (observing that "a litigant's prior agreement to a judge's expressed intention to disregard a structural limitation [on judicial power] cannot have any *legitimating* effect—*i.e.*, cannot render that disregard *lawful*"); South Dakota v. Dole, 483 U.S. 203, 210 (1987) (referring to "the range of conditions legitimately placed on federal grants").

46. *See, e.g.*, Barry Friedman, *The History of the Countermajoritarian Difficulty, Part Three: The Lesson of* Lochner, 76 N.Y.U. L. Rev. 1383, 1455 (2001).

47. Cheney v. United States Dist. Court, 542 U.S. 367, 380 (2004) (quoting Bankers Life & Casualty Co. v. Holland, 346 U.S. 379, 383 (1953)); *see also id.* (linking a "clear abuse of discretion" with "a judicial 'usurpation of power'" as the only "exceptional circumstances" warranting the issuance of a writ of mandamus to restrain a lower court (first quoting *Holland*, 346 U.S. at 383; then quoting Will v. United States, 389 U.S. 90, 95 (1967))).

48. *See, e.g.*, Bernard Schwartz, Administrative Law § 10.16 (3d ed. 1991).

49. *See, e.g.*, Helvering v. Davis, 301 U.S. 619, 640 (1937).

50. In perhaps the most basic sense, "jurisdiction is power to declare the law." *Ex parte* McCardle, 74 U.S. (7 Wall.) 506, 514 (1869).

51. *See, e.g.*, *In re* Yamashita, 327 U.S. 1, 8 (1946); Ng Fung Ho v. White, 259 U.S. 276, 284 (1922).

52. *See, e.g.*, Estep v. United States, 327 U.S. 114, 122–23 (1946) (plurality opinion).

53. *See, e.g.*, Alan M. Dershowitz, Supreme Injustice: How the High Court Hijacked Election 2000, at 174 (2001).

54. *See, e.g.*, Thornburgh v. Am. Coll. of Obstetricians & Gynecologists, 476 U.S. 747, 791 (1986) (White, J., dissenting); Planned Parenthood of Se. Pa. v. Casey, 505 U.S. 833, 951–52 (1992) (Rehnquist, C. J., concurring in the judgment in part and dissenting in part).

55. *See, e.g.*, Antonin Scalia & Bryan A. Garner, Reading Law: The Interpretation of Legal Texts 15 (2012).

56. U.S. Const. art. II, § 2, cl. 2.

57. *Id.*

58. *Id.* § 4.

59. *See* Myers v. United States, 272 U.S. 52, 110–32 (1926).

60. There are, to be sure, a few who believe that constitutional adjudication can be purged of any normative judgments. *See, e.g.*, John O. McGinnis & Michael B. Rappaport, *Original Methods Originalism: A New Theory of Interpretation and the Case against Construction*, 103 Nw. U. L. Rev. 751, 773–76 (2009).

61. Relevant cases include *Myers v. United States*, 272 U.S. 52 (holding that president must be able to remove executive officers at his discretion); *Humphrey's Executor v. United States*, 295 U.S. 602 (1935) (permitting Congress to place limitations on removal of quasi-legislative or quasi-judicial officers); *Morrison v. Olson*, 487 U.S. 654 (1988) (upholding constitutionality of restriction on president's removal of independent counsel to showings of "good cause"); and *Free Enterprise Fund v. Public Company Accounting Oversight Board*, 561 U.S. 477 (2010) (invalidating a statutory provision that limited the president's powers to remove members of one board by locating such power in another board, whose members the president could remove, but only in limited circumstances).

62. An increasing number of originalists thus distinguish between original meaning, which is the object of constitutional "interpretation" but is often vague or ambiguous, and constitutional "construction," which requires further judgment in rendering determinate what, as a matter of purely historical fact, was indeterminate. *See, e.g.*, Jack M. Balkin, *The New Originalism and the Uses of History*, 82 Fordham L. Rev. 641, 646 (2013); Lawrence B. Solum, *Originalism and Constitutional Construction*, 82 Fordham L. Rev. 453, 483 (2013).

63. *See, e.g.*, Jack M. Balkin, *The Construction of Original Public Meaning*, 31 Const. Comment. 71 (2016); Lawrence B. Solum, *Originalism and Constitutional Construction*, 82 Fordham L. Rev. 453 (2013); Randy E. Barnett, *Interpretation and Construction*, 34 Harv. J.L. & Pub. Pol'y 65, 66 (2011).

64. Chapter 6 will offer reasons to be skeptical of the claim of John O. Mc-Ginnis & Michael B. Rappaport, *Original Methods Originalism: A New Theory of Interpretation and the Case against Construction*, 103 Nw. U. L. Rev. 751 (2009), that courts can and should resolve indeterminacies by applying the interpretive methods that reasonable, well-informed judges and lawyers would have employed to gauge the meaning of a constitutional provision at the time of its enactment.

65. *See* Joseph Raz, *On the Authority and Interpretation of Constitutions: Some Preliminaries, in* Constitutionalism: Philosophical Foundations 152, 173 (Larry Alexander ed., 1998).

66. 17 U.S. (4 Wheat.) 316, 408, 411 (1819).

67. *Cf.* Joseph Raz, *The Problem of Authority: Revisiting the Service Conception*, 90 Minn. L. Rev. 1003, 1035 (2006) ("It seems implausible to think that one can be a legitimate authority however bad one is at acting as an authority.").

68. *See* Richard H. Fallon Jr., *The Core of an Uneasy Case* for *Judicial Review*, 121 Harv. L. Rev. 1693 (2008).

69. As noted in the Introduction, when judges speak in the name of the law, they need not necessarily claim that the law is morally correct, only that the law is morally binding. *See* John Gardner, *How Law Claims, What Law Claims, in* Law as a Leap of Faith 125, 139–45 (2012). But when judges and Justices speak with the authority of law, they must claim that their decisions are the most morally legitimate ones that can be made within the bounds that the law establishes.

2 Constitutional Meaning: Original Public Meaning

1. King v. Burwell, 135 S. Ct. 2480, 2500 (2015) (Scalia, J., dissenting).

2. *See, e.g.*, Lawrence B. Solum, *Communicative Content and Legal Content*, 89 Notre Dame L. Rev. 479, 498 (2013); Vasan Kesavan & Michael Stokes Paulsen, *The Interpretive Force of the Constitution's Secret Drafting History*, 91 Geo. L.J. 1113, 1132 (2003).

3. U.S. Const. amend. VIII.

4. Among other things, the Due Process Clause, which says that no one may be deprived of life, liberty, or property without due process of law, U.S. Const. amend. V, seems to contemplate that the government may deprive people of their lives, as long as it provides them with due process of law before doing so.

5. *See, e.g.*, Walton v. Arizona, 497 U.S. 639, 671 (1990) (Scalia, J., concurring in part and concurring in the judgment).

6. *See, e.g.*, Randy E. Barnett, *Trumping Precedent with Original Meaning: Not as Radical as It Sounds*, 22 Const. Comment. 257, 258–59 (2005); Randy E. Barnett, *It's a Bird, It's a Plane, No, It's Super Precedent: A Response to Farber and Gerhardt*, 90 Minn. L. Rev. 1232, 1233 (2006); Michael Stokes Paulsen, *The Intrinsically Corrupting Influence of Precedent*, 22 Const. Comment. 289, 291 (2005); Gary Lawson, *The Constitutional Case against Precedent*, 17 Harv. J.L. & Pub. Pol'y 23 (1994).

7. *See, e.g.*, Mitchell N. Berman, *Originalism Is Bunk*, 84 N.Y.U. L. Rev. 1, 24–25 (2009).

8. *See* Thomas B. Colby & Peter J. Smith, *Living Originalism*, 59 Duke L.J. 239, 244–45 (2009).

9. *See, e.g.*, Richard S. Kay, *Original Intention and Public Meaning in Constitutional Interpretation*, 103 Nw. U. L. Rev. 703, 718–26 (2009); Larry Alexander, *Originalism, the Why and the What*, 82 Fordham L. Rev. 539, 540 (2013).

10. *See generally* Paul Brest, *The Misguided Quest for the Original Understanding*, 60 B.U. L. Rev. 204 (1980).

11. *See, e.g.*, John C. Yoo, *The Judicial Safeguards of Federalism*, 70 S. Cal. L. Rev. 1311, 1374 (1997); Kurt T. Lash, *Of Inkblots and Originalism: Historical Ambiguity and the Case of the Ninth Amendment*, 31 Harv. J.L. & Pub. Pol'y 467, 467–68 (2008); *see also* Alden v. Maine, 527 U.S. 706, 716–19 (1999) (examining evidence of the "original understanding" of the Constitution's ratifiers).

12. *See* Richard H. Fallon Jr., *The Many and Varied Roles of History in Constitutional Adjudication*, 90 Notre Dame L. Rev. 1753, 1766–68 (2015).

13. *See* Joseph M. Lynch, *The Federalists and the Federalist: A Forgotten History*, 31 Seton Hall L. Rev. 18, 21–23 (2000).

14. *See id.*

15. *See, e.g.*, James J. Magee, Freedom of Expression 22–24 (2002); Lawrence Rosenthal, *First Amendment Investigations and the Inescapable Pragmatism of the Common Law of Free Speech*, 86 Ind. L.J. 1, 19–22 (2011).

16. *See* Lawrence B. Solum, *Communicative Content and Legal Content*, 89 Notre Dame L. Rev. 479, 498 (2013); Vasan Kesavan & Michael Stokes Paulsen, *The Interpretive Force of the Constitution's Secret Drafting History*, 91 Geo. L.J. 1113, 1132–33 (2003); Gary Lawson & Guy Seidman, *Originalism as a Legal Enterprise*, 23 Const. Comment. 47, 48, 72 (2006).

17. *See, e.g.*, Mark D. Greenberg & Harry Litman, *The Meaning of Original Meaning*, 86 Geo. L.J. 569 (1998).

18. *See* U.S. Const. amend. V ("No person shall be . . . deprived of life, liberty, or property, without due process of law.").

19. *See generally* Harmelin v. Michigan, 501 U.S. 957 (1991); *see also* Walton v. Arizona, 497 U.S. 639, 671 (1990) (Scalia, J., concurring in part and concurring in the judgment).

20. Michael Klarman, *An Interpretive History of Modern Equal Protection*, 90 Mich. L. Rev. 213, 252 (1991).

21. The sole prominent exception is Michael W. McConnell, *Originalism and the Desegregation Decisions*, 81 Va. L. Rev. 947 (1995).

22. Michael J. Klarman, Brown, *Originalism, and Constitutional Theory*, 81 Va. L. Rev. 1881, 1885–93 (1995).

23. 347 U.S. 483 (1954).

24. *Id.* at 489.

25. *Id.* at 492.

26. Roughly speaking, a statement's semantic or literal meaning is the meaning it would have for someone operating solely with dictionary definitions, the rules of grammar, and other general propositions bearing on how the

meaning of a sentence emerges from the combination of its elements. *See, e.g.,* Andrei Marmor, The Language of Law 22–23 (2014).

27. U.S. Const. amend. XIV § 1.

28. 163 U.S. 537 (1896).

29. *Brown*, 347 U.S. at 495.

30. The example is adapted from one offered by Mark D. Greenberg & Harry Litman, *The Meaning of Original Meaning*, 86 Geo. L.J. 569, 592 (1998).

31. *See, e.g.,* Michael W. McConnell, *Originalism and the Desegregation Decisions*, 81 Va. L. Rev. 947 (1995); Steven G. Calabresi & Michael W. Perl, *Originalism and* Brown v. Board of Education, 2014 Mich. St. L. Rev. 429.

32. *See, e.g.,* United States v. Virginia, 518 U.S. 515, 568–69 (1996) (Scalia, J., dissenting).

33. For development of an argument to this effect, see Jack M. Balkin, Living Originalism (2012).

34. U.S. Const. amend. I.

35. *See* Leonard W. Levy, Emergence of a Free Press xii–xv (1985); David A. Strauss, The Living Constitution 61 (2010).

36. *Cf.* Brown v. Entm't Merchs. Ass'n, 564 U.S. 786, 792 (2011) (explaining that the Court will not carve out additional exceptions to the prohibition against content-based regulation absent "persuasive evidence that a novel restriction on content is part of a long (if heretofore unrecognized) tradition of proscription").

37. *See, e.g.,* Michael Moore, *Moral Reality*, 1982 Wis. L. Rev. 1061; Michael S. Moore, *Moral Reality Revisited*, 90 Mich. L. Rev. 2424 (1992); *see also* Ronald Dworkin, Freedom's Law: The Moral Reading of the American Constitution 7–10 (1996).

38. *See* Steven G. Calabresi & Julia T. Rickert, *Originalism and Sex Discrimination*, 90 Tex. L. Rev. 1, 2–15 (2011).

39. *See, e.g.,* Ronald Dworkin, *Comment, in* Antonin Scalia, A Matter of Interpretation 115, 120–21 (Amy Gutmann ed., 1997); Mark D. Greenberg & Harry Litman, *The Meaning of Original Meaning*, 86 Geo. L.J. 569, 603–13 (1998).

40. Schenck v. United States, 249 U.S. 47, 52 (1919).

41. *See, e.g.,* Church of the Lukumi Babalu Aye, Inc. v. City of Hialeah, 508 U.S. 520, 533 (1993); Brown v. Entm't Merchs. Ass'n, 564 U.S. 786, 798 (2011).

42. *See, e.g.,* John F. Manning, *Textualism and Legislative Intent*, 91 Va. L. Rev. 419, 428–31 (2005).

43. *See, e.g.,* Antonin Scalia, *Common Law Courts in a Civil-Law System: The Role of United States Federal Courts in Interpreting the Constitution and Laws, in* A Matter of Interpretation 3, 17 (Amy Gutmann ed., 1997); Caleb Nelson, *What Is Textualism?*, 91 Va. L. Rev. 347, 353–57 (2005); John F. Manning, *What Divides Textualists from Purposivists?*, 106 Colum. L. Rev. 70, 79 (2006).

44. 514 U.S. 211 (1995).

45. *Id.* at 219, 221.

46. *See* Ollman v. Evans, 750 F.2d 970, 993 (D.C. Cir. 1984) (en banc) (Bork, J., concurring); Robert H. Bork, The Tempting of America: The Political Seduction of the Law 167–69 (1990).

47. *See* Frederick Schauer, *Is Law a Technical Language?*, 52 San Diego L. Rev. 501 (2015) (exploring but stopping short of embracing this possibility).

48. 22 U.S. (9 Wheat.) 1, 71 (1824).

49. For discussion of the role of presuppositions in linguistic communication, see, for example, 1 Scott Soames, Philosophical Essays: Natural Language: What It Means and How We Use It 3–130 (2008); Robert Stalnaker, *Common Ground*, 25 Linguistics & Philology 701, 701 (2002). Presuppositions can be distinguished in various ways. For example, Soames distinguishes among logical, expressive, and pragmatic presuppositions. *See* 1 Scott Soames, Philosophical Essays: Natural Language: What It Means and How We Use It 75–76 (2008); Robyn Carston, *Legal Texts and Canons of Construction: A View from Current Pragmatic Theory*, *in* 15 Law and Language: Current Legal Issues 8, 9 (Michael Freeman & Fiona Smith eds., 2013).

50. *See, e.g.*, Scott Soames, *Toward a Theory of Legal Interpretation*, 6 N.Y.U. J.L. & Liberty 231, 236–37 (2011).

51. Scott Soames, *Deferentialism: A Post-originalist Theory of Legal Interpretation*, 82 Fordham L. Rev. 597, 598 (2013).

52. *See, e.g.*, *id.* at 597–98; Scott Soames, *Toward a Theory of Legal Interpretation*, 6 N.Y.U. J.L. & Liberty 231, 236–37 (2011).

53. Soames emphasizes these distinctions, rather than denying them, *see, e.g.*, Scott Soames, *Toward a Theory of Legal Interpretation*, 6 N.Y.U. J.L. & Liberty 231, 236–37 (2011), but thinks that legal interpreters fall into confusion by failing to recognize that focus on "asserted or stipulated . . . content . . . is required by any defensible form of textualism," *id.* at 237.

54. *See* Scott Soames, *Deferentialism: A Post-originalist Theory of Legal Interpretation*, 82 Fordham L. Rev. 597, 598 (2013):

> In most standard linguistic communications, all parties know, and know they all know, the linguistic meanings of the words and sentences used, plus the general purpose of the communication and all relevant facts about what previously has been asserted or agreed upon. Because of this, what is asserted or stipulated can usually be identified with what the speaker means and what the hearers take the speaker to mean by the words used on that occasion. Applying this lesson to legal interpretation, the deferentialist looks for *what the lawmakers meant and what any reasonable person who understood the linguistic meanings of their words, the publically available facts, the recent history in the lawmaking context, and the background of existing law into which the new provision is expected to fit, would take them to have meant.* This—not the original linguistic meaning of the words they used—is the content of the law as enacted.

55. E-mail from Andrei Marmor to Richard Fallon Jr. (July 4, 2014) (on file with author).

56. *See, e.g.*, Lawrence B. Solum, *Communicative Content and Legal Content*, 89 Notre Dame L. Rev. 479, 488 (2013).

57. *See, e.g.*, *id.* at 480–84.

58. Frank Jackson, From Metaphysics to Ethics: A Defence of Conceptual Analysis 37 (1998), labels concepts of this kind as "folk concepts."

59. *See id.* (noting that, in the case of folk concepts, linguistic intuitions are relevant because "inasmuch as my intuitions are shared by the folk, they reveal the folk theory" that presumptively defines a folk concept's extension).

60. *See* Scott Soames, *Deferentialism: A Post-originalist Theory of Legal Interpretation*, 82 FORDHAM L. REV. 597, 598 (2013).

61. Jack N. Rakove, *Joe the Ploughman Reads the Constitution, or, The Poverty of Public Meaning Originalism*, 48 SAN DIEGO L. REV. 575, 586 (2011).

62. 17 U.S. (4 Wheat.) 316, 408 (1819).

63. As he put it, "general reasoning" dictates that a court, given a choice, should not adopt an interpretation of the Constitution that would render the achievement of its largest purposes "difficult, hazardous, and expensive." *Id.* at 408, 411.

64. President Andrew Jackson, Veto Message (July 10, 1832), *in* 2 A COMPILATION OF THE MESSAGES AND PAPERS OF THE PRESIDENTS 576, 582 (James D. Richardson ed., 1907).

65. *See* THE FEDERALIST NO. 37, at 229–30 (James Madison) (Clinton Rossiter ed., 1961).

66. *See, e.g.,* Scott Soames, *Toward a Theory of Legal Interpretation*, 6 N.Y.U. J.L. & LIBERTY 231, 243 (2011); Lawrence B. Solum, *Originalism and Constitutional Construction*, 82 FORDHAM L. REV. 453 (2013); Randy E. Barnett, *Interpretation and Construction*, 34 HARV. J.L. & PUB. POL'Y 65 (2011).

67. *See generally* Richard H. Fallon Jr., *Strict Judicial Scrutiny*, 54 UCLA L. REV. 1267 (2007).

3 Constitutional Meaning: Varieties of History That Matter

1. Letter from James Madison to Spencer Roane (Sept. 2, 1819), *in* 8 THE WRITINGS OF JAMES MADISON 447, 450 (Gaillard Hunt. ed., 1908); *see also* THE FEDERALIST NO. 37, at 229–30 (James Madison) (Clinton Rossiter ed., 1961).

2. Act of Sept. 24, 1789, ch. 20, § 4, 1 Stat. 73, 74–75.

3. ART. III, section 1 provides that "the judicial power of the United States, shall be vested in one Supreme Court, and in such inferior courts as the Congress may from time to time ordain and establish. The judges, both of the supreme and inferior courts, shall hold their offices during good behaviour, and shall, at stated times, receive for their services, a compensation, which shall not be diminished during their continuance in office." On the historical controversy surrounding the constitutional permissibility of circuit riding, see BRUCE ACKERMAN, THE FAILURE OF THE FOUNDING FATHERS: JEFFERSON, MARSHALL, AND THE RISE OF PRESIDENTIAL DEMOCRACY 163–76 (2005); Steven G. Calabresi & David C. Presser, *Reintroducing Circuit Riding: A Timely Proposal*, 90 MINN. L. REV. 1386, 1390–1400 (2006).

4. *See* Stuart v. Laird, 5 U.S. (1 Cranch) 299, 309 (1803).

5. *See* Steven G. Calabresi & David C. Presser, *Reintroducing Circuit Riding: A Timely Proposal*, 90 MINN. L. REV. 1386, 1399–1400 (2006); Felix Frankfurter & James M. Landis, *The Business of the Supreme Court of the United States—A Study in the Federal Judicial System*, 38 HARV. L. REV. 1005, 1033–34 (1925).

6. 17 U.S. (4 Wheat.) 316 (1819).

7. *See, e.g.*, DREW R. McCOY, THE LAST OF THE FATHERS: JAMES MADISON AND THE REPUBLICAN LEGACY 79–81 (1989); H. Jefferson Powell, *The Original Understanding of Original Intent*, 98 HARV. L. REV. 885, 940 (1985).

8. 17 U.S. (4 Wheat.) at 402.

9. 521 U.S. 898, 905 (1997) (internal quotations and citations omitted).

10. For analysis of the frequently unanalyzed notion of historical gloss, see Curtis A. Bradley & Trevor W. Morrison, *Historical Gloss and the Separation of Powers*, 126 HARV. L. REV. 411, 417–24 (2012).

11. 343 U.S. 579, 610–11 (1952) (Frankfurter, J., concurring). For arguable examples of the Supreme Court's acceptance of historical practice as constituting a gloss on constitutional meaning, see, e.g., *American Insurance Ass'n v. Garamendi*, 539 U.S. 396, 415 (2003) (affirming a presidential power to suspend pending legal claims based on "the fact that the practice goes back over 200 years, and has received congressional acquiescence throughout its history"); *Dames & Moore v. Regan*, 453 U.S. 654, 686 (1981) (finding that the president had the power to suspend claims in American courts against Iran in part on the basis of "a history of [congressional] acquiescence"); *United States v. Curtiss-Wright Export Corp.*, 299 U.S. 304, 327–28 (1936) (relying on historical practice to find that Congress could constitutionally delegate to the president the power to criminalize arms sales to countries involved in a conflict in Latin America); *The Pocket Veto Case*, 279 U.S. 655, 689 (1929) (relying in part on "long settled and established practice" to find that a bill presented to the president fewer than ten days before an intersession recess that the president neither signs nor returns does not become a law); *McCulloch v. Maryland*, 17 U.S. (4 Wheat.) 316, 401 (1819) ("A doubtful question . . . in the decision of which . . . the respective powers of those who are equally the representatives of the people, are to be adjusted . . . ought to receive a considerable impression from [the practice of the government]."). *See generally* Curtis A. Bradley & Trevor W. Morrison, *Historical Gloss and the Separation of Powers*, 126 HARV. L. REV. 411, 417–24 (2012) (examining the prevalence of the historical gloss argument in connection with debates over the scope of presidential power).

12. *See* Curtis A. Bradley & Neil S. Siegel, *Historical Practice, Textual Ambiguity, and Constitutional Adverse Possession*, 2014 SUP. CT. REV. 1 (distinguishing a "liquidation" approach from a "historical gloss" approach).

13. 134 S. Ct. 2550, 2560 (2014).

14. *See* Curtis A. Bradley & Trevor W. Morrison, *Historical Gloss and the Separation of Powers*, 126 HARV. L. REV. 411, 417 (2012); Jane E. Stromseth, *Understanding Constitutional War Powers Today: Why Methodology Matters*, 106 YALE L.J. 845, 876 (1996) (book review).

15. *See* Walz v. Tax Comm'n, 397 U.S. 664, 678 (1970).

16. *See, e.g.*, Town of Greece v. Galloway, 134 S. Ct. 1811, 1845 (2014) (Kagan, J., joined by Ginsburg, Breyer, and Sotomayor, JJ., dissenting) (agreeing with the majority on this point).

17. *See id.*

18. During the oral argument in *Noel Canning*, Justice Antonin Scalia asked the lawyer for the United States whether the Court could lawfully follow a historical practice when it contradicted the Constitution's original meaning, and

the lawyer, Solicitor General Donald Verrilli, answered in the affirmative. *See* Curtis A. Bradley & Neil S. Siegel, *Constructed Constraint and the Constitutional Text*, 64 DUKE L.J. 1213, 1265 (2015). Justice Scalia was unpersuaded. The Court's majority opinion in the case treated historical practice as authoritative, but only after describing the original meaning as ambiguous. *See id.*

19. *See id.* at 1238–68.

20. Washington v. Glucksberg, 521 U.S. 702, 720–21 (1997) (quoting Moore v. City of East Cleveland, 431 U.S. 494, 503 (1977) (plurality opinion)).

21. *See, e.g.,* Obergefell v. Hodges, 135 S. Ct. 2584, 2598 (2015) (Kennedy, J.) ("History and tradition guide and discipline [the substantive due process] inquiry but do not set its outer boundaries."); Lawrence v. Texas, 539 U.S. 558, 572 (2003) ("History and tradition are the starting point but not in all cases the ending point of the substantive due process inquiry." (quoting County of Sacramento v. Lewis, 523 U.S. 833, 857 (1998) (Kennedy, J., concurring))).

Analysis has revealed deep challenges in identifying the content of pertinent traditions, which can often be described either broadly or narrowly. In *Michael H. v. Gerald D.*, 491 U.S. 110 (1989), for example, Justices Scalia and William J. Brennan disagreed over the level of generality at which to define the fundamental right in question. Scalia characterized the claim before the Court as involving the purported parental rights of an "adulterous natural father," *id.* at 127 n.6 (plurality opinion of Scalia, J.). By contrast, Justice Brennan viewed the father as coming within a tradition of legal respect for the more general rights associated with "parenthood," *id.* at 139 (Brennan, J., dissenting). For commentary on Justices Scalia and Brennan's debate over levels of generality in defining fundamental rights, see J. M. Balkin, *Tradition, Betrayal, and the Politics of Deconstruction*, 11 CARDOZO L. REV. 1613, 1614–29 (1990); Laurence H. Tribe & Michael C. Dorf, *Levels of Generality in the Definition of Rights*, 57 U. CHI. L. REV. 1057, 1058 (1990).

22. *See* McDonald v. City of Chicago, 561 U.S. 742, 791 (2010) (Scalia, J., concurring) ("Despite my misgivings about substantive due process as an original matter, I have acquiesced in the Court's incorporation of certain guarantees in the Bill of Rights.").

23. *See* Wisconsin v. Yoder, 406 U.S. 205, 232 (1972); Meyer v. Nebraska, 262 U.S. 390, 399–401 (1923); *Glucksberg*, 521 U.S. at 724.

24. United States v. Virginia, 518 U.S. 515, 568 (1996) (Scalia, J., dissenting) (emphasis omitted).

25. *Id.* at 519 (majority opinion).

26. 388 U.S. 1, 2 (1967).

27. *See generally* David A. Strauss, *The Supreme Court, 2014 Term—Foreword: Does the Constitution Mean What It Says?*, 129 HARV. L. REV. 1 (2015).

28. *See, e.g.,* ANTONIN SCALIA & BRYAN A. GARNER, READING LAW: THE INTERPRETATION OF LEGAL TEXTS 411–12 (2012); Randy J. Kozel, *Settled versus Right: Constitutional Method and the Path of Precedent*, 91 TEX. L. REV. 1843, 1873 (2013). As discussed in Chapter 2, however, there are some originalists who insist that original meaning should always determine constitutional outcomes.

29. *See, e.g.,* Planned Parenthood of Se. Pa. v. Casey, 505 U.S. 833, 854–55 (1992):

When this Court reexamines a prior holding, its judgment is customarily informed by a series of prudential and pragmatic considerations. . . . Thus, for example, we may ask whether the rule has proven to be intolerable simply in defying practical workability, *Swift & Co. v. Wickham*, 382 U.S. 111, 116 (1965); whether the rule is subject to a kind of reliance that would lend a special hardship to the consequences of overruling and add inequity to the cost of repudiation, *e.g.*, *United States v. Title Ins. & Trust Co.*, 265 U.S. 472, 486 (1924); whether related principles of law have so far developed as to have left the old rule no more than a remnant of abandoned doctrine, see *Patterson v. McLean Credit Union*, 491 U.S. 164, 173–174 (1989); or whether facts have so changed, or come to be seen so differently, as to have robbed the old rule of significant application or justification, *e.g.*, *Burnet [v. Coronado Oil & Gas Co.*, 285 U.S. 393, 412 (1932)]* (Brandeis, J., dissenting).

30. *See id.*

31. Richard H. Fallon Jr., *The Meaning of Legal "Meaning" and Its Implications for Theories of Legal Interpretation*, 82 U. CHI. L. REV. 1235, 1251–52 (2015).

32. *See, e.g.*, McDonald v. City of Chicago, 561 U.S. 742, 791 (2010) (Scalia, J., concurring).

33. U.S. CONST. amend. I.

34. *See, e.g.*, New York Times Co. v. United States, 403 U.S. 713 (1971). For general discussion of the extension of First Amendment principles to the executive branch and the judiciary, and of the more general relationship of linguistic meaning to constitutional meaning, see Curtis A. Bradley & Neil S. Siegel, *Constructed Constraint and the Constitutional Text*, 64 DUKE L.J. 1213, 1245–46 (2015); David A. Strauss, *The Supreme Court, 2014 Term—Foreword: Does the Constitution Mean What It Says?*, 129 HARV. L. REV. 1, 30–34 (2015).

35. *See* Thomas R. Lee, *Stare Decisis in Historical Perspective: From the Founding Era to the Rehnquist Court*, 52 VAND. L. REV. 647, 662–81 (1999). Although the early history is less than perfectly consistent, Founding-era commentators generally presupposed that constitutional precedents would be treated as authoritative, *see id.* at 718, and the Marshall Court's decisions "repeatedly adverted to the binding or controlling effect of precedent," *id.* at 684. Justice Joseph Story's influential COMMENTARIES ON THE CONSTITUTION OF THE UNITED STATES actually maintained that the "conclusive effect of judicial adjudications . . . was in the full view of the framers of the Constitution," 1 JOSEPH STORY, COMMENTARIES ON THE CONSTITUTION OF THE UNITED STATES 373 (Fred B. Rothman & Co. 1991) (1833), and thus, apparently, could be seen as part of the original understanding of the Constitution. I hasten to add, however, that I do not mean to endorse, much less stake my argument on, Story's claim. *See* Richard H. Fallon Jr., *Stare Decisis and the Constitution: An Essay on Constitutional Methodology*, 76 N.Y.U. L. REV. 570, 580 n.44 (2001).

36. Michael Stokes Paulsen, *Abrogating Stare Decisis by Statute: May Congress Remove the Precedential Effect of Roe and Casey?*, 109 YALE L.J. 1535, 1578 n.115 (2000).

37. There have been occasional complaints and expressions of doubt, including a suggestion by Chief Justice Roger B. Taney that the Supreme Court might dispense with stare decisis in constitutional cases. *See* The Passenger Cases, 48 U.S. (7 How.) 283, 470 (1849) (Taney, C.J., dissenting). But Taney's suggestion came in a solitary dissent, and he subsequently appeared to apply a more standard position. *See* Thomas R. Lee, *Stare Decisis in Historical Perspective: From the Founding Era to the Rehnquist Court*, 52 Vand. L. Rev. 647, 717–18 & n.377 (1999). Although Justices have sometimes maintained that to treat precedent as wholly conclusive would violate their oaths to uphold the Constitution, their protests have addressed the weight that should attach to stare decisis, not questioned whether the doctrine should exist at all. *See* Richard H. Fallon Jr., *Stare Decisis and the Constitution: An Essay on Constitutional Methodology*, 76 N.Y.U. L. Rev. 570, 582–83 (2001).

38. 515 U.S. 200 (1995). Justices Scalia and Thomas have taken a similar stand in interpreting the Takings Clause. In *Lucas v. South Carolina Coastal Council*, 505 U.S. 1003 (1992), Justice Scalia's opinion for the Court relied on prior Court decisions to support its holding that the Takings Clause restricts "regulatory as well as physical deprivations" of property, despite historical evidence that the Clause was not originally so understood. *Id.* at 1028 n.15. Another example comes from "dormant" Commerce Clause doctrine, under which the Court sometimes invalidates *state* legislation on the ground that it interferes with Congress's power to regulate interstate commerce, even though the Commerce Clause is exclusively a grant of power to Congress and makes no reference to any prohibition against states other than those that Congress enacts. In *West Lynn Creamery, Inc. v. Healy*, 512 U.S. 186 (1994), Justice Scalia, joined by Justice Thomas, concluded that dormant Commerce Clause doctrine has no historical grounding, but he determined nevertheless that stare decisis mandated the doctrine's continued application because the Court had "decided a vast number of negative-Commerce-Clause cases, engendering considerable reliance interests." *Id.* at 209–10 (Scalia, J., concurring in the judgment).

39. *See generally* Henry Paul Monaghan, *Stare Decisis and Constitutional Adjudication*, 88 Colum. L. Rev. 723, 727–39 (1988) (listing examples of prominent doctrines that are likely inconsistent with original understanding).

40. For an important, recent discussion of conflicts among legal authorities, see Nicole Roughan, Authorities: Conflicts, Cooperation, and Transnational Legal Theory (2013).

41. *See, e.g.*, Joseph Raz, Ethics in the Public Domain: Essays in the Morality of Law and Politics 198 (1994).

42. Although I once argued otherwise, I did so based on so capacious a view of original meaning that conflicts resulting in decision based on the lexical categorization would almost never arise. *See* Richard H. Fallon Jr., *A Constructivist Coherence Theory of Constitutional Interpretation*, 100 Harv. L. Rev. 1189, 1237–1268 (1987).

43. Planned Parenthood of Se. Pa. v. Casey, 505 U.S. 833, 854 (1992).

44. 529 U.S. 765 (2000).

45. *Id.* at 778 n.8 ("We express no view on the question whether *qui tam* suits violate Article II, in particular the Appointments Clause of § 2 and the 'take Care' Clause of § 3.").

46. 462 U.S. 919 (1983).

47. *See* Obergefell v. Hodges, 135 S. Ct. 2584 (2015).

4 Law in the Supreme Court: Jurisprudential Foundations

1. U.S. CONST. art. V. Article V alternatively provides that "Congress . . . on the application of the legislatures of two-thirds of the several states, shall call a convention for proposing amendments" that would then require ratification by three-fourths of the states, but this mechanism has never been employed.

2. *See* Bruce A. Ackerman, *The Storrs Lectures: Discovering the Constitution*, 93 YALE L.J. 1013, 1017 (1984).

3. *Id.* (explaining that the Framers were undoubtedly "acting beyond their legal authority" in "claiming the right to ignore . . . the state legislatures").

4. *See* John Harrison, *The Lawfulness of the Reconstruction Amendments*, 68 U. CHI. L. REV. 375, 379 n.14 (2001).

5. *Id.* at 451–57.

6. *Id.* at 451–52.

7. *See, e.g.*, AKHIL REED AMAR, AMERICA'S CONSTITUTION: A BIOGRAPHY 366 (2005); Akhil Reed Amar, *The Consent of the Governed: Constitutional Amendment outside Article V*, 94 COLUM. L. REV. 457, 464–69 (1994); Robert G. Natelson, *Proposing Constitutional Amendments by Convention: Rules Governing the Process*, 78 TENN. L. REV. 693, 719–23 (2011); John Harrison, *The Lawfulness of the Reconstruction Amendments*, 68 U. CHI. L. REV. 375, 419–57 (2001).

8. *See* Frederick Schauer, *Amending the Presuppositions of a Constitution, in* RESPONDING TO IMPERFECTION: THE THEORY AND PRACTICE OF CONSTITUTIONAL AMENDMENT 145, 154 (Sanford Levinson ed., 1995).

9. I add the qualification concerning "minimal" legal legitimacy in deference to the traditional "natural law" view that an unjust law is "no law at all." *See* Chapter 1. Although I have resisted the strong version of that position, I accept the important point that severely unjust laws such as the proslavery provisions of the original Constitution are so defective as species of law that their defective character sets them apart from what we might think of as law in the ordinary sense.

10. *See* H. L. A. HART, THE CONCEPT OF LAW 116–17 (2d ed. 1994).

11. *Id.* at 61.

12. *See* RICHARD H. FALLON JR., IMPLEMENTING THE CONSTITUTION 111–26 (2001); Frederick Schauer, *Amending the Presuppositions of a Constitution, in* RESPONDING TO IMPERFECTION: THE THEORY AND PRACTICE OF CONSTITUTIONAL AMENDMENT 145, 156–57 (Sanford Levinson ed., 1995); Kent Greenawalt, *The Rule of Recognition and the Constitution*, 85 MICH. L. REV. 621, 654 (1987); Steven D. Smith, *Stare Decisis in a Classical and Constitutional Setting: A Comment on the Symposium*, 5 AVE MARIA L. REV. 153, 168 (2007).

13. *See* Michael Sean Quinn, *Practice-Defining Rules*, 86 ETHICS 76, 76 (1975). For other influential discussions of the concept of a practice, see ALASDAIR MACINTYRE, AFTER VIRTUE: A STUDY IN MORAL THEORY 187–88 (2d ed. 1984); Thomas Morawetz, Commentary, *The Rules of Law and the Point of Law*,

121 U. Pa. L. Rev. 859, 859–60 (1973); John Rawls, *Two Concepts of Rules*, 64 Phil. Rev. 3, 3–4 (1955).

14. *See, e.g.*, Michael Sean Quinn, *Practice-Defining Rules*, 86 Ethics 76, 76 (1975).

15. *See* Ludwig Wittgenstein, Philosophical Investigations paras. 151–53, 179–83 (G. E. M. Anscombe trans., 1953); *see also* Jules L. Coleman, The Practice of Principle: In Defence of a Pragmatist Approach to Legal Theory 80–81 (2001) (invoking the Wittgensteinian notion to explicate jurisprudential issues).

16. McDonald v. City of Chicago, 561 U.S. 742, 762–65 (2010) (explaining the Court's process of "selective incorporation" of the Bill of Rights); *see also* Gitlow v. New York, 268 U.S. 652 (1925) (incorporating right to freedom of speech); Near v. Minnesota *ex rel.* Olson, 283 U.S. 697 (1931) (incorporating right to freedom of press).

17. *See, e.g.*, Hicks v. Miranda, 422 U.S. 332, 344–45 (1975). For illuminating discussions of judicial hierarchy, see Evan H. Caminker, *Why Must Inferior Courts Obey Superior Court Precedents?*, 46 Stan. L. Rev. 817 (1994). Tara Leigh Grove, *The Structural Case for Vertical Maximalism*, 95 Cornell L. Rev. 1 (2009), offers further helpful discussion and sources on the issue of judicial hierarchy.

18. In *Texas v. Johnson*, 491 U.S. 397 (1989), the Court divided five to four, with Justice William J. Brennan writing the majority opinion striking down the flag-burning statute, and Chief Justice William Rehnquist writing the chief dissent, which chastised the majority for ignoring the "unique position" the American flag occupies "as the symbol of our Nation." *Id.* at 422 (Rehnquist, C.J., dissenting). And in *City of Erie v. Pap's A.M.*, 529 U.S. 277 (2000), the Court splintered badly, with Justice Sandra Day O'Connor writing the plurality opinion upholding the prohibition on nude dancing under intermediate scrutiny, *id.* at 296, Justice Antonin Scalia writing a concurrence in the judgment that would have upheld the nude-dancing ban as traditional morals legislation outside the scope of the First Amendment, *id.* at 310 (Scalia, J., concurring in the judgment), and Justice John Paul Stevens dissenting on the ground that the nude-dancing ban should be invalidated based on its "censorial purpose," *id.* at 326 (Stevens, J., dissenting).

19. I do not mean to deny that some interpretive rules can be derived or inferred from the Constitution. *See, e.g.*, John F. Manning, Response, *Deriving Rules of Statutory Interpretation from the Constitution*, 101 Colum. L. Rev. 1648 (2001).

20. *See* H. L. A. Hart, The Concept of Law 94–95, 100–110 (2d ed. 1994).

21. *Cf.* Frederick Schauer, *Amending the Presuppositions of a Constitution*, *in* Responding to Imperfection: The Theory and Practice of Constitutional Amendment 145, 150 (Sanford Levinson ed., 1995) ("There is no reason to suppose that the ultimate source of law need be anything that looks at all like a rule, whether simple or complex, or even a collection of rules, and it may be less distracting to think of the ultimate source of recognition . . . as a *practice*.").

22. *See* A. W. B. Simpson, *The Common Law and Legal Theory, in* OXFORD ESSAYS IN JURISPRUDENCE (SECOND SERIES) 77 (A. W. B. Simpson ed., 1973).

23. *See* H. L. A. HART, THE CONCEPT OF LAW 101 (2d ed. 1994).

24. *See id.* at 289 (characterizing his view as "similar" to that—which is quoted in the text—of PETER WINCH, THE IDEA OF A SOCIAL SCIENCE AND ITS RELATION TO PHILOSOPHY 58 (R. F. Holland ed., 1958)).

25. *See* Thomas Morawetz, *The Rules of Law and the Point of Law,* 121 U. PA. L. REV. 859, 860–64 (1973).

26. *See, e.g.,* RONALD DWORKIN, FREEDOM'S LAW: THE MORAL READING OF THE AMERICAN CONSTITUTION 7–10 (1996).

27. *See* Richard H. Fallon Jr., *Constitutional Precedent Viewed through the Lens of Hartian Positivist Jurisprudence,* 86 N.C. L. REV. 1107, 1138–39 (2008).

28. For a theoretically ambitious and highly provocative account of the nature of constitutional change in the absence of formal constitutional amendment, see 1 BRUCE ACKERMAN, WE THE PEOPLE: FOUNDATIONS (1991); 2 BRUCE ACKERMAN, WE THE PEOPLE: TRANSFORMATIONS (2000); 3 BRUCE ACKERMAN, WE THE PEOPLE: THE CIVIL RIGHTS REVOLUTION (2014) (tracing "constitutional moments" in U.S. history that unsettled inherited norms, understandings, and expectations of U.S. constitutional decision making). *Cf.* Jack M. Balkin & Sanford Levinson, *Understanding the Constitutional Revolution,* 87 VA. L. REV. 1045, 1067–83 (2001) (explaining that constitutional change occurs over time primarily because of "partisan entrenchment"—that is, a history of presidents appointing members of their own party to the federal judiciary).

29. Emphasizing shifting understandings and theoretical debates among judges and Justices, Professor Ronald Dworkin argued forcefully that Hart's picture of law as a system of "rules" was fundamentally misconceived. Instead, Dworkin asked us to think of law as an "interpretive concept" the application of which required a "protestant attitude" in identifying the applicable law of any particular community. *See* RONALD M. DWORKIN, LAW'S EMPIRE 410–13 (1986). Without delving into the details of the Hart-Dworkin debate, I would emphasize that, at the end of the day, even Dworkin offers us—ineluctably, I believe—a practice-based theory of law. As I said previously, the term "rules of recognition" may be misleading, but the fundamental point for our purposes remains unshaken: the foundations of law, including American constitutional law in the Supreme Court, lie in socially grounded practices of recognition and their acceptance by judges and Justices, among others.

30. *See* RICHARD H. FALLON JR. ET AL., HART AND WECHSLER'S THE FEDERAL COURTS AND THE FEDERAL SYSTEM 47 (7th ed. 2015).

31. *See generally* Frederick Schauer, *Easy Cases,* 58 S. CAL. L. REV. 399 (1985).

32. *See* SUP. CT. R. 10(a) (listing as a compelling reason to grant certiorari the fact that "a United States court of appeals has entered a decision in conflict with the decision of another United States court of appeals on the same important matter").

33. *See* Plessy v. Ferguson, 163 U.S. 537 (1896); United States v. Butler, 297 U.S. 1 (1936); Hepburn v. Griswold, 75 U.S. 603 (1870).

34. *See* Cass R. Sunstein, *Unanimity and Disagreement on the Supreme Court,* 100 CORNELL L. REV. 769, 780 (2015). For the 2013 term, the unanimity rate reached 62 percent. *Id.* at 783–84.

35. 163 U.S. 537 (1896).

36. *Cf.* MICHAEL J. KLARMAN, FROM JIM CROW TO CIVIL RIGHTS 22 (2004) (explaining that "*Plessy* was easy" because "traditional legal sources" supported the ruling, and because it "simply mirrored the preferences of most white Americans").

37. In *Planned Parenthood of Southeastern Pennsylvania v. Casey,* 505 U.S. 833, 863 (1992), for example, the majority opinion affirmed, "We think *Plessy* was wrong the day it was decided."

38. *See, e.g.,* DANIEL KAHNEMAN, THINKING FAST AND SLOW (2011); Dan M. Kahan, *The Supreme Court, 2010 Term—Foreword: Neutral Principles, Motivated Cognition, and Some Problems for Constitutional Law,* 125 HARV. L. REV. 1 (2011).

39. 163 U.S. 537, 551 (1896).

40. Charles Black, *The Lawfulness of the Segregation Decisions,* 69 YALE L.J. 421, 422 n.8 (1960).

41. RONALD M. DWORKIN, LAW'S EMPIRE 3–4, 13 (1986).

42. As Professor Jamal Greene has written, the American "anticanon" of constitutional law—consisting of cases such as *Dred Scott, Plessy, Lochner,* and *Korematsu*—"embodies a set of propositions that all legitimate constitutional decisions must be prepared to refute." Jamal Greene, *The Anticanon,* 125 HARV. L. REV. 379, 380 (2011).

43. *See* ANTONIN SCALIA & BRYAN A. GARNER, READING LAW: THE INTERPRETATION OF LEGAL TEXTS (2012) (endorsing a set of fifty-seven "valid canons," *id.* at 9, while explicitly disclaiming thirteen "falsities"); William N. Eskridge Jr., *The New Textualism and Normative Canons,* 113 COLUM. L. REV. 531, 536 (2013) (book review) (purporting to identify 187 interpretive canons).

44. *See* H. L. A. HART, THE CONCEPT OF LAW 289 (2d ed. 1994) (approvingly citing PETER WINCH, THE IDEA OF A SOCIAL SCIENCE AND ITS RELATION TO PHILOSOPHY 58 (R. F. Holland ed., 1958)).

45. *See* Randy E. Barnett, *Trumping Precedent with Original Meaning: Not as Radical as It Sounds,* 22 CONST. COMMENT. 257, 258–59 (2006); Randy E. Barnett, *It's a Bird, It's a Plane, No, It's Super Precedent: A Response to Farber and Gerhardt,* 90 MINN. L. REV. 1232, 1233 (2006); Gary Lawson, *The Constitutional Case against Precedent,* 17 HARV. J.L. & PUB. POL'Y 23, 30 (1994); Michael Stokes Paulsen, *The Intrinsically Corrupting Influence of Precedent,* 22 CONST. COMMENT. 289, 291 (2005).

46. *Cf.* Jack Knight & Lee Epstein, *The Norm of Stare Decisis,* 40 AM. J. POL. SCI. 1018, 1021–22 (1996) (noting that the Justices feel constrained from overruling too many cases by an apprehension that the public would find too much instability in constitutional law to be unacceptable).

47. *See* Miranda v. Arizona, 384 U.S. 436 (1966).

48. 530 U.S. 428, 443 (2000). The Court explained that stare decisis "carries such persuasive force that we have always required a departure from precedent to be supported by some special justification." *Id.* (quoting United States v. Int'l

Bus. Machs. Corp., 517 U.S. 843, 856 (1996) (internal quotation marks omitted)).

49. *See generally* Richard H. Fallon Jr., *Constitutional Precedent Viewed through the Lens of Hartian Positivist Jurisprudence*, 86 N.C. L. REV. 1107, 1148–50 (2008) (characterizing precedents that "have generated settled expectations that preclude their being overruled" as "superprecedents").

50. *See generally* RICHARD H. FALLON JR., IMPLEMENTING THE CONSTITUTION 82 (2001).

51. On the history of the emergence of the strict scrutiny test, see Richard H. Fallon Jr., *Strict Judicial Scrutiny*, 54 UCLA L. REV. 1267 (2007); Stephen A. Siegel, *The Origin of the Compelling State Interest Test and Strict Scrutiny*, 48 AM. J. LEGAL HIST. 355 (2006).

52. *See* RICHARD H. FALLON JR., IMPLEMENTING THE CONSTITUTION 81 (2001).

53. *See, e.g.*, Planned Parenthood of Se. Pa. v. Casey, 505 U.S. 833, 854–55 (1992), which is quoted in relevant part in Chapter 3.

54. *See* JULES L. COLEMAN, THE PRACTICE OF PRINCIPLE: IN DEFENCE OF A PRAGMATIST APPROACH TO LEGAL THEORY 100 (2001).

55. *See* David L. Shapiro, *Mr. Justice Rehnquist: A Preliminary View*, 90 HARV L. REV. 293, 296–97 (1976).

56. For example, Chief Justice Rehnquist is widely credited with overseeing a "federalism revolution" that would have been nearly unimaginable during his early years on the Supreme Court. *See generally* Richard H. Fallon Jr., *The "Conservative" Paths of the Supreme Court's Federalism Decisions*, 69 U. CHI. L. REV. 429, 429–32 (2002).

57. *Cf.* Morrison v. Olson, 487 U.S. 654, 697–734 (1988) (Scalia, J., dissenting), *with* Free Enter. Fund v. Pub. Co. Accounting Oversight Bd., 561 U.S. 477 (2010) (Roberts, C.J.) (adopting, in significant part, Justice Scalia's dissent in *Morrison* as controlling law).

58. *See, e.g.*, Dep't of Transp. v. Ass'n of Am. R.Rs., 135 S. Ct. 1225, 1240–55 (2015) (Thomas, J., concurring in the judgment) (writing separately to call into question the legitimacy of the Court's modern separation of powers and nondelegation jurisprudence).

59. *See generally* NOAH FELDMAN, SCORPIONS (2010).

60. *See, e.g.*, RICHARD H. FALLON JR., IMPLEMENTING THE CONSTITUTION 5, 42 (2001).

61. *See* H. W. PERRY JR., DECIDING TO DECIDE: AGENDA SETTING IN THE UNITED STATES SUPREME COURT 198–215 (1991); Tonja Jacobi & Matthew Sag, *Taking the Measure of Ideology: Empirically Measuring Supreme Court Cases*, 98 GEO. L.J. 1, 16 n.73 (2009); Mark Tushnet, *Themes in Warren Court Biographies*, 70 N.Y.U. L. REV. 748, 764 n.86 (1995).

62. *See* Tom Ginsburg, *The Global Spread of Constitutional Review*, *in* THE OXFORD HANDBOOK OF LAW AND POLITICS 81, 85 (Keith E. Whittington et al. eds., 2008) (describing how the "model of a designated constitutional court became the basis of the post–World War II constitutional courts in Europe").

5 Constitutional Constraints

1. CHARLES EVANS HUGHES, *Speech before the Elmira Chamber of Commerce, May 3, 1907, in* ADDRESSES OF CHARLES EVAN HUGHES, 1906–1916, at 179, 185 (2d ed. 1916).

2. For a recent, sophisticated argument that coercion is normally a central feature of law and legal systems, see FREDERICK SCHAUER, THE FORCE OF LAW (2015). *See also* Danny Priel, *Sanction and Obligation in Hart's Theory of Law*, 21 RATIO JURIS 404 (2008); Nicos Stavropolous, *The Relevance of Coercion: Some Preliminaries*, 22 RATIO JURIS 339 (2009).

3. THE FEDERALIST No. 51 (James Madison) (Clinton Rossiter ed., 1961).

4. I use the term "external constraints" more broadly than Madison did. Madison contrasted "internal" constraints, which were those established and enforced within the federal government, typically by one branch against another, with "external" constraints, which originated outside the federal government's tripartite structure. *See id.* at 320–23. As I explain more fully later, I use the term "external constraint" to embrace both of Madison's categories of the internal and the external. For my purposes, the pertinent contrast is between constraints rooted in norms ("normative constraints"), on the one hand, and those rooted in concerns about adverse consequences ("external constraints"), on the other.

5. *See* STEPHEN HOLMES, PASSIONS AND CONSTRAINT 163 (1995).

6. For discussions of this topic, see, for example, NUNO GAROUPA & TOM GINSBURG, JUDICIAL REPUTATION: A COMPARATIVE THEORY (2015); LAWRENCE BAUM, JUDGES AND THEIR AUDIENCES 10–14 (2006); LEE EPSTEIN & JACK KNIGHT, THE CHOICES JUSTICES MAKE 9–10 (1998); Barry Friedman, *The Politics of Judicial Review*, 84 TEX. L. REV. 257 (2005); Richard A. Posner, *What Do Judges and Justices Maximize? (The Same Thing Everybody Else Does)*, 3 SUP. CT. ECON. REV. 1 (1993).

7. Philosophers sometimes distinguish between "constitutive rules," which "create or define new forms of behavior," and "regulative rules," which "regulate a pre-existing activity, an activity whose existence is logically independent of the rules." JOHN R. SEARLE, SPEECH ACTS 33–34 (1969); Christopher Cherry, *Regulative Rules and Constitutive Rules*, 23 PHIL. Q. 301 (1973). For criticism of the view that regulative and constitutive rules are truly distinct, see JOSEPH RAZ, PRACTICAL REASON AND NORMS 108–11 (1990).

8. On the constitutive function of constitutions, see, e.g., STEPHEN HOLMES, PASSIONS AND CONSTRAINT 163 (1995); Ernest A. Young, *The Constitution outside the Constitution*, 117 YALE L.J. 408 (2007). Andrei Marmor, *Legal Conventionalism*, 4 LEGAL THEORY 509 (1998), similarly argues that the jurisprudential concept of a "rule of recognition," which I discussed in Chapter 4, should be regarded as a "constitutive convention."

9. For an interesting discussion of the related issue of how the breadth and significance of judicial opinions tend to be influenced by the ideological cohesion of the Justices forming the majority, see Nancy Staudt, Barry Friedman, & Lee Epstein, *On the Role of Ideological Homogeneity in Generating Consequential Constitutional Decisions*, 10 U. PA. J. CONST. L. 361 (2008).

10. The Supreme Court in Conference (1940–1985), at 118 (Del Dickson ed., 2001).

11. U.S. Const. art. III, § 1.

12. *See, e.g.,* Stump v. Sparkman, 435 U.S. 349, 356 (1978).

13. U.S. Const. art. II, § 4; *see also* The Federalist No. 81, at 453 (Alexander Hamilton) (Clinton Rossiter ed., 1961) ("There never can be danger that the judges, by a series of deliberate usurpations on the authority of the legislature, would hazard the united resentment of the body intrusted with it, while this body was possessed of the means of punishing their presumption, by degrading them from their stations.").

14. U.S. Const. art. III, § 2, cl. 2. With Congress having regulated the Court's appellate jurisdiction since the 1789 Judiciary Act, the Court's current appellate jurisdiction is almost entirely governed by statute. *See* 28 U.S.C. §§ 1251–59 (2012). Although it is almost universally agreed that some possible statutory limitations on the Court's jurisdiction would violate the Constitution, the bounds on congressional power have seldom been tested and remain much debated. *See* Richard H. Fallon Jr. et al., Hart and Wechsler's the Federal Courts and the Federal System 319–22 (7th ed. 2015).

15. *See* William E. Leuchtenburg, The Supreme Court Reborn: The Constitutional Revolution in the Age of Roosevelt 84–85, 96–97, 112–21, 142–43, 216–20 (1995); Rafael Gely & Pablo T. Spiller, *The Political Economy of Supreme Court Constitutional Decisions: The Case of Roosevelt's Court-Packing Plan,* 12 Int'l Rev. L. & Econ. 45 (1992).

16. *See* Joseph Alsop & Turner Catledge, The 168 Days 135 (1938).

17. *See, e.g.,* Kenneth Einar Himma, *Making Sense of Constitutional Disagreement: Legal Positivism, the Bill of Rights, and the Conventional Rule of Recognition in the United States,* 4 J.L. & Soc'y 149, 154 (2003); McNollgast, *Politics and the Courts: A Positive Theory of Judicial Doctrine and the Rule of Law,* 68 S. Cal. L. Rev. 1631, 1641–47 (1995).

18. *Cf.* William Baude, *The Judgment Power,* 96 Geo. L.J. 1807, 1862 (2008) (arguing that the judicial power to bind the president applies only when a court is acting within its jurisdiction).

19. *See* Frederick Schauer, *The Supreme Court, 2005 Term—Foreword: The Court's Agenda—and the Nation's,* 120 Harv. L. Rev. 4 (2006).

20. *But cf.* Daryl Levinson, *Empire-Building Government in Constitutional Law,* 118 Harv. L. Rev. 915 (2005) (challenging the premise that government officials characteristically seek to expand the power of the institutions in which they serve).

21. *See* Keith E. Whittington, Political Foundations of Judicial Supremacy: The Presidency, the Supreme Court, and Constitutional Leadership in U.S. History 31–40 (2007) (summarizing well-known episodes of actual and threatened presidential defiance of judicial authority).

22. For a vivid account of the relevant history, see Bruce A. Ackerman, The Failure of the Founding Fathers: Jefferson, Marshall, and the Rise of Presidential Democracy (2005).

23. U.S. Const. art. III, § 1.

24. 5 U.S. (1 Cranch) 299 (1803).

25. 5 U.S. (1 Cranch) 137 (1803).

26. *See* Richard H. Fallon Jr., Marbury *and the Constitutional Mind: A Bicentennial Essay on the Wages of Doctrinal Tension*, 91 CALIF. L. REV. 1, 16–20 (2003).

27. *See* BRUCE A. ACKERMAN, THE FAILURE OF THE FOUNDING FATHERS: JEFFERSON, MARSHALL, AND THE RISE OF PRESIDENTIAL DEMOCRACY 182–86 (2005).

28. 17 F. Cas. 144 (C.C.D. Md. 1861). For a detailed analysis of the decision in *Ex parte Merryman* and its aftermath, see DANIEL A. FARBER, LINCOLN'S CONSTITUTION 17, 157–63, 188–95 (2003).

29. *See* DANIEL A. FARBER, LINCOLN'S CONSTITUTION 159, 194 (2003).

30. 317 U.S. 1 (1942).

31. *See* Daniel J. Danelski, *The Saboteurs' Case*, 1996 J. SUP. CT. HIST. 61, 69.

32. *See* Richard H. Fallon Jr. & Daniel J. Meltzer, *Habeas Corpus Jurisdiction, Substantive Rights, and the War on Terror*, 120 HARV. L. REV. 2029, 2078–79 (2007); *see also* Andrew Kent, *Judicial Review for Enemy Fighters: The Court's Fateful Turn in* Ex parte Quirin, *the Nazi Saboteur Case*, 66 VAND. L. REV. 153, 231–32 (2013) (canvassing the ways in which public opinion and executive pressure shaped the Court's approach).

33. Brown v. Bd. of Educ. (II), 349 U.S. 294, 301 (1955); *see* MICHAEL J. KLARMAN, FROM JIM CROW TO CIVIL RIGHTS: THE SUPREME COURT AND THE STRUGGLE FOR RACIAL EQUALITY 312–20 (2004).

34. THE FEDERALIST No. 51, at 322 (James Madison) (Clinton Rossiter ed., 1961).

35. *Id.*

36. *See, e.g.*, KEITH E. WHITTINGTON, POLITICAL FOUNDATIONS OF JUDICIAL SUPREMACY: THE PRESIDENCY, THE SUPREME COURT, AND CONSTITUTIONAL LEADERSHIP IN U.S. HISTORY 4 (2007); Mark A. Graber, *Constructing Judicial Review*, 8 ANN. REV. POL. SCI. 425, 425 (2005).

37. On departmentalism and its history, see LARRY KRAMER, THE PEOPLE THEMSELVES: POPULAR CONSTITUTIONALISM AND JUDICIAL REVIEW (2004).

38. *See* KEITH E. WHITTINGTON, POLITICAL FOUNDATIONS OF JUDICIAL SUPREMACY: THE PRESIDENCY, THE SUPREME COURT, AND CONSTITUTIONAL LEADERSHIP IN U.S. HISTORY 25 (2007). *See generally* RAN HIRSCHL, TOWARDS JURISTOCRACY: THE ORIGINS AND CONSEQUENCES OF THE NEW CONSTITUTIONALISM (2004) (describing conditions under which vulnerable political elites in other nations have chosen to establish robust schemes of judicial review to protect the then-prevailing elite's values).

39. *See, e.g.*, KEITH E. WHITTINGTON, POLITICAL FOUNDATIONS OF JUDICIAL SUPREMACY: THE PRESIDENCY, THE SUPREME COURT, AND CONSTITUTIONAL LEADERSHIP IN U.S. HISTORY 134–52 (2007); Mark A. Graber, *The Nonmajoritarian Difficulty: Legislative Deference to the Judiciary*, 7 STUD. AM. POL. DEV. 35, 38 (1993). Congress and the president may also be happy to see dominant national visions enforced against the states, *see* KEITH E. WHITTINGTON, POLITICAL FOUNDATIONS OF JUDICIAL SUPREMACY: THE PRESIDENCY, THE SUPREME COURT, AND CONSTITUTIONAL LEADERSHIP IN U.S. HISTORY 105–7 (2007), and to delegate to the courts a number of issues possessing low political salience, *see id.* at 121.

40. *See* Richard H. Fallon Jr., *Constitutional Precedent Viewed through the Lens of Hartian Positivist Jurisprudence*, 86 N.C. L. Rev. 1107, 1141–42, 1150 (2008).

41. *See* Robert A. Dahl, Democracy and Its Critics 190 (1989); Robert G. McCloskey, The American Supreme Court 224 (1960); Kevin T. McGuire & James A. Stimson, *The Least Dangerous Branch Revisited: New Evidence on Supreme Court Responsiveness to Public Preferences*, 66 J. Pol. 1018 (2004).

42. President Roosevelt appointed Justices Hugo L. Black, Stanley Reed, Felix Frankfurter, William O. Douglas, Frank Murphy, James F. Byrnes, Robert H. Jackson, and Wiley B. Rutledge, and also elevated Justice Harlan Fiske Stone to Chief Justice.

43. For analyses of the Warren Court's liberal legacy, see generally Morton J. Horwitz, The Warren Court and the Pursuit of Justice (1998); The Warren Court in Historical and Political Perspective (Mark Tushnet ed., 1993).

44. *See* Brandenburg v. Ohio, 395 U.S. 444 (1969); Gideon v. Wainwright, 372 U.S. 335 (1963); Miranda v. Arizona, 384 U.S. 436 (1966).

45. *See* Chris Hickman, *Courting the Right: Richard Nixon's 1968 Campaign against the Warren Court*, 36 J. Sup. Ct. Hist. 287, 292 (2011).

46. *See generally* Michael J. Graetz & Linda Greenhouse, The Burger Court and the Rise of the Judicial Right (2016).

47. Social scientists commonly equate the Court's institutional legitimacy with what they call "diffuse support" among the public, as reflected in opinion surveys of whether the Court is a generally trustworthy decision maker whose rulings therefore deserve respect or obedience. *See, e.g.*, James L. Gibson et al., *Measuring Attitudes toward the United States Supreme Court*, 47 Am. J. Pol. Sci. 354, 356–58 (2003).

48. Thomas M. Keck, The Most Activist Supreme Court in History: The Road to Modern Judicial Conservatism 277 (2004).

49. *See* Jon Elster, *Social Norms and Economic Theory*, 3 J. Econ. Persp. 99, 103–4 (1989).

50. *See* Matthew C. Stephenson, *Legal Realism for Economists*, 23 J. Econ. Persp. 191, 205 (2009) (arguing from a legal-realist perspective that good lawyering is valuable because "legal advocates make specifically *legal* arguments as a way of lowering the cost to the judge of reaching the advocate's preferred outcome by, in essence, doing some of the judge's work").

51. For a classic historical and sociological study, see Kai T. Erikson, Wayward Puritans (1966).

52. For leading statements of the "attitudinal model," see Jeffrey A. Segal & Harold J. Spaeth, The Supreme Court and the Attitudinal Model 228 (1993); Jeffrey A. Segal & Harold J. Spaeth, The Supreme Court and the Attitudinal Model Revisited (2002).

53. Jeffrey A. Segal & Harold J. Spaeth, The Supreme Court and the Attitudinal Model 65 (1993).

54. Cass R. Sunstein, *Unanimity and Disagreement on the Supreme Court*, 100 Cornell L. Rev. 769, 784 (2015).

55. *See* Thomas M. Keck, *Party, Policy, or Duty: Why Does the Supreme Court Invalidate Federal Statutes?*, 101 Am. Pol. Sci. Rev. 321, 336 (2007).

56. *Id.*; *see also* Rachel E. Barkow, *Originalists, Politics, and Criminal Law on the Rehnquist Court*, 74 Geo. Wash. L. Rev. 1043, 1045 (2006) (arguing that Rehnquist Court decisions involving Sixth Amendment rights to trial by jury in criminal cases, which often resulted from an alliance between liberal and originalist Justices, "provide a concrete and important example of the power of law and legal methodology—and not simply politics—in Supreme Court decision making").

57. *See, e.g.,* Ronald Dworkin, Freedom's Law: The Moral Reading of the American Constitution 7–10 (1996).

6 Constitutional Theory and Its Relation to Constitutional Practice

1. John Rawls maintained that only "public reasons" could have a legitimate role in political argument and decision making, paradigmatically including constitutional adjudication. *See* John Rawls, Political Liberalism 213–54 (1993). By "public reasons," he roughly meant reasons that would register as reasons within an overlapping consensus of reasonable moral and political views within a particular community. Ronald Dworkin argued for a different restriction. *See* Ronald Dworkin, Law's Empire 225–26, 243–44, 338–39 (1986). According to him, the Justices should rely directly only on political principles that would figure in the morally best, rationalizing account of the content of prior legally authoritative texts and decisions. In his view, such principles are already immanent in American law. Other views are also plausible.

2. Moral philosophers frequently draw a distinction between the "rational," which can be understood in purely instrumental, self-interested terms, and the "reasonable," which imports a disposition to behave in ways that give due consideration to the interests of others. *See, e.g.,* John Rawls, Political Liberalism 49 n.1 (1993) ("Knowing that people are rational we do not know the ends they will pursue, only that they will pursue them intelligently. Knowing that people are reasonable where others are concerned, we know that they are willing to govern their conduct by a principle from which they and others can reason in common; and reasonable people take into account the consequences of their actions on others' well-being" (citing W. M. Sibley, *The Rational versus the Reasonable*, 62 Phil. Rev. 554, 560 (1953)); T. M. Scanlon, What We Owe to Each Other 191–92 (1998) (suggesting that rationality entails a simple capacity for means-ends analysis, while reasonableness involves "tak[ing] others' interests into account").

3. *See generally* H. Jefferson Powell, Constitutional Conscience (2008) (calling for a requirement of good faith in constitutional adjudication as an aspect of "constitutional conscience"). For a valuable examination of the largely antithetical notion of bad faith in constitutional argument, see David E. Pozen, *Constitutional Bad Faith*, 129 Harv. L. Rev. 885 (2016).

4. *See* Abbe R. Gluck, *The Federal Common Law of Statutory Interpretation: Erie for the Age of Statutes*, 54 Wm. & Mary L. Rev. 753 (2013); Abbe R. Gluck, *Intersystemic Statutory Interpretation: Methodology as "Law" and the Erie Doctrine*, 120 Yale L.J. 1898 (2011).

5. In a variety of contexts, it is systematically mistaken to judge decision making by a multimember institution, such as the Supreme Court, by the standards that would apply to decision making by a single individual. *See, e.g.,* ADRIAN VERMEULE, THE SYSTEM OF THE CONSTITUTION (2011); Frank H. Easterbrook, *Ways of Criticizing the Court,* 95 HARV. L. REV. 802, 811–13 (1982).

6. *See, e.g.,* J. HARVIE WILKINSON III, COSMIC CONSTITUTIONAL THEORY: WHY AMERICANS ARE LOSING THEIR INALIENABLE RIGHT TO SELF-GOVERNANCE (2012).

7. Stephen E. Sachs, *Originalism as a Theory of Legal Change,* 38 HARV. J.L. & PUB. POL'Y 817 (2015), advances two bracing arguments to the contrary. First, Professor Sachs argues that originalism is a positive theory of what American law simply is—namely, the set of legal norms that were either established by or in place at the time of the Founding, unless they have been validly changed since the Founding. Second, he maintains that the law in place at the Founding contained adequate methodological and interpretive principles to resolve all questions that might subsequently arise if one just follows original principles. The first of these claims seems to me to be either false or radically underdetermined if asserted as a simple matter of fact. One might be able to argue that originalism is the normatively best theory among the set of candidates that fit the plain facts of American constitutional practice even plausibly well. If so, there might be a normative case for embracing originalism. But to say that our practice simply is pervasively originalist, and that anyone who fails so to recognize has made a factual error, is far too strong. *See generally* David A. Strauss, *The Supreme Court, 2014 Term—Foreword: Does the Constitution Mean What It Says?,* 129 HARV. L. REV. 1 (2015). The second claim, that the prescription just to follow the law could furnish all of the guidance that one needs in order to resolve hard cases, is plausibly true only if one understands applicable legal principles as counseling the exercise of relatively open-ended moral judgment in order to resolve indeterminacies. Although someone exercising moral judgment in this way would be acting pursuant to or in accordance with the law, to say she was "just following the law" would be more misleading than descriptively informative.

8. Lawrence B. Solum, *Originalism and Constitutional Construction,* 82 FORDHAM L. REV. 453, 456 (2013).

9. *See* Thomas B. Colby & Peter J. Smith, *Living Originalism,* 59 DUKE L.J. 239, 244–45 (2009) (describing originalism as a "smorgasbord of distinct constitutional theories"). For a more sympathetic overview of originalism's history and variations, see Lawrence B. Solum, *What Is Originalism? The Evolution of Contemporary Originalist Theory, in* THE CHALLENGE OF ORIGINALISM: THEORIES OF CONSTITUTIONAL INTERPRETATION 12 (Grant Huscroft & Bradley W. Miller eds., 2011).

10. *See, e.g.,* Lawrence B. Solum, *Originalism and Constitutional Construction,* 82 FORDHAM L. REV. 453 (2013); Randy E. Barnett, *Interpretation and Construction,* 34 HARV. J.L. & PUB. POL'Y 65, 66 (2011).

11. *See* James B. Thayer, *The Origin and Scope of the American Doctrine of Constitutional Law,* 7 HARV. L. REV. 129 (1893).

12. For a modern defense of the Thayerian position, see ADRIAN VERMEULE, JUDGING UNDER UNCERTAINTY 230–88 (2006).

13. *See* DAVID A. STRAUSS, THE LIVING CONSTITUTION (2010) (analogizing constitutional interpretation to common-law interpretation).

14. *See id.* at 37–40.

15. *See* David A. Strauss, *The Supreme Court, 2014 Term—Foreword: Does the Constitution Mean What It Says?*, 129 HARV. L. REV. 1, 21 (2015).

16. *Id.* at 39, 44.

17. *See* DAVID A. STRAUSS, THE LIVING CONSTITUTION 43–46 (2010).

18. *See id.* at 44.

19. PHILIP BOBBITT, CONSTITUTIONAL FATE: THEORY OF THE CONSTITUTION 9–119 (1982); PHILIP BOBBITT, CONSTITUTIONAL INTERPRETATION 12–13 (1991).

20. *See* PHILIP BOBBITT, CONSTITUTIONAL INTERPRETATION 170 (1991).

21. *See* RONALD M. DWORKIN, FREEDOM'S LAW: THE MORAL READING OF THE AMERICAN CONSTITUTION 7–10 (1996); RICHARD POSNER, LAW, PRAGMATISM, AND DEMOCRACY (2003); RICHARD POSNER, OVERCOMING LAW 531–51 (1995); Richard A. Posner, *Pragmatic Adjudication*, 18 CARDOZO L. REV. 1 (1996); Richard A. Posner, *Legal Pragmatism Defended*, 71 U. CHI. L. REV. 683 (2004).

22. *See, e.g.*, RICHARD A. POSNER, DIVERGENT PATHS: THE ACADEMY AND THE JUDICIARY 320 (2016).

23. *See, e.g.*, KEITH WHITTINGTON, CONSTITUTIONAL INTERPRETATION: TEXTUAL MEANING, ORIGINAL INTENT, AND JUDICIAL REVIEW 61–62 (1999); Antonin Scalia, *Originalism: The Lesser Evil*, 57 U. CIN. L. REV. 849 (1989).

24. Antonin Scalia, *Response, in* A MATTER OF INTERPRETATION 129, 145 (Amy Gutmann ed., 1997).

25. *See* RONALD M. DWORKIN, FREEDOM'S LAW: THE MORAL READING OF THE AMERICAN CONSTITUTION 7–10 (1996).

26. *See* DAVID A. STRAUSS, THE LIVING CONSTITUTION 52–53 (2010). *See generally* LEONARD W. LEVY, EMERGENCE OF A FREE PRESS (1985) (finding it doubtful that the Founding generation understood the Free Speech Clause as doing more than barring systems of administrative censorship or "prior restraints").

27. *See* Citizens United v. FEC, 558 U.S. 310, 385–88 (2010) (Scalia, J., concurring); *see also* Brown v. Entm't Merchs. Ass'n, 564 U.S. 786, 792 (2011) (Scalia, J.).

28. *See, e.g.*, Steven G. Calabresi & Julia T. Rickert, *Originalism and Sex Discrimination*, 90 TEX. L. REV. 1, 2–15 (2011). *But cf.* Michael B. Rappaport, *Originalism and the Colorblind Constitution*, 89 NOTRE DAME L. REV. 71 (2013) (defending, from an originalist viewpoint, a Fourteenth Amendment prohibition on race-based discrimination).

29. *See* Joseph M. Lynch, *The Federalists and the Federalist: A Forgotten History*, 31 SETON HALL L. REV. 18, 21–23 (2000).

30. *See* Chisholm v. Georgia, 2 U.S. (2 Dall.) 419 (1793).

31. *See, e.g.*, JAMES F. SIMON, WHAT KIND OF NATION: THOMAS JEFFERSON, JOHN MARSHALL, AND THE EPIC STRUGGLE TO CREATE A UNITED STATES 49–76 (2002).

32. By contrast, Professors John O. McGinnis and Michael B. Rappaport have proposed to resolve indeterminacies by applying the interpretive methods that reasonable, well-informed judges and lawyers would have employed to gauge the meaning of a constitutional provision at the time of its enactment. *See* John O. McGinnis & Michael B. Rappaport, *Original Methods Originalism: A New Theory of Interpretation and the Case against Construction,* 103 Nw. U. L. Rev. 751, 751 (2009). But this move only postpones the problem if, as others have argued, reasonable people of the Founding era disagreed about matters of interpretive methodology.

33. *See* The Federalist No. 37, at 229–30 (James Madison) (Clinton Rossiter ed., 1961); Letter from James Madison to Spencer Roane (Sept. 2, 1819), *in* 8 The Writings of James Madison 450 (Gaillard Hunt. ed., 1908).

34. *See, e.g.,* William Baude, *Is Originalism Our Law?,* 115 Colum. L. Rev. 2349, 2358–61 (2015).

35. *See* Antonin Scalia, *Response, in* A Matter of Interpretation 129, 140 (Amy Gutmann ed., 1997).

36. *See, e.g.,* Stephen E. Sachs, *Originalism as a Theory of Legal Change,* 38 Harv. J.L. & Pub. Pol'y 817 (2015).

37. *See, e.g.,* Antonin Scalia & Bryan A. Garner, Reading Law: The Interpretation of Legal Texts 413 (2012).

38. The originalist Justices Scalia and Clarence Thomas joined part of a precedent-based opinion interpreting the Fifth Amendment in this way in *Adarand Constructors, Inc. v. Pena,* 515 U.S. 200, 215–18 (1995).

39. Duncan Kennedy, *The Hermeneutic of Suspicion in Contemporary American Legal Thought,* 25 Law & Critique 91 (2014).

40. *See* Jeffrey A. Segal & Harold J. Spaeth, The Supreme Court and the Attitudinal Model 228 (1993); Jeffrey A. Segal & Harold J. Spaeth, The Supreme Court and the Attitudinal Model Revisited (2002).

41. *See* Jeffrey Toobin, The Nine: Inside the Secret World of the Supreme Court 103 (2007).

42. *See* Henry Paul Monaghan, *Stare Decisis and Constitutional Adjudication,* 88 Colum. L. Rev. 723, 734, 744–45 (1988); David A. Strauss, The Living Constitution 12, 15 (2010).

43. *See, e.g.,* Van Orden v. Perry, 545 U.S. 677, 700 (2005) (Breyer, J., concurring in the judgment) ("While the Court's prior tests provide useful guideposts . . . no exact formula can dictate a resolution to . . . fact-intensive cases [under the Establishment Clause]."); Stephen Breyer, Active Liberty: Interpreting Our Democratic Constitution (2005) (disclaiming any intention to "present a general theory of constitutional interpretation," *id.* at 7, and counseling "against category boundaries that are too rigid or fixed and against too mechanical an application of those categories" in constitutional doctrine, *id.* at 43).

44. 134 S. Ct. 2550 (2014). U.S. Const. art. II, § 2, cl. 3 provides, "The President shall have Power to fill up all Vacancies that may happen during the Recess of the Senate, by granting Commissions which shall expire at the End of their next Session." The dispute in *Noel Canning* involved the meaning of "the Recess."

45. Larry Alexander, *Telepathic Law*, 27 Const. Comment. 139, 149 (2010), argues that the idea of "legal intuitions" (as distinguished from unvarnished moral intuitions) makes sense only, if at all, "in cases where the original meaning is unclear and where we think considerations of policy or justice strongly favor one possible meaning over the other." Consistent with the argument of Chapter 2, however, even modestly well-informed observers can have a legal intuition that there may be multiple candidates to count as the original meaning of constitutional language. And as Chapter 3 further argued, "precedential" meaning is sometimes a further plausible candidate. Under these circumstances, the idea of morally influenced legal intuitions seems to me to be wholly intelligible and unproblematic, even if the intuitions may not always bear up under further reflection and research.

46. *See generally* John Rawls, A Theory of Justice 20–22, 48–53 (1971).

47. *See id.* at 20. Although Rawls coined the term "reflective equilibrium" and introduced it into moral and political philosophy, Nelson Goodman, Fact, Fiction, and Forecast 64 (4th ed. 1983) had previously (1955) advanced a similarly coherentist method of justification of our practices of inductive and deductive logic: "*A rule is amended if it yields an inference we are unwilling to accept; an inference is rejected if it violates a rule we are unwilling to amend.* The process of justification is the delicate one of making mutual adjustments between rules and accepted inferences; and in the agreement achieved lies the only justification needed for either."

48. *See* John Rawls, A Theory of Justice 20–21 (1971).

49. *See* Mitchell N. Berman, *Reflective Equilibrium and Constitutional Method: Lessons from John McCain and the Natural-Born Citizenship Clause, in* The Challenge of Originalism: Theories of Constitutional Interpretation 246 (Grant Huscroft & Bradley Miller eds., 2011). There are significant differences as well as similarities between Berman's theory and mine. Among the differences, my thesis is more global and possibly more normative than Berman's: whereas he develops his thesis largely as an argument against originalism, I seek to explain why even originalists likely employ a Reflective Equilibrium Theory in developing the details of their theories. *See also* Vicki C. Jackson, *Conclusion: Gender Equality and the Idea of a Constitution: Entrenchment, Jurisdiction, and Interpretation, in* Constituting Equality: Gender Equality and Comparative Constitutional Law 312, 318 (Susan H. Williams ed., 2009) ("A good theory in this universe of feminist epistemologies is one that grows out of and is recursively refined by its interactions with facts, experiences, and interpretations of those experiences from the perspectives of women.").

I defended a first-order constitutional theory that relied on the concept of equilibrium among considerations pertinent to the correct resolution of individual cases in Richard H. Fallon Jr., *A Constructivist Coherence Theory of Constitutional Interpretation*, 100 Harv. L. Rev. 1189 (1987). The second-order theory that I advance here is consistent with but does not depend on that first-order theory.

50. *See* T. M. Scanlon, Being Realistic about Reasons 77 (2014).

51. *See* Jeff McMahan, *Moral Intuition, in* The Blackwell Guide to Ethical Theory 103, 110 (Hugh LaFollette & Ingmar Persson eds., 2013).

52. Michael W. McConnell, *Originalism and the Desegregation Decisions*, 81 VA. L. REV. 947, 952 (1995).

53. *See* MICHAEL J. KLARMAN, FROM JIM CROW TO CIVIL RIGHTS: THE SUPREME COURT AND THE STRUGGLE FOR RACIAL EQUALITY 295–308 (2004) (discussing the evolving thinking of Justices Felix Frankfurter and Robert H. Jackson, who initially thought school segregation morally wrong but probably constitutionally permissible, but who ultimately joined the *Brown* majority in invalidating school segregation).

54. For an illuminating discussion of the general phenomenon of reversals of position on issues of institutional authority, often driven by merits bias or sheer opportunism, see Eric A. Posner & Cass R. Sunstein, *Institutional Flip-Flops*, 94 TEX. L. REV. 485 (2016).

55. For a classic explication and defense of the ideal of candor in judicial decisions, see David L. Shapiro, *In Defense of Judicial Candor*, 100 HARV. L. REV. 731 (1987).

56. The principle of charity calls for interpretations of another's words or texts that, in situations of possible doubt, "maximize the truth or rationality in the subject's sayings." SIMON BLACKBURN, THE OXFORD DICTIONARY OF PHILOSOPHY 62 (1994).

57. *See, e.g.*, JOHN RAWLS, POLITICAL LIBERALISM 49 n.1 (1993); T. M. SCANLON, WHAT WE OWE TO EACH OTHER 191–92 (1998).

58. JOHN RAWLS, POLITICAL LIBERALISM 49 n.1 (1993).

59. *See, e.g.*, Benjamin C. Zipursky, *Reasonableness in and out of Negligence Law*, 163 U. PA. L. REV. 2131, 2149–2150 (2015).

60. *See, e.g.*, Alan D. Miller & Ronen Perry, *The Reasonable Person*, 87 N.Y.U. L. REV. 323, 391 (2012).

61. *See* JOHN RAWLS, POLITICAL LIBERALISM 8 n.8 (1993); John Rawls, *The Independence of Moral Theory*, 48 PROC. & ADDRESSES OF THE AM. PHIL. ASS'N 5 (1974–1975). At the very minimum, Rawls's conception of wide reflective equilibrium contemplates a need to specify the "the original position" from which representative individuals would choose principles of justice from behind a "veil of ignorance" as part of the same process of equilibration from which substantive judgments about individual cases and statements of general principles of political morality also emerge. *See* JOHN RAWLS, A THEORY OF JUSTICE 17–22, 136–42 (1971).

62. JOHN RAWLS, POLITICAL LIBERALISM 137 (1993).

63. For discussion of some of the issues involved in working out a conception of the rule of law, see Richard H. Fallon Jr., *"The Rule of Law" as a Concept in Constitutional Discourse*, 97 COLUM. L. REV. 1 (1997).

64. On the need for compromise among the Justices in order to produce majority opinions, see Richard H. Fallon Jr., *The Supreme Court, 1996 Term—Foreword: Implementing the Constitution*, 111 HARV. L. REV. 54, 59–60 (1997).

65. For a valuable discussion of ways in which judicial opinions can be minimalist or maximalist, see CASS R. SUNSTEIN, ONE CASE AT A TIME: JUDICIAL MINIMALISM ON THE SUPREME COURT (1999).

66. *See generally* WHAT *BROWN V. BOARD OF EDUCATION* SHOULD HAVE SAID: THE NATION'S TOP LEGAL EXPERTS REWRITE THE LANDMARK CIVIL RIGHTS DECISION (Jack M. Balkin ed., 2001).

7 Sociological, Legal, and Moral Legitimacy: Today and Tomorrow

1. *See, e.g.,* Jeffery J. Mondak, *Policy Legitimacy and the Supreme Court: The Sources and Contexts of Legitimation,* 47 Pol. Res. Q. 675, 676–77 (1994); James L. Gibson et al., *Measuring Attitudes toward the United States Supreme Court,* 47 Am. J. Pol. Sci. 354, 356–58 & n.4 (2003) (citing David Easton, A System Analysis of Political Life 273 (1965)).

2. *See* Joseph Daniel Ura, *Backlash and Legitimation: Macro Political Responses to Supreme Court Decisions,* 58 Am. J. Pol. Sci. 110, 111 (2014); James L. Gibson, *The Legitimacy of the U.S. Supreme Court in a Polarized Polity,* 4 J. Empirical Legal Stud. 507, 533 (2007); Lawrence Baum & Neal Devins, *Why the Supreme Court Cares about Elites, Not the American People,* 98 Geo. L.J. 1515, 1552–53 (2010); James L. Gibson et al., *Measuring Attitudes toward the United States Supreme Court,* 47 Am. J. Pol. Sci. 354, 361 (2003); Tom R. Tyler & Gregory Mitchell, *Legitimacy and the Empowerment of Discretionary Legal Authority: The United States Supreme Court and Abortion Rights,* 43 Duke L.J. 703, 781 (1994).

3. For the polling data, see *Supreme Court,* Gallup, http://gallup.com/poll /4732/Supreme-Court.aspx (last accessed July 17, 2017). On comparisons with Congress and the president, see Marc J. Hetherington & Joseph L. Smith, *Issue Preferences and Evaluations of the U.S. Supreme Court,* 71 Pub. Opinion Q. 40, 41 (2007).

4. *See Supreme Court,* Gallup, http://gallup.com/poll/4732/Supreme -Court.aspx (last accessed July 17, 2017).

5. *See id.* In July 2016, the Court's approval rating tied a record low, with only 42 percent of Americans approving, compared with 52 percent who disapproved. The numbers for September 2016 showed a slight rebound, but Gallup still recorded that only 45 percent of Americans approved of the way that the Court was doing its job, compared with 47 percent who disapproved. *See id.;* Jeffrey M. Jones, *U.S. Supreme Court Job Approval Rating Ties Record Low,* Gallup (July 29, 2016), http://www.gallup.com/poll/194057/supreme-court-job -approval-rating-ties-record-low.aspx.

6. *See Supreme Court,* Gallup, http://gallup.com/poll/4732/Supreme -Court.aspx (last accessed July 17, 2017). In 2016, this number improved slightly, with 61 percent reporting either a "fair amount" or "great deal" of confidence in the federal courts. *See id.*

7. *See id.*

8. *See, e.g., Negative Views of Supreme Court at Record High, Driven by Republican Dissatisfaction,* Pew Res. Ctr. (July 29, 2015), http://www.people-press .org/2015/07/29/negative-views-of-supreme-court-at-record-high-driven-by -republican-dissatisfaction/ (reporting that "seven-in-ten Americans . . . say that in deciding cases, the [J]ustices of the Supreme Court 'are often influenced by their own political views' "); *Opinions of the Supreme Court,* N.Y. Times (June 7, 2012), http://www.nytimes.com/interactive/2012/06/08/us/politics/opinions-of -the-supreme-court.html (76 percent believe the Justices "sometimes let personal or political views influence their decisions").

9. For a brilliant and occasionally haunting development of this theme, see Robert M. Cover, *Violence and the Word*, 95 YALE L.J. 1601 (1986); Robert M. Cover, *The Supreme Court, 1982 Term—Foreword: Nomos and Narrative*, 97 HARV. L. REV. 4 (1983).

10. *See generally* FREDERICK SCHAUER, THE FORCE OF LAW 89–92 (2015) (explaining that government officials tend to believe that their vision of good policy is coterminous with the bounds of the Constitution). Recent social scientific findings highlight the delegitimation effects that result when members of the public perceive ideological mismatch between themselves and the Court. *See, e.g.*, Brandon L. Bartels & Christopher D. Johnston, *On the Ideological Foundations of Supreme Court Legitimacy in the American Public*, 57 AM. J. POL. SCI. 184, 197 (2013).

11. Among political scientists, Dino P. Christenson & David M. Glick, *Chief Justice Roberts's Health Care Decision Disrobed: The Microfoundations of the Supreme Court's Legitimacy*, 59 AM. J. POL. SCI. 403, 415 (2015), find that public accounts of the Supreme Court as political have significant deleterious effects on perceptions of legitimacy, so that "people who got bad news on both fronts—that is, read about the non-legal influences on the Court and came to see the Court as less congruent with their views than they previously believed—exhibited especially large legitimacy losses." *See also* Brandon L. Bartels & Christopher D. Johnston, *On the Ideological Foundations of Supreme Court Legitimacy in the American Public*, 57 AM. J. POL. SCI. 184, 197 (2013) ("The Court's legitimacy in the mass public is significantly influenced by individuals' perceived ideological disagreement with the Court's policymaking."); Mark D. Ramirez, *Procedural Perceptions and Support for the U.S. Supreme Court*, 29 POL. PSYCHOL. 675, 676 (2008) (noting that "although the Court may lose support with unfavorable decisions, it appears unable to generate support with favorable decisions," and concluding that overall perceptions of the Court's legitimacy are dependent on media framing). Not all political scientists are so gloomy, with Professor James L. Gibson offering a repeated voice of optimism. *See, e.g.*, James L. Gibson & Michael J. Nelson, *Change in Institutional Support for the US Supreme Court: Is the Court's Legitimacy Imperiled by the Decisions It Makes?*, 80 PUB. OPINION Q. 622, 624 (2016) (finding, in conclusions "run[ning] strongly counter to recent scholarship," that "the Court's legitimacy is *not* overly sensitive to its constituents' dissatisfaction with its decisions" (emphasis added)).

12. *See* JOHN RAWLS, POLITICAL LIBERALISM 217 (1993).

13. Thomas W. Merrill, *Originalism, Stare Decisis and the Promotion of Judicial Restraint*, 22 CONST. COMMENT. 271, 274 (2005), explains that the term can refer variously to "fidelity to the original meaning of the Constitution," "fidelity to prior precedent," and "a style of judging that produces the fewest surprises."

14. *See, e.g.*, Jeremy Waldron, *The Core of the Case against Judicial Review*, 115 YALE L.J. 1346, 1387–89 (2006).

15. *See* Richard H. Fallon Jr., *The Core of an Uneasy Case for Judicial Review*, 121 HARV. L. REV. 1693 (2008).

16. *See* James B. Thayer, *The Origin and Scope of the American Doctrine of Constitutional Law*, 7 HARV. L. REV. 129, 144 (1893).

17. *See, e.g.*, Church of the Lukumi Babalu Aye, Inc. v. City of Hialeah, 508 U.S. 520, 533 (1993).

18. *See, e.g.*, FCC v. Beach Commc'ns, Inc., 508 U.S. 307, 313–15 (1993).

19. *See* Richard H. Fallon Jr., *Strict Judicial Scrutiny*, 54 UCLA L. Rev. 1267, 1306–8 (2007).

20. *See, e.g.*, Pamela S. Karlan, *The Supreme Court, 2011 Term—Foreword: Democracy and Disdain*, 126 Harv. L. Rev. 1, 12 (2012).

21. *See* James B. Thayer, *The Origin and Scope of the American Doctrine of Constitutional Law*, 7 Harv. L. Rev. 129, 144 (1893); *see also* Sylvia Snowiss, Judicial Review and the Law of the Constitution 188–90 (1990) (describing the prevalence of the clear-mistake rule at the Founding and explaining that Thayer's revival of that rule in the late 1800s "gained impressive support on and off the Court").

22. *See* New State Ice Co. v. Liebmann, 285 U.S. 262, 284 (1932) (Brandeis, J., dissenting) (arguing for deference to state legislatures such that a "presumption of validity attends [their] enactment[s]"). The era took its name from *Lochner v. New York*, 198 U.S. 45 (1905), which invalidated a statute setting maximum hours for bakery workers.

23. For example, Pamela S. Karlan, *The Supreme Court, 2011 Term— Foreword: Democracy and Disdain*, 126 Harv. L. Rev. 1, 12 (2012), chastises the current Court for combining "a very robust view of its interpretive supremacy with a strikingly restrictive view of Congress's enumerated powers."

24. Like the rest of us, the Justices may have a strong psychological disposition to see things as they would like things to be. *See* Dan M. Kahan, *The Supreme Court, 2010 Term—Foreword: Neutral Principles, Motivated Cognition, and Some Problems for Constitutional Law*, 125 Harv. L. Rev. 1, 6–8 (2011). Kahan draws on psychological literature that prominently includes Ziva Kunda, *The Case for Motivated Reasoning*, 108 Psychol. Bull. 480 (1990); Christopher K. Hsee, *Elastic Justification: How Unjustifiable Factors Influence Judgments*, 66 Organizational Behav. & Hum. Decision Processes 122 (1996); Maurice E. Schweitzer & Christopher K. Hsee, *Stretching the Truth: Elastic Justification and Motivated Communication of Uncertain Information*, 25 J. Risk & Uncertainty 185 (2002).

25. *See, e.g.*, Robert Barnes, *Justice Kennedy: The Highly Influential Man in the Middle*, Wash. Post (May 13, 2007), http://www.washingtonpost.com/wp-dyn /content/article/2007/05/12/AR2007051201586.html.

26. 558 U.S. 310 (2010).

27. Nat'l Fed'n of Indep. Bus. v. Sebelius, 567 U.S. 519 (2012) (Scalia, Kennedy, Thomas, and Alito, JJ., dissenting).

28. Obergefell v. Hodges, 135 S. Ct. 2584 (2015).

29. 347 U.S. 483 (1954). On the balance of legal arguments available to the Justices in *Brown*, see generally Michael J. Klarman, From Jim Crow to Civil Rights: The Supreme Court and the Struggle for Racial Equality (2004).

30. Korematsu v. United States, 323 U.S. 214 (1944).

31. John Hart Ely, Democracy and Distrust (1980).

32. *See, e.g.*, Laurence H. Tribe, *The Puzzling Persistence of Process-Based Constitutional Theories*, 89 Yale L.J. 1063, 1064 (1980).

33. Lochner v. New York, 198 U.S. 45, 76 (1905) (Holmes, J., dissenting).

34. *See id.* at 75–76.

35. *See* THE ESSENTIAL HOLMES: SELECTIONS FROM THE LETTERS, SPEECHES, JUDICIAL OPINIONS, AND OTHER WRITINGS OF OLIVER WENDELL HOLMES, JR. 107 (Richard A. Posner ed., 1992).

36. *See, e.g.,* Abrams v. United States, 250 U.S. 616, 624 (1919) (Holmes, J., dissenting); Gitlow v. New York, 268 U.S. 652, 672 (1925) (Holmes, J., dissenting).

37. *See* Nat'l Fed'n of Indep. Bus. v. Sebelius, 567 U.S. 519 (2012). Chief Justice Roberts held that Congress lacked power to enact the purchase mandate under the Commerce Clause, but he voted to uphold the statutory penalties for those who failed to buy insurance as permissible under Congress's power to impose taxes.

38. *See, e.g.,* Van Orden v. Perry, 545 U.S. 677 (2005). In casting the decisive vote not to require the removal of a long-standing Ten Commandments display from the grounds of the Texas State Capitol, Justice Breyer explained that "absolutism" in requiring "the government to purge from the public square all that in any way partakes of the religious" would "tend to promote the kind of social conflict the Establishment Clause seeks to avoid." *Id.* at 699.

39. President Barack Obama's nomination of Merrick Garland, which the Republican Senate majority refused to bring to a vote, furnished a model in this respect.

40. *See* RAN HIRSCHL, TOWARDS JURISTOCRACY: THE ORIGINS AND CONSEQUENCES OF THE NEW CONSTITUTIONALISM (2004); Matthew C. Stephenson, *"When the Devil Turns . . .": The Political Foundations of Independent Judicial Review,* 32 J. LEGAL STUD. 59 (2003).

41. *See* Douglas H. Ginsburg, *Delegation Running Riot,* REGULATION, Winter 1995, at 83, 84 (reviewing DAVID SCHOENBROD, POWER WITHOUT RESPONSIBILITY: HOW CONGRESS ABUSES THE PEOPLE THROUGH DELEGATION (1993)); *see also* RANDY E. BARNETT, RESTORING THE LOST CONSTITUTION: THE PRESUMPTION OF LIBERTY (2004); RICHARD A. EPSTEIN, HOW PROGRESSIVES REWROTE THE CONSTITUTION (2006).

42. William Baude, *Is Originalism Our Law?,* 115 COLUM. L. REV. 2349 (2015); *see also* Stephen E. Sachs, *Originalism as a Theory of Legal Change,* 38 HARV. J.L. & PUB. POL'Y 817 (2015) (advancing a positive theory of originalism as "our law").

43. *See* Eric J. Segall, *The Constitution According to Justices Scalia and Thomas: Alive and Kickin',* 91 WASH. U. L. REV. 1663 (2014).

44. *Cf.* Antonin Scalia, *Originalism: The Lesser Evil,* 57 U. CIN. L. REV. 849, 862–64 (1989) (defending originalism over nonoriginalism but acknowledging that his commitment to originalism might prove "faint-hearted"). Justice Scalia subsequently repudiated his embrace of faintheartedness regarding originalism. *See* JAMES E. FLEMING, FIDELITY TO OUR IMPERFECT CONSTITUTION 2 n.11 (2015).

45. *See, e.g.,* CASS R. SUNSTEIN, RADICALS IN ROBES 131 (2005); Jed Rubenfeld, Essay, *Affirmative Action,* 107 YALE L.J. 427, 431–32 (1997); Stephen A. Siegel, *The Federal Government's Power to Enact Color-Conscious Laws: An Originalist Inquiry,* 92 NW. U. L. REV. 477, 481 (1998).

46. *See, e.g.,* Lawrence v. Texas, 539 U.S. 558, 587 (2003) (Scalia, J., dissenting).

47. *See* Eric A. Posner & Cass R. Sunstein, *Institutional Flip-Flops,* 94 Tex. L. Rev. 485, 500–504 (2016).

48. *See generally* Richard H. Fallon Jr., *Interpreting Presidential Powers,* 63 Duke L.J. 347, 351 (2013) (advocating a methodology for the interpretation of executive powers that includes a discontinuity between ordinary and extraordinarily high-stakes cases).

49. Charles L. Black Jr., The People and the Court: Judicial Review in Democracy 34 (1960).

Acknowledgments

In writing this book, I have drawn on ideas developed in a number of articles that I have written over the past dozen years. These include *Legitimacy and the Constitution*, 118 Harv. L. Rev. 1789 (2005); *Constitutional Precedent Viewed through the Lens of Hartian Positivist Jurisprudence*, 86 N.C. L. Rev. 1107 (2008); *Constitutional Constraints*, 97 Cal. L. Rev. 975 (2009); *The Many and Varied Roles of History in Constitutional Adjudication*, 90 Notre Dame L. Rev. 1753 (2015); *The Meaning of Legal "Meaning" and Its Implications for Theories of Legal Interpretation*, 82 U. Chi. L. Rev. 1235 (2015); and *Arguing in Good Faith about the Constitution: Ideology, Methodology, and Reflective Equilibrium*, 84 U. Chi. L. Rev. 123 (2017).

In working on the book and in thinking about the issues that it addresses, I have also benefited enormously from the help of many friends, colleagues, and students, most of whose names I shall not attempt to recite. My work and their contributions have spanned too many years. But special thanks for helping me think through one or another issue go to Ahson Azmat, Curt Bradley, Rosalind Dixon, Heather Gerken, Andrew Gold, Vicki Jackson, David Law, Frank Michelman, Martha Minow, Bernhard Nickel, Stephen Sachs, Fred Schauer, Neil Siegel, Larry Solum, David Strauss, Cass Sunstein, Amanda Tyler, Adrian Vermeule, and Lloyd Weinreb.

Josh Halpern, Ephraim McDowell, Steve Schaus, and Max Schulman have provided outstanding research assistance. They are only the latest in a chain of superb research assistants, stretching back over many years, who have helped me develop and sharpen ideas that this book deploys and pushes in new directions. Among those to whom I owe the largest debts are Elizabeth Barchas Prelogar, Niko Bowie, Elissa Hart-Mahan, Steven Horowitz, Max Rosen, and Joshua Segal.

My editor, Thomas LeBien, offered both general and specific guidance that greatly improved the book. So did two anonymous reviewers.

As always, I also want to express my deepest gratitude to my wife, Jenny, for her patience and support.

During the period when the ideas for this book began to congeal, I lost my mother, Jean Murray Fallon, who inspired me more deeply than anyone else I have ever known, and my incomparable friend, colleague, and collaborator Daniel J. Meltzer. I cannot imagine two more admirable human beings. I dedicate this book to their memories.

Index

Abrams v. United States (1919), 212n36
abuse of discretion, 39–40
Adams, John, 112
Adarand Constructors, Inc. v. Pena (1995), 79
affirmative action, 5, 12, 79, 115, 123, 163, 172
Alden v. Maine (1999), 186n11
Alien and Sedition Acts, 50, 66, 139
American Insurance Ass'n v. Garamendi (2003), 190n11
Appointments Clause, 42–43
Article I, 50, 66, 95, 139
Article II, 42–43, 81
Article III, 56, 73, 110, 112, 139
Article V, 37, 83–84, 87
Article VII, 84
Articles of Confederation, 84–85
Atkins v. Virginia (2002), 6
attitudinal model of judicial decision making, 122, 140

Bank of the United States, 50, 66, 71, 73, 139
baseball, 88, 91, 107–108, 136
Berman, Mitchell, 143
Bill of Rights, 78, 89, 140, 141
Black, Charles, 96, 174
Bobbitt, Philip, 135–136

Bolling v. Sharpe (1954), 37–38
Bowers v. Hardwick (1986), 6
Brandenburg v. Ohio (1969), 202n44
Breyer, Stephen, 74, 142, 165
Brown v. Board of Education (*Brown I*) (1954), 8, 19, 20, 37, 110, 114, 117, 152, 162, 164; and originalism, 52–53, 141; as precedent and theoretical constraint, 100–101, 145, 146
Brown v. Board of Education (*Brown II*) (1955), 201n33
Brown v. Entertainment Merchants Ass'n (2011), 187n36, 187n41, 205n27
Bush v. Gore (2000), 2–3, 11, 20–21, 40–41, 156, 172, 179n4

certiorari process, 94
Cheney v. United States District Court (2004), 183n47
Chisholm v. Georgia (1793), 205n30
Church of the Lukumi Babalu Aye, Inc. v. City of Hialeah (1993), 187n41, 211n17
Citizens United v. FEC (2010), 4, 5, 9, 11, 162, 205n27
City of Erie v. Pap's A.M. (2000), 195n18
Civil War, 113, 119; pre-war legal regime, 30
consent: and legitimacy, 25–27, 34; and Reconstruction amendments, 84

constitutional constraints, 17, 105–109;
external constraints, 105, 109–120;
normative constraints, 105, 120–123
constitutional meaning, 15, 43, 47–70,
71–82, 101, 139–140; contextual
meaning, 51, 52–53, 57, 59–60, 138,
140, 145, 146; and history, 71–82;
intended meaning, 51, 56–57, 59, 61,
62–63; interpreted or precedential
meaning, 64, 78, 98, 99, 101, 128, 131,
139, 140, 152; and linguistic meaning,
57–65, 88, 139; literal or semantic
meaning, 51, 53–55, 59, 60, 62, 146;
moral conceptual meaning, 51, 55,
57, 60, 138; reasonable meaning, 51,
55–56, 61, 65–67, 98; Time One (T1)
meanings, 71–72, 75–82, 101, 127, 129,
142; Time Two (T2) meanings, 71–72,
72–82, 101, 122, 128, 129, 131; Time
Three (T3) meanings, 71–72, 77–82;
and vagueness or indeterminacy, 65–68
construction, 43–44, 67, 76–78, 134, 139,
147, 168; distinguished from interpretation, 43, 67, 134, 139
contextual meaning. See constitutional
meaning
Cooper v. Aaron (1958), 8, 178nn22–23
Cynical Realism, 14, 171
Cynical Realists, 2, 97, 169–171. See also
Cynical Realism

Dames & Moore v. Regan (1981), 190n11
Davis, Kim, 9
democracy, 29, 45, 57, 157, 167; and
legitimacy, 29
Democratic-Republicans, 67, 112
departmentalism, 115
Department of Transportation v. Association
of American Railroads (2015), 198n58
Dickerson v. United States (2000), 99
Douglas, William, 109
Due Process Clause, 4, 5, 10–12, 37,
75–76, 78, 79, 89, 100, 140; of the Fifth
Amendment, 5, 10, 11, 12, 37, 75–76,
79, 100, 140; of the Fourteenth
Amendment, 4, 10, 11, 75–76, 78, 89,
100, 140
Dworkin, Ronald, 38, 97, 123

Eighth Amendment, 48, 51–52, 65, 138
Ely, John Hart, 163

Equal Protection Clause, 5, 11, 37, 52–57,
64, 65, 67, 71, 76, 79, 84, 95, 101, 135,
138; and the Fifth Amendment, 5, 37;
and gender discrimination, 71, 76, 135,
138; and racial discrimination, 5, 37,
52–57, 71, 76, 79, 95, 101, 138
Establishment Clause, 74–75, 165
Estep v. United States (1946), 184n52
Ex Parte Merryman (1861), 113
Ex Parte Quirin (1942), 113–114
external constraints. See constitutional
constraints

Fainthearted Commitments Hypothesis,
170–173
FCC v. Beach Communications, Inc. (1993),
211n18
Federalist Papers, 15, 66, 105
Federalists, 67, 112–113, 139
Fifth Amendment, 5, 12, 37, 52, 79, 140;
and capital punishment, 52; and due
process, 5, 12, 37, 79, 140
First Amendment, 4, 11, 50, 54–55, 57,
67, 74, 78, 89–90, 100, 138–139. See also
Alien and Sedition Acts; Establishment
Clause; Free Speech Clause
Fourteenth Amendment, 4–5, 52–55, 65,
67–68, 78, 84–85, 87, 89, 140. See also
Due Process Clause; Equal Protection
Clause
Framers, 5, 16, 49, 54, 57, 81, 83, 87, 134
Free Enterprise Fund v. Public Company
Accounting Oversight Board (2010), 184n61
Free Speech Clause, 50, 57
Freytag v. Commissioner (1991), 183n45

Gaddafi, Muammar, 22
Gibbons v. Ogden (1824), 58
Gideon v. Wainwright (1963), 202n44
Gitlow v. New York (1925), 195n16, 212n36
good faith: in constitutional argument,
11–13, 19, 96, 109, 126–127, 130–132,
137, 141, 144–153, 161, 163, 168–169,
171, 173–174; and joining opinions,
151–153; and legitimacy, 130–132, 137,
141; and prior mistakes, 144–146
Green v. County School Board (1968), 179n3

Hamilton, Alexander, 15, 50, 66, 139
Harmelin v. Michigan (1991), 186n19
Hart, H. L. A., 16, 86

Helvering v. Davis (1937), 184n49
Hepburn v. Griswold (1870), 196n33
Hercules, Judge, 38
Hicks v. Miranda (1975), 195n17
historical gloss, 74–75, 81, 131, 146
Hitler, Adolf, 21, 24, 30
Holmes, Oliver Wendell, 55–56, 164
Hughes, Charles Evans, 105
Humphrey's Executor v. United States
  (1935), 184n61

*Immigration and Naturalization Service v.
  Chadha* (1983), 81
intended meaning. *See* constitutional
  meaning
interpreted meaning. *See* constitutional
  meaning
Iran, 108, 111, 119

Jackson, Andrew, 66
Jefferson, Thomas, 50, 66, 112–113, 115,
  119, 139
judicial restraint, 134, 159–165, 166
judicial review, 1, 45, 113, 116, 159–165,
  166
Judiciary Act of 1789, 73
Judiciary Act of 1802, 112
jurisdiction to decide, 39–40

Keck, Thomas, 122–123
Kennedy, Anthony, 6, 162, 172
King v. Burwell (2015), 185n1
Korematsu v. United States (1944), 183n39,
  211n30

Lawrence v. Texas (2003), 5–6, 191n21,
  213n46
legal legitimacy. *See* legitimacy
Legal Realism, 1, 2
legitimacy, 20–46, 155–174; desiderata for
  Supreme Court decision making,
  41–46, 127–132; forward-looking and
  backward-looking aspects, 44, 58, 69,
  72, 82, 101, 103, 122, 127–132, 147–148;
  ideal versus minimal, 24–35; legal
  legitimacy, 21, 35–41; moral legitimacy,
  21, 22–35; sociological legitimacy, 21,
  22–24, 156
Libya, 22
linguistic meaning. *See* constitutional
  meaning

liquidation through practice, 72–77, 81,
  131, 146
literal or semantic meaning. *See*
  constitutional meaning
living constitutionalism, 17, 69, 125, 132,
  134–136
Lochner v. New York (1905), 160, 211n22,
  212n33
Loving v. Virginia (1967), 76
Lucas v. South Carolina Coastal Council
  (1992), 193n38

Madison, James, 15, 66, 72–73, 77, 80,
  105, 112–114, 119, 139; and the
  Federalist Papers, 15, 66, 105; and
  liquidation, 72–73, 77, 80
Marbury v. Madison (1803), 113
Marshall, John, 44, 58, 66, 73, 112–113,
  119
Marshall, Thurgood, 122
McConnell, Michael, 145
McCulloch v. Maryland (1819), 44, 66, 73,
  190n11
McDonald v. City of Chicago (2010), 191n22
meaning. *See* constitutional meaning
Meyer v. Nebraska (1923), 191n23
Michael H. v. Gerald D. (1989), 191n21
Miranda v. Arizona (1966), 99, 118,
  202n44
money, constitutionality of paper money,
  79, 95, 99, 116, 141
moral conceptual meaning. *See* constitu-
  tional meaning
moral legitimacy. *See* legitimacy
moral reading of the Constitution, 136.
  See also Dworkin, Ronald
Morrison v. Olson (1988), 184n61, 198n57
Myers v. United States (1926), 184n59,
  184n61

Nazism: and moral legitimacy, 30; and
  reflective equilibrium, 149, 150; and
  sociological legitimacy, 21
Near v. Minnesota ex rel. Olson (1931),
  195n16
New Deal, 110–111, 117, 168
New State Ice Co. v. Liebmann (1932),
  211n22
New York Times Co. v. United States (1971),
  192n34
NFIB v. Sebelius (2012), 211n27, 212n37

NLRB v. Noel Canning (2014), 74, 142
normative constraints. *See* constitutional
constraints
North Korea, 28, 35
Nozick, Robert, 25

Obama, Barack, 2
Obamacare, 157–158, 161
Obergefell v. Hodges (2015), 4, 9, 11,
191n21, 194n47, 211n28
Ollman v. Evans (1984), 187n46
originalism, 5, 17, 43, 47–50, 67–70, 76,
79, 125, 130, 132, 133–134, 135,
137–141, 146, 168, 169, 172, 173.
See also constitutional meaning;
original public meaning
original public meaning, 4, 11, 12, 47–70,
75, 101, 131, 134, 137, 138

*Planned Parenthood of Southeast Pennsyl-
vania v. Casey* (1992), 9, 184n54,
191n29, 193n43, 197n37, 198n53
Plato, 25
Plaut v. Spendthrift Farm, Inc. (1995), 56
Plessy v. Ferguson (1896), 53, 95–96
politically constructed bounds of judicial
power, 17, 114–120. *See also* judicial
review
Posner, Richard, 169
practices: and meaning, 72–75, 80–81;
and the Supreme Court, 95, 96–103,
119, 125–154, 167–174; and theories of
law, 16, 87–92
precedent: and originalism, 134, 139–140;
and Supreme Court practice, 98–101
precedential meaning. *See* constitutional
meaning
principle of interpretive charity, 148, 171
Printz v. United States (1997), 73

Rakove, Jack, 65
Rawls, John, 18, 25–28, 133, 143, 149–151;
and legitimacy, 25–28; method of
reflective equilibrium, 143, 149–151
reasonable meaning. *See* constitutional
meaning
reasonableness, 26, 40–41, 50, 56, 65–66,
129, 142, 149–150; and constitutional
meaning, 56, 65; distinguished from
rationality, 149; and legitimacy, 26,
40–41, 129; and originalism, 50, 65–66;

and reflective equilibrium, 142,
149–150
Reconstruction, 5, 84–85
reflective equilibrium, 127, 143–144,
150–151; narrow versus wide, 150–151
Reflective Equilibrium Hypothesis,
170–173
Reflective Equilibrium Theory, 18, 126,
142–154, 164, 170, 173
Rehnquist, William, 4, 102, 122
respect: and legitimacy, 8, 11–13, 23–26,
29–33, 34, 38, 128; and legitimate legal
authorities, 136, 147–148; and
reasonableness, 129
Roberts, John, 165
Roe v. Wade (1973), 4, 9, 11, 13, 20–21,
40–41, 101, 104, 110, 158
Roosevelt, Franklin, 110, 113, 117, 118,
119
Roper v. Simmons (2005), 6
Rousseau, Jean-Jacques, 25
rule(s) of recognition, 16–17, 90–96,
99–108, 119–123, 128, 131, 132, 168.
See also practices

Scalia, Antonin, 2, 4, 47, 102; and
originalism, 52, 57, 76, 79, 138, 139,
141
Schenck v. United States (1919), 187n40
Second Amendment, 157
slavery, 27, 31, 36, 60, 84, 150
Soames, Scott, 62–67
Social Security, constitutionality of, 79,
95, 99, 101, 111, 116, 117, 119, 141
sociological legitimacy. *See* legitimacy
Solum, Lawrence, 134, 139
South Dakota v. Dole (1987), 183n45
state sovereign immunity, 139
Stevens, John Paul, 4
Strauss, David, 134–135
strict scrutiny, 68, 79, 89, 100, 160
Stuart v. Laird (1803), 112–113, 189n4
Stump v. Sparkman (1978), 200n12
substantive due process, 40, 75, 78

Taney, Roger, 113
Texas v. Johnson (1989), 195n18
The Passenger Cases (1849), 193n37
The Pocket Veto Case (1929), 190n11
Thirteenth Amendment, 84–85, 87
Thomas, Clarence, 79, 102

Thornburgh v. American College of Obstetricians & Gynecologists (1986), 184n54

Toobin, Jeffrey, 2–3

Town of Greece v. Galloway (2014), 190n16

United States v. Butler (1936), 196n33

United States v. Curtiss-Wright Export Co. (1936), 190n11

United States v. Virginia (1996), 76, 187n32

Van Orden v. Perry (2005), 206n43, 212n38

Vermont Agency of Natural Resources v. United States ex rel. Stevens (2000), 81

Walton v. Arizona (1990), 185n5

Walz v. Tax Commission (1970), 190n15

Warren, Earl, 53, 117

Warren Court, 117–118, 160, 168

Washington, George, 50, 73

Washington v. Glucksberg (1997), 191n20, 191n23

Weber, Max, 22, 86

West Lynn Creamery, Inc. v. Healy (1994), 193n38

Wisconsin v. Yoder (1972), 191n23

Wittgenstein, Ludwig, 88

Youngstown Sheet & Tube Co. v. Sawyer (1952), 74